The Philosophy of the Environment

THE PHILOSOPHY OF THE ENVIRONMENT

Edited by
T. D. J. Chappell

EDINBURGH UNIVERSITY PRESS

© The contributors, 1997
© Introduction and Chapters 1,
2, 5, 6, 7, 8: Edinburgh University
Press, 1997

Edinburgh University Press Ltd
22 George Square, Edinburgh

Typeset in Garamond by
Bibliocraft, Dundee,
and printed and bound in Great Britain

A CIP record for this book is
available from the British Library

ISBN 0 7486 0911 3 (paperback)

CONTENTS

Contributors   vi

Introduction
    Timothy Chappell: Respecting Nature – Environmental
    Thinking in the Light of Philosophical Theory   1

1. Stephen R. L. Clark: Platonism and the Gods of Place   19
2. Holmes Rolston III: Nature for Real: Is Nature a Social Construct?   38
3. Ronald W. Hepburn: Trivial and Serious in Aesthetic
    Appreciation of Nature   65
4. John Haldane: 'Admiring the High Mountains':
    The Aesthetics of Environment   78
5. Mary Midgley: Sustainability and Moral Pluralism   89
6. Timothy Chappell: How to Base Ethics on Biology   102
7. Timothy L. S. Sprigge: Respect for the Non-Human   117
8. Kate Rawles: Conservation and Animal Welfare   135
9. J. Baird Callicott: Whaling in Sand County:
    The Morality of Norwegian Minke Whale Catching   156
10. Dale Jamieson: Zoos Revisited   180

Index   193

CONTRIBUTORS

J. Baird Callicott is Professor of Philosophy at the University of North Texas, USA.

Timothy Chappell is Lecturer in Philosophy at the University of Manchester, UK.

Stephen Clark is Professor of Philosophy at the University of Liverpool, UK.

John Haldane is Professor of Philosophy in the Department of Moral Philosophy, and Head of the School of Philosophical and Anthropological Studies at the University of St Andrews, UK.

Ronald Hepburn was, until his retirement, Professor of Philosophy at the University of Edinburgh, UK.

Dale Jamieson is Professor of Philosophy at the University of Colorado at Boulder, USA.

Mary Midgley was, until her retirement, Senior Lecturer in Philosophy at the University of Newcastle upon Tyne, UK.

Kate Rawles is Lecturer in Philosophy at the University of Lancaster, UK.

Holmes Rolston III is Professor of Philosophy at the State University of Colorado, USA.

Timothy Sprigge is Professor Emeritus and Endowment Fellow in the Department of Philosophy, University of Edinburgh, UK.

INTRODUCTION: RESPECTING NATURE – ENVIRONMENTAL THINKING IN THE LIGHT OF PHILOSOPHICAL THEORY

Timothy Chappell

The core question of this volume – the one which gives it its focus and its unity – is the question of how more or less informal thinking about environmental matters can be made to mesh with a whole philosophical theory or outlook.

One reason why this question is interesting is the obvious tension between the immediate and urgent imperatives of practice and the rather differently demanding imperatives of theory – the tension, as we might say, between the bottom-up and the top-down. Working from the bottom up, we may begin with what strikes us as of immediate practical concern, and try to work towards a more general view which makes sense of that immediate concern in the light of a broader or deeper set of considerations. Working from the top down, we may begin with the attempt to develop some such set of very general considerations into a consistent and cogent system of thought, and then look to see what issues from that system – what such a system says *ought* to be of immediate practical concern. But clashes between the two approaches are evidently possible, and reconciling them satisfactorily is not easy, but difficult enough to be a philosophically interesting task.

There is another reason why we might find the issue an interesting one. Despite the present flourishing of environmental philosophy it is still, unfortunately, not that unusual for thinking about the environment and formal philosophical theory to pass each other by. One conventional picture, which remains more common among philosophers than is often admitted, assumes that 'environmental philosophy' could only mean environmental *ethics*, and then takes it that the relationship of environmental ethics to ethics in general is analogous to that of ethics to philosophy in general – the relationship being, in this picture, something like that of an afterthought or bolt-on extra ('philosophy *ad hoc*', as Holmes Rolston III puts it in Chapter 2).

It is the remit of this volume to challenge such views. To ask how systematic thinking about environmental matters might mesh with a *whole* philosophical theory is naturally to refer to a philosophical theory which includes not just ethics, but also metaphysics, epistemology, aesthetics, philosophy of mind, philosophy of science, history of philosophy and so on.

Is such an all-in approach even possible? In part the answer to that question has to be 'Try it and see'. One good test of whether it is possible is to consider the attempts to run that sort of approach in particular areas which are represented by the essays in this volume. If they work, then clearly this approach is feasible.

Before turning to those essays, we may also mention some more general considerations which suggest that there ought to be more interchange between environmental philosophy and such central areas of conventional philosophy as, say, metaphysics and epistemology. To begin with, consider the word 'environment' itself. What is the environment, or an environment? The French etymology of the word suggests that our environment is whatever is *environ de nous*: that is, our environment is whatever we see around us in performing a turn or veer (*en virant*) through 360 degrees. But what is revealed by such a look around is not only, or even most commonly, known to philosophers as the 'environment'. They also call it 'the external world'.

Now this (it will no doubt be said) is a merely etymological point. But even aside from etymology, there seem to be illuminating connections between philosophers' uses of the two terms 'environment' and 'external world'.[1] 'Environment' tends in practice to be used merely as the correlative of 'environmental philosophy' – to indicate simply whatever it may be that environmental philosophers are interested in. A similar point can be made about 'external world', a term which is often used merely as the correlative of (a certain sort of) epistemology and metaphysics – to indicate whatever it may be that those who study these topics are interested in. When the terms are thus used, it is clear that the crucial question remains open: why shouldn't what environmental philosophers are interested in be just the same thing as what students of metaphysics and epistemology are interested in, only seen in a different light?

If we recognise that there is a sense in which environmental philosophy and conventional metaphysics are 'two takes on the same thing', then we will also recognise that there is a sense in which the external world *is* the environment. That recognition can have beneficial effects for philosophers working in both areas. On the one side, it may help environmental philosophers to see how the environmental issues which concern them are more than bolt-on extras to philosophy. They will be enabled to see that those issues are, rather, of absolutely central importance to philosophy, and are involved in or interwoven with most of philosophy's most fundamental questions. On the other side, the thought may prompt more 'conventional' metaphysicians and epistemologists to notice and query two deep-rooted assumptions which still seem to underlie far too much post-Cartesian epistemology and metaphysics. (That these assumptions also underlay nearly all Western ethical attitudes to the environment from at least the sixteenth to the twentieth century is, by now, hardly news.)

These two assumptions come in the form of (related) metaphors or pictures. One may be called the picture of perception or knowledge as 'consumption': it is the idea that 'the external world' is, so to speak, no more than value-neutral material awaiting our appropriation and consumption when we perceive it or theorise about it. The other is the picture of perception or knowledge as 'conquest': this sees the external world as a sort of unoccupied territory or unclaimed continent which is to be conquered, colonised and civilised by our perception and conceptualisation of it – by us, the would-be 'masters and possessors of nature'.

We – and our metaphysics and epistemology – can perhaps be helped to get beyond these pictures by the realisation that 'the external world' which so much mainstream philosophy is still implicitly aiming to control and manipulate is to a very large degree *simply identical* with 'the environment' which so much environmental ethics is now explicitly aiming to protect and defend. At any rate it seems certain that we badly need to get beyond such pictures, given their inherent aggression and acquisitiveness: as Bertrand Russell put it, 'Greatness of soul is not fostered by those philosophies which assimilate the universe to man.'[2]

One essay in the present collection which takes very seriously the idea of exploring the terrain between environmental philosophy's usual concerns and those of metaphysics and epistemology is Chapter 2, Holmes Rolston III's discussion of 'nature for real'. Professor Rolston's enquiry begins from a post-Kantian predicament. His question is whether we can claim to have any real access to a natural world which has value in and of itself, or whether we rather have to accept the claim that the whole idea of nature and its value is no more than a product of human thinking and conceptualisation – a 'social construct'. In various ways that claim is exactly what all sorts of different writers have recently been tending towards. Rolston cites Alexander Wilson's claim that 'Humans and nature construct each other': such claims are, of course, part of the stock in trade of postmodernist thought, which has insisted relentlessly on the absence of any sort of determinate or objective 'given' from almost every area of enquiry, in a way strongly reminiscent of a possible sceptical reading (or extension) of the programme of Kant's *First Critique*.

But it is not only postmodernists like Derrida or Rorty who have been tending towards seeing nature as a social construct. Even philosophers from such solidly analytic backgrounds as Hilary Putnam have been finding it important to insist that 'there isn't a ready-made world' – that *we* are involved, in some crucial ways, in the constitution of *our* reality.[3] But then if this way of thinking is correct – if the environment is not something 'out there', over against us, which we can know about in its own right – then what can we say about the environment's *value*? As Rolston puts it, 'We cannot correctly value what we do not to some degree correctly know.' So what entitles us to make ethical or aesthetic claims about what we do not even have real epistemic access to? Carefully and patiently, Rolston teases out an exploration of these disquieting arguments and of what might count as an answer to them, and a re-establishment of some sort of 'nature for real' which is at least objective enough to be the locus of objective values. For, as he himself concludes, 'If we cannot have that much truth, we have not only lost a world, we have become lost ourselves . . . the epistemic crisis is as troubling as the environmental crisis, and the one must be fixed before the other can.'

Rolston's search for an understanding of a reality 'out there' is, as I say, expressive of a post-Kantian predicament. It is also recognisably post-Platonic. One theme of Rolston's essay is the question of *the reality of natural kinds*. Rolston is inclined to oppose Putnam's claim that '*We* cut up the world into objects when we introduce one or another scheme of description', because it seems to Rolston that the way the world comes to us necessarily excludes certain sorts of 'cutting up'. In Plato's famous phrase some possible divisions of reality 'divide it at the joints' (*Phaedrus* 265e). Other possible divisions do not, and a correct understanding of reality (or the external world, or 'the environment') is bound to make discriminations against these divisions and in favour of the divisions that do get the world right, by picking out all and only those kinds which are *real* or *natural*.

So Plato repeatedly argues – this is one of the central points of his famous 'theory of Forms'. The theme of the reality of natural kinds also comes up in Chapter 1, Stephen Clark's 'Platonism and the gods of place', in which Clark emphasises the importance of this Platonic theme for the environmentalist. In fact, he argues, the notion of real kinds or types has two particular sorts of importance to environmental philosophy. First, it is the importance of that notion which explains why we should think it a bad thing if some real kind like the dodo is 'lost' by extinction. As Clark puts it: 'It is precisely because things here *ought* to embody form, that the loss of any such successful form must be an occasion for regret . . . admiring virtue, exactly, requires us to wish virtue to be embodied; admiring the dodo (for example) requires us to regret its absence'.

Second, the notion of a real kind is the notion of a standard against which particular examples of that kind may be measured. Without such a notion, Clark argues, there is no place for the idea that a given example of any kind might have anything *wrong* with it. Deficiency is always deficiency compared with the standards set by the notion of the kind. So if the notion of real kinds is wholly absent from our thinking, all we can have to say about how it is with particular things is the vacuous remark that 'everything is an exactly perfect example of one unique type' – itself. Hence we will never be able to recognise the possibility of defect at all. Again, suppose the notion of kinds that we hold is not a notion of *real* kinds but merely (as Locke would say) of *nominal* kinds, of Putnamesque humanly-imposed categories which do not, for anything we know, match reality in any genuine or non-arbitrary way. Plato and Clark would argue that in that case too we will be unable to recognise the possibility of real defects in particular things; all we will be able to acknowledge is the possibility that particular things may be deficient *from one conceivable point of view* (yet not from another which is equally conceivable), or that they may not seem to be as *we* would like them to be. Plainly this is not all we mean by talking, as we do, of the defects of things. Such talk implies that the thing, itself, is not as it ought to be, in itself – not just perspectivally, and not just relative to our wants or interests, but in full and plain fact. As Plato and Clark hold, there is insufficient room for this idea in any metaphysics short of full Platonism – the metaphysics that takes such real kinds as Dodo actually to exist in themselves, as changeless and timeless realities, and as guarantors to other things (like particular dodos) of their reality.

Of course if this sort of Platonism is true, then there is a sense in which real kinds like Dodo cannot be lost. Even if all the particular dodos which exemplify the real kind Dodo happen to die, we still have the real kind itself: it is just for this reason that the Platonist regards the real kinds themselves as being of transcendent value. But now aren't we getting towards the kind of Platonism which environmentalists have so often decried – the kind of Platonism which says that it is *only* 'the world of the Forms' which has value, that the particular embodiments of those Forms don't matter in themselves, and so that the whole of the world of nature – i.e. the environment (or external, physical world) – is really beneath a philosopher's notice? Recently Plato has been much castigated by environmentalists for an attitude to nature which is said to be dualist and improperly intellectual, and hence ecologically harmful. So, for example, the American Vice-President Al Gore has written of the 'Platonic assumptions' that 'man is separate from the world of nature', and that humans are 'disembodied spiritual intellects' with little or no concern for the natural world except in so far as it exemplifies those patterns or templates of reality which Plato calls the Forms.

Clark wants to challenge this way of understanding the history of philosophy. He wants to show that, on the contrary, Platonism is not an anti-natural (and so anti-environmental) asceticism, but in fact is uniquely well equipped to provide us, not only with the right sort of ethical and aesthetic approach to the natural world about us, but also with an adequate metaphysical and epistemological basis for our philosophy of value. Clark believes that Plato's thought is misjudged by environmentalists, and that Platonism constitutes one important strand in ecological thought: 'It is because some things don't change that we can appreciate what does; it is because the things that change are never everything that should be that we can live with change, while still acknowledging a difference between decay and process.'

This sort of engagement with the history of philosophy, and in particular with classical philosophy, is also evident in Chapter 4 – John Haldane's '"Admiring the high mountains": the aesthetics of environment'. At first sight Haldane may seem almost at one with the postmodernists discussed by Rolston's essay in his readiness to acknowledge that 'The "aesthetics of the environment" is like "the politics of the home" – a term of art invented to label a set of concerns and an associated field of academic study each developed over time and out of particular cultural histories.' For all that Haldane is happy to turn to such emphatically 'premodern' authorities as Aristotle and Aquinas for the outline of a philosophical structure for understanding the nature of aesthetic experience in general, which he then applies to the aesthetics of nature in particular. The working out of this approach proves to commit Haldane to certain views about natural forms or types or kinds which are strikingly reminiscent of (some of) the theses which Clark advances in Chapter 1 in his discussion of Platonism. As Haldane writes:

> An objectivist [about aesthetics] . . . might hold that the objects of environmental aesthetic experience are natural forms, by which I mean, primarily, the forms of organisms and derivatively those of non-organic entities. Something of this view is suggested by . . . Aquinas in his discussions of beauty. He explicitly denies the

claim that something is beautiful simply because we like it, insisting by contrast that our appreciation is directed towards the beauty of things, and that a thing is beautiful to the extent that it manifests its proper form or structure . . .

Haldane goes on to argue not only that 'Forms are real, mind-independent entities, there to be discovered and contemplated' (contrast Rolston and Putnam), but also – in the next sentence – that 'the question of whether one member of a natural kind better realises the species' common nature is one that it makes sense to ask and one which informed attention can hope to answer' (contrast Clark's Platonist view of the form of a species or kind as the standard or benchmark for members of that species or kind).

Like Haldane, Ronald Hepburn too is happy – in his contribution, Chapter 3 – to apply considerations drawn from the general study of aesthetics to the special case of environmental aesthetics. Hepburn is himself the author of a classic paper – 'Contemporary aesthetics and the neglect of natural beauty'[4] – which has served as a manifesto for the general project of bringing the environment within the purview of aesthetic consideration, whence it had long and dismissively been excluded. His present paper, 'Trivial and serious in aesthetic appreciation of nature', is a further exploration of that same project.

Hepburn's central concern in Chapter 3 is to show that the aesthetic appreciation of nature can seriously, and not just trivially, *matter*. The importance of establishing this thesis in our present predicament must be obvious:

> When we seek to defend areas of 'outstanding natural beauty' against depredations, it matters greatly what account we can give of . . . how its value can be set alongside competing . . . values . . . If we wish to attach very high value to the appreciation of natural beauty, we must be able to show that more is involved in such appreciation than the pleasant, unfocused enjoyment of a picnic place, or a fleeting and distanced impression of countryside through a touring-coach window.

Now Hepburn readily admits that the aesthetic experience of nature *can* be trivial, as can aesthetic experience of any other sort; and he produces considerations designed to give us some feel for what might make such experience trivial. In part, his suggestion is that such experience is trivial when 'it distorts, ignores, suppresses truths about its objects, feels and thinks about them in ways that falsify how nature really is'. (At once we should notice the objective reference of these remarks.) Elsewhere Hepburn also says this:

> It is nature, nature's own forms, that we seek to contemplate; and the more serious our engagement, the more earnest will be our regard for, and our respect for, the integrity and the proper modes of being of the objects in nature themselves, animate and inanimate.

'Nature's own *forms*': Hepburn is, I think, not a Platonist (nor an Aristotelian), and so does not here mean quite the same as Clark or Haldane when he uses the word 'form'. Nonetheless it is at least evident that, for Hepburn as much as for these others, the idea of a nature which is 'for real' is a necessary presupposition of his views about what can make aesthetic experience of nature more than trivial.

But as Hepburn recognises, his idea that serious aesthetic experience or enjoyment of nature must involve attention to the realities of nature is under obvious threat from the kind of subjectivising or relativising of the human viewpoint which is also Rolston's concern. Hepburn diagnoses part of the attraction of such moves as coming from the modern tendency to want to unmask, undermine or ironise any viewpoint which seems to offer us, or invite us to feel, what Hopkins called 'the world's splendour and wonder'.[5] Notoriously, this belittling and trivialising tendency itself seems to be just one more viewpoint waiting to be undermined or unmasked. It is never easy to see how perspectivalism, taken seriously, can avoid undermining *itself* as well as everything else.

Besides the threat of relativism, there is another way in which attachment to the notion of the reality of nature may seem vulnerable. Nature is after all a harsh and unforgiving mistress, as human experience has always shown, and as the modern understanding of evolutionary theory now confirms. It is natural to feel that, in Hume's famous words,[6] 'the whole presents nothing but the idea of a blind nature, impregnated by a great vivifying principle, and pouring forth from her lap, without discernment or parental care, her maimed and abortive children!' Hepburn himself concedes that 'There is no doubt that to perceive [the vulnerability and brevity of individual life] is to be closer to the truth of things than not to.' So how can we admit the truth that there is in such bleaker views of nature, without losing the idea that nature can also rightly and seriously be seen as both *good* (an ethical adjective) and *wonderful* (an aesthetic adjective)? If we found that we could not keep both of these thoughts, then might that justify our taking some other line, for instance a 'formalist' or 'impressionistic' approach, which concerns itself not with 'how things actually are' in nature but only with 'the sensuous surfaces' of things? Hepburn is sceptical about the possibility of taking refuge in any such alternative, in particular because of its abandonment of the constraints suggested by consideration of 'how things really are'. He thinks it would be better simply to say that there is a *balance* to be found between the extremes of bleakness and sentimentality, and leave it at that. After all, Hume notwithstanding, not *every* increase in the gloominess of our view of nature is an increase in its truthfulness.

An attractive feature of Hepburn's discussion is his desire not to do what so many philosophers seem to want to do – to streamline or oversimplify issues by subsuming as many of them as possible under the smallest possible number of simple and allegedly all-embracing first principles. Clearly this desire is shared by other contributors to this volume. It is particularly evident in Mary Midgley's contribution, Chapter 5: 'Sustainability and moral pluralism'. Midgley's essay is the first in the order of the volume to be concerned directly with issues of environmental *ethics* – which she addresses in the course of discussing much wider ethical issues raised by our heritage of Enlightenment moral thinking. Her essay is then (among other things) an engagement with the history of philosophy, like Clark's and Haldane's contributions.

It is also an attack on the 'evidently mistaken search for a single all-purpose "moral theory"' – a search in which the notions of leading Enlightenment thinkers like Kant and Hobbes are still very prominent. Like some other recent ethicists, in particular Bernard Williams,[7] Midgley argues against the very idea of such a search. When we are concerned with the really big questions of ethics, 'the notion that there is just one right set' of moral principles for solving them all is (she argues) 'a mere distraction' – as indeed is the idea that any one answer to a given question of ethics must, if it is *a* right answer, therefore be considered *the* right answer. 'If somebody asks . . . "Why, really, shouldn't I kill you?" many people will be somewhat stuck for an answer. This is not (as cocky graduate students tend to think) because these people don't know the answer, but because they know too many answers. Such general queries make no sense unless we know just why they are being asked.'

Midgley's contention is then that Enlightenment thinking has left us with an unduly narrow conception of what it is to do ethics or moral philosophy. A second and related contention which Midgley also advances is that Enlightenment thinking has also left us with an unduly narrow conception of what can be a proper object of moral concern in its own right. 'Since the Renaissance,' she writes, 'there has been a deliberate effort to exclude from concern everything non-human, and many supposedly non-rational aspects of human life as well . . . This is still the unquestioned creed expressed in the ministries and offices from which our society is run.' Midgley's thesis is that it is from this conception of what moral concern ought to be that there has arisen the emphasis in current political debate about the environment on the anthropocentric (and indeed economically conditioned) notion of 'sustainability'. Sustainability alone, says Midgley, is not enough to motivate the kind of changes that are necessary to secure the continued well-being of our planet (even at its obviously sub-optimal, indeed sub-minimal, present level).

It is not that sustainability is a notion without appeal or use. It is rather that, for one thing, sustainability is only *one* sort of appeal, and we need lots of different sorts (for example – Midgley's example – an appeal to a sense of outrage). And for another, the roots of the idea of sustainability seem to be in something like Hobbes' notion that we begin moral philosophy by thinking of individual self-interest, and only arrive at any more generous notions than that by extension and analogy from the individual case. Appeals to sustainability then are just appeals to self-interest on an 'immensely public, long-term scale'. But such appeals in fact have less of a realistic chance of success than they are often thought to have, given the proximity and obviousness of what they ask the individual to surrender, and the distance and nebulousness of what they offer in return; as Midgley insists against theorists like Adam Smith, unfortunately human self-interest is typically *not* 'enlightened'. But anyway, even if such appeals did succeed, they would still bring us back to the Enlightenment conceptions of rationality and anthropocentrism which we are now finding increasingly philosophically unsatisfactory.

Philosophical dissatisfaction with one Enlightenment conception in particular is the starting point for my own contribution to the volume, Chapter 6, 'How to base ethics on biology'. My concern is with the concept of a *person*, a concept which is now used by a large variety of writers on ethics (including environmental ethics) as the key determinant of moral status or lack of it. If one's whole philosophical development has been nurtured by, for instance, Descartes' conception of the self, and/or Kant's notion of the pure will's essentially rational (but not essentially human) agency, then the notion that it is *persons*, not *human beings*, which are of overriding moral importance is likely to seem an entirely natural one. Natural but, as I argue, deeply misleading for at least two sorts of reason: one to do with ethics, the other to do with metaphysics.

The ethical problem with this sort of use of the notion of persons is that the opposition *person/non-person* suggests a picture according to which (as we might put it) only two 'weights' of moral significance occur – one and zero. Everything is either a person and therefore fully morally significant in its (his/her?) own right, or else is not a person and has no (direct?) moral significance whatever. But this picture, I argue, is inadequate to say many things that we want to say. In the first place, it legitimises – historically, has always legitimised – attitudes of aggression, consumption and domination towards everything else on the parts of those who are pleased to dub themselves persons. In the second place, the proposal that we give even loosely metaphorical *weights* to different moral statuses suggests a procedure which has come to be suspected by many serious philosophers of being no more than a way of giving a specious 'scientific' respectability to our own mere prejudices. Third, even if we can make good non-question-begging sense of the metaphor of moral weighting, we are likely to think, if we are also environmentally concerned, that the personhood criterion of moral significance simply gets the weightings in question wrong. No self-respecting 'Green' can swallow the idea that the mattering of the various sorts of animals is contingent on their being *persons*, since so many of the animals that 'Greens' want to say matter quite patently are not persons. The problem becomes even more acute if 'Greens' also want to say, as they regularly and rightly do, that some *habitat* or other matters. The idea that the ground of *this* sort of mattering *has* to be in some sort of animism seems absurd.

So even those who defend the personhood criterion are, when they reflect on the matter, unlikely to want to stay committed to the desperately implausible claim that only persons have direct moral significance. They may decide instead that what they want to say is that only persons have *rights*. But then we should ask: what is the difference between having rights and having any other sort of moral significance? Is there really any more than a verbal difference between, for example, the following claims?

1. X has a moral status such that causing X pain is wrong because unresponsive to that moral status.
2. X has rights such that causing X pain is wrong because contrary to those rights.

We may reasonably doubt whether any serious distinction in moral status is introduced to the debate by bringing in talk of 'rights'. Rights-talk seems to mark a distinction without a difference. But so – I argue – does person-talk. This is my second main point: that the notion of personhood is not only ethically questionable, but also metaphysically unfounded. 'Person' does not pick out any sort of natural kind. Hence the answer to the question what anything is, is never best or most fundamentally given by saying that it is (or isn't) a person.

This in turn brings me to a further ethical conclusion: since ethics (including environmental ethics) should base itself on what is really there, on what is metaphysically real, it should not base itself on personhood. Rather it should base itself on the real natural kinds to which individual animals are correctly to be assigned: which means on biological species such as *Homo sapiens*, *Panthera leo*, *Panthera tigris*, and so forth. It is the different intrinsic natures of these kinds which should be seen as grounding their different sorts of intrinsic value. The key idea connecting nature and value here is the Aristotelian notion of 'well-being': the notion of living well or flourishing as a creature of a given kind. Since well-being is differently specified relative to different species, this notion can happily accommodate a far greater – though certainly not a limitless – range of different sorts of moral significance than can be recognised within the conceptual straitjacket of the personhood criterion.

My claim is then that the correct basis for an environmental ethics is, unsurprisingly, in biology not in biologically (and metaphysically) baseless fabrications like the idea that 'person' might be the name of any metaphysically important category of existent. My reason for this claim is a possibly more surprising claim. It is that *environmental* ethics should be based this way because ethics *in general* should be based this way – on the metaphysical facts. Mistakes about metaphysics are neither necessary nor sufficient conditions of mistakes about ethics. Nonetheless they do tend to produce them, and in some cases seem very closely correlated with them: the case of the personhood criterion of moral significance or of rights being a case in point.

Plainly Chapter 6 shares with Chapter 1 to 4 a concern with the notion of a natural kind and with 'what is really there' in the natural world. In its desire to get ethical thought away from preoccupation with the notion of a person, Chapter 6 is also concerned like Chapter 5 to broaden, enrich and complicate ethical *theory* about the environment in ways that bring it more into line with how *in practice* we naturally and instinctively think about the environment.

A third theme which Chapter 6 brings out is one which has come out already in a very obvious way in Midgley's discussion in Chapter 5 of the official scepticism sometimes expressed about the notion of nature's intrinsic value; the same theme is I think also latent throughout Hepburn's and Rolston's discussions. This theme is the notorious problem of the 'is/ought gap' – the problem of how if at all we can defensibly argue from metaphysical claims about how things are, to ethical claims about how things ought to be.

In Chapter 7 Timothy Sprigge advances the bold claim that those who know what human beings or animals *are* know that human beings (or animals) have rights. From this remark it is evident already that Sprigge too is concerned not only with rights, but also with the problem of the is/ought gap. As he sees it, it is blindness about the ontology of animal reality which lies behind the cruelty to animals inherent in such practices as deliberately burning cats, or throwing donkeys off towers, or vivisection, or factory farming. That is, Sprigge contends that it is precisely *factual* ignorance (whether willed or not) which normalises such practices: for Sprigge, anyone who understood what was *really going on* in cat-burning *could not* condone it.

One may sometimes have the sense that unfortunately there are people who know perfectly well what cruelty is and yet engage in it. For all that, Sprigge's is an intuitively attractive claim. For one thing, it helps us to explain how it is that *simple description* of what is done, say, to rhesus monkeys or rabbits in cosmetics laboratories can often be all that is needed to change people's attitudes to such practices – and to explain it without assuming that any sort of 'emotive' appeal is being illicitly relied upon. But how could mere description have that effect on anyone who took at all seriously the doctrine of the is/ought gap?

Notice that it is central to Sprigge's case to claim that there is no real difference in the basic grounds on which we should condemn man's inhumanity to animals and man's inhumanity to man. The basic ground is just that animals too, like other humans, are other consciousnesses. How different then is Sprigge's account of what grounds moral significance from the species-based criterion offered by Chapter 6 and also suggested in different ways by Chapters 1, 2 and 9? Here we should note Sprigge's view that what we need to solve detailed problems as to what is morally acceptable in the treatment of animals by man is a sympathetic grasp of what it is like to be any such animal, a phenomenology of the life-worlds of other species. Now of course there are going to be different phenomenologies for different species, so evidently Sprigge does have *some* use for the notion of species as the ground of differences in moral status. However, for Sprigge, such differences between species are not (as they are for me in Chapter 6) the fundamental ethical given, in the light of which further adjustments may be made to accommodate moral considerations about such phenomena as sentience. For Sprigge, it is exactly the other way round: the fundamental criterion of moral significance is sentience; thoughts about species-membership are morally important, if at all, only *after* the question of sentience has been considered.

This explains why Sprigge is not prepared automatically to extend the same sort of moral considerability as is captured by saying that humans and other animals have 'rights' to the non-sentient species in the world – even though Sprigge is happy to concede that there may be other kinds of considerability or value present in what is not sentient. For Sprigge it would (it seems: but there is a qualification coming) just be a mistake to empathise with a tree or an ecosystem, to ask what it was like to be such things, or to suppose that these things have phenomenologies of their own. And this, he holds, is precisely why such things do not have value in the same way as sentient animals do. Inanimate nature may have aesthetic value, or what Sprigge calls 'inner' value, the value of its own secret life; it may even have 'mystical' value such as Wordsworth sensed at Tintern Abbey; but it does not have moral value in the way that any centre of sentience does.

Sprigge's sentience criterion of moral significance seems very different from the personhood criterion which I criticise in Chapter 6. For one thing, it is very much less *demanding* than most versions of the personhood criterion. Nonetheless it has at least one important affinity with the personhood criterion: namely that it draws a firm and exclusive line between the morally significant and the morally insignificant, on the basis of a criterion to do with anything's mental life. (This is not to say that Sprigge admits no cases where it is not clear whether we have a case of sentience or not – but his inclination seems to be to put this sort of vagueness down to our ignorance rather than to anything in the nature of such cases.)

Here, however, it is relevant to point out that Sprigge is both an idealist and a panpsychist, and that there is a sense in which his panpsychism leads him towards a different conclusion about the value of 'the non-sentient' from that dictated by his idealism. One reason why, given Sprigge's views, what seems non-sentient cannot have the same sort or weight of moral value as the sentient is surely because of the ontological dependence of the non-sentient on the sentient in Sprigge's idealism. As he puts it at one point, 'If there were no creatures with suitable sense-organs, the panorama they find beautiful *simply would not exist*' (my italics). (Notice here the parallel and connection between Sprigge's ethical view that only centres of sentience have moral significance in their own right, and his metaphysical view that only centres of sentience exist in their own right[8] – a connection which of course brings us back once again to the theme of the is/ought gap.) On the other hand, Sprigge's panpsychism is, of course, precisely the view that there is some sort of sentience *in everything*. So why doesn't this lead Sprigge to say that everything is morally significant if what is sentient is morally significant?

The answer to this is, first, that it does lead *Sprigge* in that direction – but he assumes (probably justifiably) that most of his readers are not panpsychists, and challenges them to square any sort of deep-ecological approach which may attract them with the denial of panpsychism. But, second, Sprigge adds this qualification:

> I suspect that, even for the panpsychist, where it is not the welfare of individual organisms in question, but the alleged value of units such as total ecosystems . . . appeal must be mainly to aesthetic value. For, even if there is a world of inner feeling in nature, we must remain so ignorant of its character . . . that we can hardly take the values realised there into account in our moral reckonings.

In his discussion Sprigge is, of course, entering a long-running and sometimes heated debate in environmental philosophy between animal welfare campaigners and conservation campaigners – between those who are concerned with the prevention of animal suffering, and those who are concerned with the well-being of the entire world ecosystem even if promoting that overall involves causing animal suffering (e.g. by culling). The (at first sight) firm line which Sprigge wanted to draw between the sentient and the non-sentient seems at least initially to commit him to taking sides in this debate with the animal rights campaigners. In Chapter 8, 'Conservation and animal welfare', Kate Rawles also discusses this dispute, but unlike Sprigge, she seems much more inclined simply to arbitrate, or even just to describe and explore, the dispute than to join one or the other side.

As Rawles sees it, the two sides of the argument are divided on four main issues. First, something I have also noted: animal welfarists typically draw a line *somewhere* between what is morally significant and what isn't. Rawles calls this the 'no-trespass view of morality', since it implies that there is one area of moral space in which we may do what we like, and another in which we must not violate rights. (Compare the personhood criterion's absolute divide between persons and non-persons, and Sprigge's apparently absolute divide between the sentient and the non-sentient.) By contrast, conservationists typically want to value *everything there is without exception*. They do not necessarily want to value it all in the same way, but they do still want to put everything in nature (which, surely, means *everything*: cp. my remarks above about 'the environment' and 'the external world') on the positive side of the line between moral significance and insignificance. This seems to be the sort of view that, for instance, Rolston, Clark and Callicott would favour.

Second, as Rawles notes, animal welfarists typically proceed by fixing on one morally significant characteristic (or on a small and related group of such features), and then emphasise the moral (and indeed logical) requirement that we treat all bearers of that feature *alike* or *consistently*. (Thus, for example, for Sprigge, anything sentient is morally significant in its own right, and nothing else is.) They appeal to our intuitions about the importance of consistency, whereas conservationists tend to appeal to different intuitions, usually about the intrinsic goodness of certain things. For example, conservationists often appeal to our intuitions about the intrinsic goodness of saving rare species or ecologies, and want to say that those intuitions can justify us in actions which might seem radically inconsistent to the animal welfarist. Take a policy of killing off predators to protect a rare species from extinction. The radical welfarist is likely to see such a policy as telling us to cause one lot of suffering to this bunch of animals to prevent another lot of suffering from happening to that bunch of animals, where the amount of suffering prevented is not even necessarily a larger amount than the amount caused. Clearly, the intuition that 'all animals are equal' cannot on its own make any sense of such policies.

Third and fourth, and most obviously of all, conservationists and animal welfarists disagree over the relative importance of (on the one hand) ecosystems and the species or populations which they contain, and (on the other) of individual animals of those species or populations. This is partly a matter of metaphysics (the third difference): how *metaphysically* justifiable is the welfarist's implied belief that the individual animal is the basic reality, the basic unit of existence? It is also partly a matter of ethics (the fourth difference): how *morally* justifiable is the ethical approach which highlights the individual, not the species? (Notice again that the evidently correct idea that these two disagreements are connected with each other implies a need to say something about the is/ought gap.)

The culling of red deer in such places as the Highlands of Scotland provides a clear example to focus our thoughts about this last, ethical disagreement. The conservationist typically justifies the killing of large numbers of individual red deer on the ground that, unless they are killed, the whole of the Highland ecosystem will be degraded, so that it will be better in the long run if some individual animals are killed now. But the animal welfarist will object to this. For him the cruelty involved in killing the individual animals outweighs the advantages to the environment of having a cull.

Of course, the environmentalist might go further, and point out that the cull is not just advantageous for the environment *as opposed to* the individual red deer. Since the red deer are themselves one part of the environment in question, the cull must also be advantageous to the red deer themselves – to the red deer population, that is, not to the individuals, and in the long run, not in the short term. Animal welfarists are likely to resist this kind of response. First, they may do so on the ground that the importance of the well-being of the red deer population cannot override the importance of the well-being of individual red deer. Second, they may point out that the same sort of argument would justify culling not only red deer but humans too. Since the latter is clearly an outrageous proposal, and since there are no relevant differences between humans and deer, so must the former be.

One thing that is striking about this debate is the way in which people turn out to be on unexpected sides of it. Most leading animal welfarists are utilitarians (Sprigge himself is; so is Peter Singer; Tom Regan is a counter-example), whereas many leading conservationists are not utilitarians; some conservationists (such as myself) are positively anti-utilitarian. Now it is characteristic of utilitarianism to set an overall aim of 'utility maximisation', and then argue that whatever promotes that overall aim is the right thing to do, and that the idea of restricting or constraining the pursuit of the good by building into our ethics a theory of rights is a strictly secondary exercise. But look at the way the debate goes between animal welfare and conservation. In this debate we have non-utilitarian conservationists setting an overall goal of the well-being of the whole environment (see, for example, Callicott's citation of Aldo Leopold in Chapter 9), and then arguing that the suffering of particular animals can be justified if it helps achieve that goal. Opposing them we have utilitarian animal welfarists apparently arguing that *no* considerations about the overall well-being of the environment could possibly justify particular animals' suffering.[9] This seems a curious reversal of what we might have expected to happen!

The conflict between the animal welfarist's emphasis on individuals and the conservationist's emphasis on wholes might be resoluble in a number of ways. (One such way has already been suggested by Stephen Clark in Chapter 1: his thesis is that it is within the framework of a Platonist philosophy that we can best make sense of the mattering *both* of individuals *and* of wholes like species.) Rawles's tentative conclusion is that that conflict is deep, and so not obviously eliminable, but that perhaps the way forward is to see how the systems of ethical thought that we already have might be extended or enriched. (Cp. Midgley in Chapter 5.) Perhaps what we need, Rawles suggests, is 'to supplement or replace the conceptual apparatus of conventional ethical theory'. This brings me to Callicott's and Jamieson's papers, Chapters 9 and 10. For Jamieson's paper on zoos brings out in another way the depth and intransigence of the conflict between the conservationist viewpoint and the animal welfarist viewpoint, while Callicott's essay is precisely concerned with an attempt to extend and supplement the kinds of moral thought that we have.

Callicott begins with a contrast between what he calls a 'land ethic' and a 'sea ethic' – one ethical approach which applies to life on dry land, and another which applies to life in the deeps: 'If one wants to make an informed moral judgement about commercial whaling, one should consult the *sea* ethic, not the *land* ethic.' The very idea of such a contrast would have seemed strange to Enlightenment moral philosophers like Kant or Locke or Hobbes: for their grounding assumption is that ethics is naturally and necessarily something which applies everywhere if it applies anywhere. But Callicott is adamant that we should not start from this assumption, but from quite another point:

> The land ethic has its limits . . . Nearly three-quarters of the (misnamed) planet Earth is covered by water. Elsewhere I have argued that the land ethic would be utterly incapable of providing moral guidance should we human beings discover, and be in a position to affect, life on Mars[10] . . . Why? Because the linchpin of the land ethic is . . . the 'community concept'. And, by definition, we human beings are not evolutionarily akin or ecologically related to unearthly forms of life. We would share no community with them.

The 'community concept' to which Callicott refers here is Aldo Leopold's notion of a *biotic* community – an interdependent ecology of different sorts of animals which naturally live together, feeding with each other and indeed on each other. And that should be enough to show how profoundly different Callicott's conceptual foundations are from those presupposed by the Enlightenment moralists. Callicott does not take it, as those thinkers usually did (Hume is an exception), that genuinely different systems of ethics could emerge only as aberrations – as distortions of 'pure practical reason' or as misunderstandings of 'one's own best interests'. For Callicott different systems of ethics emerge *by nature* from different evolutionary histories and different ecological scenarios: 'We should expect the ethics correlative to these very different kinds of communities to be correspondingly very different.' I argued in Chapter 6 that ethics had to be based upon biology: Callicott takes this same thought far further than me, though also in different directions.

Part of his project is reminiscent of Midgley's in Chapter 5. Callicott wants to show that many arguments which might be drawn from the land ethic cannot on their own explain why – as many of us intuitively think – there is something profoundly wrong with practices like whaling. For many of the arguments drawn from the land ethic, whether holistic or individualist in emphasis, would have to do with ideas like sustainability; but such ideas do not provide the materials needed by the opponent of whaling. On the other hand, of course, if there is a sea ethic, then we – as land creatures – have no access to it. (At least, not yet.) So the conclusion of Callicott's sensitive and imaginative dialectic is that the arguments against whaling have to be made out by analogy with *some* moves which are familiar from our thinking within the land ethic. To him, two issues are particularly crucial.

First, there is the issue of whether or not what we hunt in the seas are members of a prey species. Notice the connection with the idea of natural well-being here: Callicott's idea is evidently that if being hunted is a natural part of some creature's life, then total freedom from being hunted cannot be a necessary part of that creature's natural well-being, and is therefore not necessarily morally due to it. (Evidently Callicott is no vegetarian; he even entertains the possibility that being hunted might be something that a prey species actually enjoys.)

However, as Callicott notes, it is unclear how decisive this criterion is. After all, most of the whales which whalers hunt are also hunted at least by killer whales (orcas), if not by other species as well. Again, we might even see *the whalers* as being a class of natural predators on the whales: as usual, it all depends what we mean by 'natural'. Callicott then turns to the second crucial issue: which is that of the whales' *intelligence*.

> 'To look upon commercial whaling with approval seems to me like looking with approval on a horde of cunning but illiterate vandals looting and plundering the art galleries of an ancient and peaceful civilisation in the name of gathering fuel for cooking fires. Should we be killing beings who may be, for all we know, the most highly evolved form of intelligent life on the planet?'

Callicott describes in some detail the sophistication and even civilisation of which whales may well be capable, and appeals to this sort of fact about whales, above all else, as grounding their moral importance.

That Callicott's dialectic moves him towards such considerations is natural enough. To consider whales in this sort of light is to try and work out what will be important in their environment, from their point of view: indeed it is to come as close as we might to formulating at least some fragments of a sea ethic, an ethic of natural well-being distinctively designed for sea creatures. But it is also to see whales in a light which might have been suggested by other lines of thought too (Callicott himself raises the question of whether this sort of reason for valuing whales is truly a land-ethical one): compare Sprigge's injunction to us to try and imagine what it would be like to be such a creature. Thus the most important considerations which Callicott adduces against hunting whales get their strength and resonance from their accord not only with his own but with other moral first principles as well. The notion of an ethics which is based upon the natural well-being, within their natural environment, of the creatures in question is only part of the argument which Callicott wants to give; at least some of his argument could be rewritten in other terms.

Callicott's argument is a case for the particular moral importance of the welfare of certain animals – the whales. Nonetheless this argument fits into the framework of a system of ethics which seems at bottom conservationist rather than animal-welfarist: witness Callicott's willingness to allow the hunting of species that are naturally hunted. By contrast Dale Jamieson's 'Zoos revisited', Chapter 10, is markedly closer to an animal-welfarist position than to a conservationist one (where, that is, such emphases clash in the kind of way which Rawles explores in Chapter 8). Jamieson's central contention, which he has argued before[11] and is now defending again from recent critics, is that zoos are a bad thing because there is a moral presumption against keeping animals in captivity. He writes that 'If animals have any moral standing at all then it is plausible to suppose that keeping them in captivity is presumptively wrong, since an interest in liberty is central to most morally significant creatures.'

In writing thus it is plainly the moral standing of *individual* animals with which Jamieson is primarily concerned: this is why his position is to be classified as an animal-welfarist one rather than a conservationist one. We see further consequences of this fact when he goes on to consider attempts to justify the suffering or privation of individual animals by saying that it is 'for the sake of the species', e.g. for such conservationist purposes as a captive breeding programme like that run at Jersey

Zoo in the Channel Islands:[12] he describes this plea as a sacrifice of 'the interests of the lower-case gorilla for those of the upper-case Gorilla'. Jamieson's thought is the nominalistic one that no abstraction could be as valuable as a real live, flesh-and-blood-and-black-fur gorilla. But the species *Gorilla* is just such an abstraction, and so, Jamieson concludes, those who would urge us (like Clark, or like myself) to take such 'abstract' just as seriously as real live animals are overdoing it more than a little. For him it is just a fallacy to think that we have obligations to species as well as to 'the individual animals themselves'. The fallacy in question, according to Jamieson, is that of 'attributing to species the properties of individual creatures' (though I am not sure that even such a resolute Platonist about species as Clark would recognise such a claim as a necessary part of his own position). What matters morally, for Jamieson, is what matters for Sprigge in Chapter 7: that there is something it is like to be an animal. By contrast, of course, there is nothing it is like to be a species.

Here we see again the importance to our other and more general views about the ethics of nature of our specific views about what a natural kind or species is. Jamieson's position rests upon two claims. The first is that evolutionary theory entails nominalism about species: i.e. the view that, in Darwin's words, we should look upon 'the term species, as one arbitrarily given for the sake of convenience to a set of individuals closely resembling one another'. The second claim is that, since (by the first claim) species are not metaphysically basic, neither are they ethically basic: a claim which, to say it one more time, shows how important some uses of Is can be to determining how we ought to use Ought. For Jamieson what we ought to be doing is not trying to preserve species like Gorilla, but making room on the earth for individual gorillas to flourish in the wild.

I have explored some ways in which the different essays interconnect: now it is time to allow my readers to go on to find interconnections of their own. Let me conclude simply by expressing my gratitude to my contributors, whose promptitude and creativity have made this editor's life enviably easy; and to Ms Jane Feore of Edinburgh University Press, whose enthusiasm and organisational skills have made the present volume not only possible, but actual.

T. D. J. Chappell
Manchester University
December 1996

NOTES

1. For some of these connections between philosophical outlooks and attitudes to the environment/external world, and for more reasons for thinking that the 'etymological point' is not *merely* etymological, cp. Descartes, *Discourse on the Method* Part VI: '. . . au lieu de cette philosophie spéculative, qu'on enseigne dans les écoles, on en peut trouver une pratique, par laquelle, connaissant la force & les actions du feu, de l'eau, des astres, & de tous les corps *qui nous environnent*, aussi distinctement que nous connaissons les divers métiers de nos artisans, nous les pourrions employer en mesme façon a tous les usages auxquels ils sont propres, & ainsi nous rendre *comme maîtres & possesseurs de la nature*' (emphases added). I am grateful

to John Cottingham's essay 'Medicine, virtues and consequences' (in D. Oderberg and J. Laing (eds), *Human Lives*, London. Macmillan, 1997) for drawing this passage and some of the connections it makes to my attention.

2. Bertrand Russell, *The Problems of Philosophy* (Oxford: Oxford University Press, 1967), p. 92.

3. A turn of phrase which may prompt the retort: if 'ours' then not really *reality*, and if 'reality' then not really *ours*.

4. First published in Hepburn's collection *Wonder and other essays* (Cambridge. Cambridge University Press, 1973). Extensively reprinted.

5. Gerard Manley Hopkins, 'The Wreck of the Deutschland', Part One.

6. Hume, *Dialogues concerning Natural Religion* (London, Penguin Classics, 1940), XI.

7. See Bernard Williams, *Ethics and the Limits of Philosophy* (London: Fontana, 1985), p. 117: 'Critical reflection should look for as much shared understanding as it can find on any issue, and use any ethical material that, in the context of the reflective discussion, makes some sense and commands some loyalty . . . Theory typically uses the assumption that we probably have too many ethical ideas . . . our major problem now is actually that we have not too many but too few, and we need to cherish as many as we can.'

8. Strictly speaking, in fact, Sprigge's view is that there is only one centre of sentience.

9. Animal welfarists may also protest (2) that they simply do not know what is meant by the overall good of the environment. Or they may say (3) that, even if we can know what it is, to attempt to bring about that overall good is 'playing God', a kind of cosmic presumption. (On this latter point the animal welfarists are in fact at one with certain 'deep ecologists', who hold (4) that humans are mistaken to think that they can or should try to influence or control nature, even to repair damage done to it: a view for which Jamieson's talk of 'technofixes' in Chapter 10 shows some sympathy.) Again, notice that there are standard objections to the utilitarianism which so many animal welfarists accept which are precise analogues of (2)–(4).

10. Cp. my discussion of Mary Anne Warren in Chapter 6.

11. See Dale Jamieson, 'Against zoos', in P. Singer (ed.), *In Defence of Animals* (New York. Harper & Row, 1985).

12. Are the animals in Jersey Zoo *suffering*, or undergoing privation, as a result of the zoo's captive breeding programme? Jamieson takes it that they must be, just by being in a zoo.

1

PLATONISM AND THE GODS OF PLACE

Stephen R. L. Clark

INTRODUCTION

Environmentalists and other New Age theorists commonly attack 'the Platonic
assumption' that we are and should be something separate from the living Earth.
My argument is that, on the contrary, Platonism – which is, sacramental theism – is
the best available metaphysic for an ecologically sensitive consciousness. It has been
Platonists who have most often argued for our duties toward other animals and the
rest of the living Earth, and Platonism that allows us to respect the beauties of that
Earth without imagining either that things-as-they-are are perfect as they are, or that
they exhaust the possibilities of beauty.

ICON OF EARTH

It is possible that the one lasting achievement of the late twentieth-century space race
was to photograph the Earth from orbit. That image, of a clouded, blue and silver
bubble against a darkened sky, has decorated the walls of offices and student bedrooms
ever since. A thought that had been confined to readers of science fiction infected
almost all of us – or all the 'Western world' at least. We all live within a single, beautiful
and isolated world; we are all terrestrials. The defensive strategy of Mutual Assured
Destruction was hence revealed for what it was: namely, mutual assured destruction.
Whatever our quarrels, whatever our deeply felt ideals and mutual antagonisms, we
are all children of Earth. Whatever our very human conceit may tell us of the deep
significance of *human beings*, that image warns us that we occupy a moment in Earth's
history, and in the world's. We are *all* terrestrials: and 'we' means more than humans.

The image of Earth as a single living globe coincided with another, and more
abstract, image, hitherto confined to ecomystics (and science fiction writers): the

Earth can best be conceived as a living system, sustaining itself as best it can through change and chance. Living creatures are not just a scum upon a fundamentally unliving sphere: they have so modified the Earth in which we live that everything about it (the composition of the air, the soil and water; the movement of tectonic plates; the global temperature) is created and sustained by biological processes. The Earth is the product, quite as much as the producer, of the living things (perhaps especially the bacterial things) that live within it (see Lovelock 1979, 1988). All this, for which there are some fairly convincing arguments, is made real to us (and more convincing than most arguments can be) simply by the sight of the Earth from orbit.

As Chesterton so often emphasised: we need to go away from home to be able to look back and love it. Seeing the Earth, and so ourselves, from outside, we can realise who and what we are. Thesrealisation may have come just in time. We need to understand, not merely intellectually but viscerally, that pollution cannot be contained, that 'when we spit upon the Earth, we spit upon ourselves',[1] that those who would seek luxury, or even safety, at *whatever* cost, will end by hurting everyone. This new religious movement – since 'religious' is exactly what it is – takes many forms. It is usual to decry 'traditional' or 'monotheistic' or 'Judaeo-Christian' or 'Western' religious attitudes, and to advocate instead the reinvention or rediscovery of more 'pagan' sensibilities. Celtic, Amerindian or Aboriginal mythologies are pillaged for new insights: 'the white man', we are told, neglects the Earth our Mother because he has imagined that there is another world, and that his destiny is to be redeemed from this. The 'truth', it now emerges, is that this world here, the living Earth, is all we have or need. Our duty is to care for 'her', or at the very least not to hurt her. Some such would-be pagans have begun to talk of 'stewardship';[2] most deny that human beings have any such large office. A few have become so confident of the Earth's divinity that they deny that we could even hurt her: everything we do is part of her rich pattern – and that includes industrialists and agribusiness. All are convinced that 'Platonism' and associated ideas have been our ruin. 'The Platonic assumption', so Al Gore reports, is that 'man is separate from the world of nature', that we are, or should be, 'disembodied spiritual intellect[s] hovering above the material world', and 'therefore' feeling no concern for it (Gore 1992, p. 249).[3] Just in time we found the living Earth our Mother, and simultaneously realised that 'abstract intellect' is not enough. An ecologically valuable wisdom is to be found among the 'simple', not the civilised; we learn about the Earth, and our fellow-residents, through empathetic love, not numbers.

Or as an older philosopher said:

> The land is our ancestral home and we must cherish it even more than children cherish their mother; furthermore, the Earth is a goddess and mistress of mortal men, and the gods and spirits already established in the locality must be treated with the same respect.

The thinker in question, of course, was Plato (*Laws* V.740),[4] and my concern is to show that 'Platonism' has been hopelessly misjudged.

DESPISING THIS WORLD HERE

I will confess my sympathy with much that Gore and others say. After all, I too am moved by the sight of Earth from orbit. I too find Lovelock's Gaia hypothesis scientifically persuasive and emotionally attractive – though I am unsure what ethical or political morals it supports. I too believe that present (and historical) attempts to distance ourselves from 'nature', or to claim a dignity immensely greater than we are prepared to recognise in others, are both irrational and harmful. On the other hand, I must reject the popular account of Platonism, and the Abrahamic religions (see Clark 1993a). So far from requiring us to despise, dismantle, desert or damage the real living Earth, Platonism (and the Abrahamic religions that were so strongly influenced by Platonism) require us to respect it. The very 'pagan' mythologies and practices that have been invoked to support the new religious sensibility are, in their essence, Platonic. What Chief Seattle almost certainly did not say, Neo-Platonists actually did:

> In their weariness the people of that time (so Trismegistus prophesied) will find the world nothing to wonder at or to worship. This All – good thing that never had nor has nor will have its better – will be endangered. People will find it oppressive and scorn it. They will not cherish this entire world, a work of god beyond compare, a glorious construction, a bounty composed of images in multiform variety. . . Every divine voice will grow mute in enforced silence. The fruits of the earth will rot; the soil will no more be fertile; and the very air will droop with gloomy lethargy.[5]

Confirmed Platonists have been the very people who have maintained the long tradition of reverence for matter and material things. Why have they been misinterpreted, to the point that Gore can claim (on the basis of his reading of environmentalist and other 'New Age' thinkers[6]) that Bacon 'echoes' Plato in supposing that 'human intellect could safely analyse and understand the natural world without reference to any moral principles defining our relationship and duties to both God and God's creation' (Gore 1992, p. 256)? On the contrary, Plato taught us that no one understands the world who does not see its beauty (see Clark 1995a), and that technical and moral knowledge cannot be divided. A 'good' craftsman is not just a technical expert, but one who seriously intends the 'good' of what he works on (*Republic* 1.347d ff.). A true lover seeks not to possess or to control the beloved, but to discover beauty (*Symposium*).

Briefly: to be is to be something. To be something is to embody, though perhaps ineptly, some one form of the many forms which shape, or are shaped in, the mosaic of the divine intellect. Every individual thing, that is, is a more or less distorted embodiment or reflection of that intellect. 'The realities we see are like shadows of all that is God. The reality we see is as unreal compared to the reality in God as a coloured photograph compared to what it represents . . . This whole world is full of shadows' (Cardenal 1974, pp. 83, 99). For everything, the something that it ought to be, by which it is measured, is what it is, in a sense, already. Things as they are are neither wholly what they should and must be (as the Stoics said) nor wholly disconnected from what should be (as modernist divisions between Fact and Value must imply). We best understand things when we see what form of beauty it is that they are aiming (or are aimed) at. Correspondingly, no one can be a genuine expert in any craft who lacks the wisdom to see what really is of benefit: which is to say, what really is worth admiring.

How 'beautiful' the world is, and where that beauty lies, have certainly been matters for dispute. Burnet, writing in his *Sacred Theory* in 1691 suggests that earth and moon alike 'are both . . . the image or picture of a great Ruine, and have the true aspect of a World lying in its rubbish' (Burnet 1965, p. 91): a few years later even ruins and rubbish dumps were regarded with respect, not merely because they might remind us of the unshattered whole, but because, in their ruinous condition, they revealed fresh 'beauties' or 'sublimities'. The Beautiful and the Sublime are different, it is said: Beauty lies in the world of human, humane order, and the Sublime in the wild woods and mountains that owe us no obedience. But Platonists may doubt the distinction. The greatest of late antique philosophers, Plotinus, did not equate the beautiful with the tame and orderly, but with the forms of life, no one of which was sufficient to represent Beauty Itself (see *Ennead* I.6.37 f.) – on which, more hereafter.

The charge against Platonists, that they 'despise the world', is rather like the charge against another, related sect of philosophers, that Stoics despise 'feeling'. Platonists and Stoics together are supposed to praise a cold, unfeeling intellectualism, and to believe that 'wise men' (it is significant that 'wise men' and 'wise women' are, traditionally, rather different sorts of thing) have no interest in material affairs. The charge is unjust, but it is worth noticing that the same charge is made against Platonists, who supposedly divided the material or the experienced world from the real or intellectual world, and against the Stoics, who said that only bodies had any causal powers at all, and that human beings were ineradicably part of the one world. The Stoics, not the Platonists, insisted that non-human animals were merely means,[7] though they agreed with Plato that 'the world does not exist for the sake of man, but man for its sake'.[8] Our metaphysical assumptions may influence our moral and political beliefs, but there is no simple relationship of the kind some New Age thinkers see. Spinoza and the Stoics were monists, and scornful of the interests of animals. Plato and his followers were – in a way – dualists (though not Cartesian dualists), and deeply respectful of the earth and all its residents. In his rejection of the interests of animals Augustine was influenced by the Stoics, not by Plato. Until this century, the one substantial work by a 'professional philosopher' in defence of the non-human was by a Platonist (namely, Porphyry's *On Abstinence from Eating Flesh*).[9] The Stranger, presumably with Plato's approval, mocks the simple division between Human and Non-Human (*Politicus* 263c ff.). Humans may have distinctive traits, but 'non-humans' no more identifies a genuine class than 'non-umbrellas'. Meat-eating, for Plato and for Platonists, as well as for the author of the Book of Genesis, is a later corruption of an earlier, saner habit.

The Stoics had a bad effect on Western attitudes to animals, though they did little more than offer poor excuses for what people were doing anyway. So also did Descartes. But even if (as I believe) they were entirely wrong in what they said of animals (roughly: that they had no minds, and didn't matter), neither Stoics nor Descartes should be blamed for everything. So far from thinking that we were wholly separate from the world, Descartes wrote as follows:

> Though each of us is a person distinct from others whose interests are accordingly in some way different from those of the rest of the world, we must still think that none of us could subsist alone and each one of us is really one of the many parts of the universe, and more particularly a part of the earth, the state, the society, the family to which we belong by our domicile, our oath of allegiance and our birth. (Descartes 1970, p. 172)

Stoics similarly urged us to remember who we were: family members, fellow citizens, fellow human beings (Epictetus, *Discourses* 2.10: Long and Sedley 1987, I, p. 364 (59Q)). And so far from urging us to be 'unfeeling', they insisted that 'feeling', especially the feeling of 'belonging', was the root of decency.

Cicero, speaking for the Stoics and for many another philosopher, declared that it took an arrogant lunacy to imagine that human beings were the best or most important things there were.[10] It was the magnificently ordered cosmos itself, filled with an enormous variety of beauties, that deserved our chief attention. Kim Stanley Robinson, devising arguments against the terraforming of Mars, states: 'We are not lords of the universe. We're one small part of it. We may be its consciousness, but being the consciousness of the universe does not mean turning it all into a mirror image of us. It means rather fitting into it as it is, and worshipping it with our attention' (Robinson 1993, p. 214). The speech is Stoic in its inspiration. As they said: 'The end is living in agreement with nature' (Long and Sedley 1987, I, p. 394ff. (63)).

In brief, even Cartesian dualism or Stoic rationalism did not have quite the moral implications now imputed to them. All such traditional philosophers would be likely to agree that 'material goods' were relatively unimportant. This was not offered as an excuse for looting them, but (precisely) for managing without them. It has been simple greed, not philosophical detachment, that has poisoned earth, air and water, and inflicted pain and death on animals of our own and other species. Philosophers, as Epictetus saw them, put aside their personal advantage, and struggle to see things as they really are. Maybe they 'despise material things': but if they do, they do not simultaneously seek them out. No one could sensibly conclude that *we* despise material things: our problem is that we all want them far too much, at far too great a cost. The best and original city, so Plato taught, was 'the city of pigs' (so-called), in which people had simple tastes that could be satisfied locally, and without embarking on a military adventure (see Clark 1995c).

However ridiculous, the confusion has been with us for centuries. 'Vegetarians' have (often simultaneously) been accused of Manichaean distaste for bodily realities, and anti-nomian delight in such bodily functions as the animals enjoyed. Sympathising with 'animals' to the extent of not wishing to deprive them of lives that they found good betrayed a sneaking wish to live an 'animal' life. Abstaining from flesh-foods betrayed a wish to be dissociated from the natural order, a wish to be something more than 'animal'. Orthodox opinion demanded simultaneously that we despise non-human animals and appreciate their flesh.

'Love', as Aristotle pointed out, is an ambiguous term. Those who 'love' wine do not therefore wish it well, but that they should drink it (*Nicomachean Ethics* 8.1159b 29 ff). All too often 'loving' something means only that we wish to keep or caress or eat it. 'Befriending' it means something rather different. Kings make tools or organs of their 'friends' – and for that very reason have no 'friends' at all (Aristotle, *Politics* 3.1287b 29 ff.; see 1.1253b 28 ff.). Conversely, those who truly befriend another are prepared to let that other be, and seem 'unloving' only to those who do not understand. So the instruction, common to Platonists and Stoics alike, that we should be 'detached' from our material concerns is quite compatible with being 'friends' of the embodied beings we would otherwise make use of. Followers of Aphrodite Pandemos, in Plato's allegorical interpretation, desire to possess the object of their passion. Followers of Aphrodite Ouranios are transformed by the beauty that they see, and wish their friends the same. What is to be despised is not the bodily being we would befriend, but our own bodily desire which will, if we allow it, destroy or hurt our 'friend'. 'Sexual love is an effort to gain friendship resulting from the appearance of beauty; and it is not directed at intercourse, but at friendship', at any rate if one is wise (Diogenes Laertius, *Lives of the Philosophers* 7.130)![11] To the unwise (which is all of us almost all the time) the wise will *seem* unfeeling.

Consider the official who came to Epictetus for advice on family matters, notably that 'when [his] daughter was ill and was thought to be in danger [he] could not bear to be near her, but fled away from her, until someone brought [him] news that she was well' (Epictetus, *Discourses* 1.11). So great was his family affection! Epictetus has no difficulty demonstrating to this (literally) *pathetic* parent that a genuine affection would not thus leave its object 'desolate and helpless'. Genuine feeling is at one with reason, and directed to the real good of its object: 'feelings' of the other kind we should control.

> It may be that vice, depravity and crime are nearly always, or even perhaps always, in their essence, attempts to eat beauty, to eat what we should only look at . . . If [Eve] caused humanity to be lost by eating the fruit, the opposite attitude, looking at the fruit without eating it, should be what is required to save it. (Weil 1959, p. 121)

Someone who wishes only to make use of a landscape, plant or animal is missing its main use, which is simply to be appreciated as it is. It is the wise who truly own the world, the Stoics said, because it is they who see it as the gods do: 'He is the true possessor of a thing who enjoys it and not he that owns it without the enjoyment of it.'[12] In a more romantic century Berkeley could insist that the world of sense experience, 'that purple sky, those wild but sweet notes of birds, the fragrant bloom upon the trees and flowers, the gentle influence of the rising sun . . . and a thousand nameless beauties of nature inspire the soul with secret transports.'[13] Maybe Berkeley delighted more in the phenomena than the ancients did: their admiration was rather for the beauty of form than of appearance. But they shared the notion that such admiration was appropriate, and different from instrumental reason.

TYPES AND PARTICULARS

But surely Plato wants us to admire the Type, not the Particular: Beauty itself rather than this beautiful boy or that beautiful landscape? A love so abstract cannot concern itself with details. What does it matter, to a Platonist, that landscapes change or species perish? They were only vehicles or reminders of an imperishable beauty, and our task is to remember *that*. A Platonic lover does not wish to possess individuals – but only because he wishes to possess, and so to become, the Form that briefly animated them. Once that is done, he can discard the individuals who first reminded him.

Platonic Love, it has been argued, is not directed at individual persons, or individual places. It is the Type that matters, not the Token. Worse still, the Type does not depend on Tokens for its being: dodos may perish, not the Dodo. If it is the Dodo only that deserves our love, then we don't need dodos. If it is Virtue alone that deserves our praise, then we don't need virtuous persons (especially if no one's *really* virtuous). It may seem to follow that Platonists have damaged the environment after all: people who don't mind about the everyday particulars, the tokens, because the type is everlasting do great damage.

To this there are three responses: first, to insist that a decent and reliable environmentalism is indeed concerned for types, not tokens; second, to point out that what we call 'individuals' are types as well; and third, to observe that loving beauty (and so wishing to be beautiful) precisely requires us to live 'in beauty', and never make things worse.

First: in praise of types. There is something offensive, to a 'modern' environmentalist sensibility, about destroying species (even though almost all the species there have ever been are now extinct, and have left no descendants). Killing the last passenger pigeon or cutting down the last *Sequioa sempervivens* is reckoned wrong even by those who do not object to killing common pigeons or cutting down some common shrub. A species, in the modern scientific sense, is only a reproductively isolated population of possibly dissimilar beings. But the popular idea of a species is of a set of creatures that variously embody a significant type. Maybe, in principle, the very same type could be embodied, in the future, in creatures of a different descent, but this is vanishingly unlikely. Once the dodo population is sufficiently depleted, there will never again be dodos: that special form of life will never appear again, and the world, to that extent, will be the poorer.

Even people unconcerned with species show a similar devotion to the type. Every particular thing, to be at all, has to be *something*, and so some *sort* of thing. Every particular thing is reckoned more or less defective, damaged, diseased by the degree it varies from the imagined *type*. Some moralists may manage to admire each single thing for what it, singly, is (or should be), as though – like Aquinas's angels – each of us was a species. Most of us, though conscious that there is no single idea of (say) human perfection, and therefore no one who is what any *human* should be, will nonetheless assess each other by how far we manage to approximate to some reasonable notion of perfection. Perfect pigs, horses, pine trees are not much easier to define, but we still insist on recognising some such things as being genuinely imperfect, as having been damaged by acid rain or mineral deficiencies or viral infections.

It may be true that Platonists believe that all such types are timeless, and so impervious to change or loss. That is really what we all believe, if we believe in types at all. If it were not true that there was a timeless type that its examples variously and defectively embody, we would be compelled to agree that every single thing is perfectly, exactly, what it 'is': there would be nothing over and above the mere empirical reality. It is because some tokens stray too far from 'their' defining type that we can see their failings. If the type were not impervious to change, then changes in the tokens could not be measured against anything but the commoner, accidental pattern of whatever 'tokens' were being surveyed together. Platonists merely agree in principle to what we all assume in practice. It does not follow that they need not regret the loss of some great type. The material world exists to embody form, and exists because it does. It is precisely because things here *ought* to embody form that the loss of any such successful form must be an occasion for regret, even if we may believe that other forms remain or will return. Admiring virtue, exactly, requires us to wish virtue to be embodied; admiring the Dodo (for example) requires us to regret its absence (perhaps its untimely absence).

> Asking myself why I approved the beauty of bodies, whether heavenly or earthly, and what resource I had for making a consistent judgement on mutable things and saying 'This ought to be so, and that ought not to be so' – asking myself, then, why I made these judgements, I discovered the unchanging and true eternity of truth above my mutable mind.[14]

Actually, even the loss – to us – of some great form may be endured. We need not suppose that all forms must be always present in the world: forms that may be eternally compresent in *eternity* may not be compatible with each other here below. If there were ever to be large mammals, the period of the dinosaurs must pass; if our children are ever to have a time to work with, we must die. The real problem for the environmentally conscious is that so many forms are being lost that the whole terrestrial biosphere is losing necessary forms – like a painting deprived of common pigments, shapes or textures. Among such necessary items are ones that, on their own, we might dislike: it does not follow that the world can gladly live without them. The most beautiful world is one that best embodies the whole range of types, or the largest compossible set of them. A depleted world is a defective mirror of the timeless types. Plato does not blame the deforestation of Attica on human action (*Critias* 111c): it is still a loss.

Does it follow that Platonists and modern environmentalists agree in their contempt for 'mere' individuals? If only the survival of a species, or the 'integrity of a biosphere', concerns us, it seems to follow that any number of 'individuals' can be sacrificed for the greater good of the whole. If what 'really matters' is only what I have in common with all other humans (or worse still, only what I do not have in common, and thereby mark myself as ill or damaged or distraught), then my own individual survival does not really matter. There will be plenty more to show off their humanity, and do it better.

But here too a Platonist may disagree: granted that my humanity is something that I share with many; granted even that there may be better examples, better tokens, of that type. But 'my' being one and the same creature from one moment to another is just as much a matter of form or type. 'Stephen' is the name of an embodied type as easily as 'Human'. There are certainly 'forms of individuals', since there is no sense in reckoning that there are individuals at all, except imaginary point-particulars, if there are no ways of being 'the same' at different times and places. It follows that a Platonist, admiring types, can also admire individuals: individuals *are* types. It is a loss to the world, even if true believers in reincarnation may doubt that it is a permanent loss, when any individual dies. To die is to depart from here. Once again: without a definite type it makes no sense even to think that someone really is departed. All that happens, on that account, is that 'we' are not counting things together as we once did. The decision not to do so is, exactly, arbitrary. And once again, it may be the *untimely* departure that we most regret.

It is commonly believed – by Gore, for example – that 'the World of Forms' is somewhere else than 'here'. Looking away from the particulars the philosopher catches sight of something far more beautiful, more real. There is perhaps some truth in this description, as there is also truth in the claim that natural historians (in antiquity and the Middle Ages) were interested only in such details as could be given an anagogical or moralising gloss (see Clark 1995a). But this is not because Plato and his followers were strictly 'dualists': there is only one real world, refracted and distorted by our sense. The separation or dissociation that Plotinus, for example, asks of us is not, of course, 'a journey for the feet' (*Enneads* I.6.8.23–5): the Other World is not a place apart from Here, beyond the moon or past the vault of heaven. 'If you are looking for the place where the soul is [once it has left the body], you must look for the place where [substance and reality and the divine] are; but in looking you must not look for it with your eyes or in the way you look for bodies' (*Enneads* IV.3.24.27–29). Our senses tell us that we are each the centre of the universe, that what is sensually (even more than sensibly) present to us is most real, that there are weeds, pests, pets and useful tools all round us. 'The world of my daily doings is a world structured by my active presence, and unintelligible it seems without it . . . The most powerful realisation that stands out in the dusk is that *all this is not so*' (Kohak 1984, pp. 73; see Clark 1991, pp. 218 f.). Opening the eyes of our intellect we can be brought to see that the world is not entirely ours, not bounded by our needs and likings, not what *seems* to be. 'Looking away' is not turning from one real, inferior thing to another, superior thing: it is remembering the real world that explains and is reflected in the egocentric illusion.

Again: the more we concentrate on what is 'merely particular' the closer we are to nothing much at all. 'Matter' conceived as something without form is nothing. All the matter that we actually confront is form (Plotinus, *Enneads* V.8.7.23). To see clearly we need to see the form embodied or reflected or refracted in the world. To perceive the world truly is like catching sight of the complete picture from myriad reflections in a broken mirror. Lacking enough reflections to construct the whole we lose sight of truth. Gazing only at the different reflections, as if they were independently real, we are as misled. To see the world clearly, and to see it whole, is to be aware of the Unseen from which the Visible takes shape: the whole set of forms from which those visible here-now (both species-forms embodied in many instances at a time, and individual-forms embodied in many occasions over time) are just a selection. The Visible World, once properly conceived, is a reflection, a segment, a suggestion of the Unseen Whole. We do not see it right until we see that what is here-now is something timelessly real, the same in many different times and places, Seen and Unseen.

So Platonists won't regret any one type's invisibility? Like the Stoic sage, they will not quite 'regret' it, will not wish the world was quite unlike its actual reality (and every species and individual a permanent entity, in time). But Platonists are much more likely than the Stoic sage to recognise the real presence of such timeless types, and to hope that the world here-now will carry on reflecting the Unseen. Platonists, so far from *not* being concerned for individuals, are almost the only philosophers to believe that there are real *individuals* to love at all.

'A GIANT OUT OF THE DESERT'

So Stoic 'apatheia', Platonic 'detachment' and 'the theory of Forms' have all been misunderstood. Their object is to perfect love, not to despise it. Everything that we ordinarily imagine to be 'real' is no more than a dream, a reflection, or (as Socrates proposes in the *Phaedo*) a puddle on the surface of the real world. This is a recognition vital to environmentalists. As long as we are persuaded that the world we ordinarily see is all the truth we need, we shall simply disbelieve all warnings of its imminent collapse. Even though we know very well that our present situation (here in 1996, in the developed West) is utterly unlike the world of even fifty years ago, or worlds just round the corner, we can hardly help assuming that our present state is final. Obviously, we just *can't* run out of water, fuel or food: change is usually so slow, and our memories so manipulable, that the present state, whatever it may be, seems to have been here for ever. Knowing, or feebly repeating, that this is untrue has very little effect. Reminding ourselves continually of past or distant danger may be a necessary discipline – but one just as likely to leave our lives unchanged.[15]

Those who deny or forget the existence of a real world different from what we choose to say and see are wholly vulnerable to manipulation.

> It appeared there had even been demonstrations to thank Big Brother for raising the chocolate ration to twenty grammes a week. And only yesterday, he reflected, it had been announced that the ration was to be *reduced* to twenty grammes a week. Was it possible that they could swallow that, after only twenty-four hours? Yes, they swallowed it. (Orwell 1954, p. 50; see Clark 1992)

Should true philosophers insist that they are cosmopolitans, citizens only of the one world-city, having no allegiance to particular persons, places or societies? Neither this person here (namely, Stephen) nor any of its personal connections has any greater standing in the world than any other creature. That is an axiom of any reasonable science, as much as any reasonable ethics. 'For those who wake there is one common world, but sleepers are turned aside to their own private one' (Heraclitus 22B89 in

Diels and Krantz 1994; see Clark 1991, p. 51). The catch in such a programme is that attempts to realise it are almost always hypocritical. The claim to speak for the one world, to have the only rational account of things, turns out to be a cover for some one, very particular, vision. Imperialists imagine that the worlds of those they conquer are in obvious error. The one true way of looking at things turns out to be identical with the prejudices of an arrogantly educated class (see Clark 1995b). 'What every sensible person thinks' turns out to be what nanny thought or taught. The 'superstitious' boundaries or rituals or taboos of native cultures are habitually displaced by 'bureaucratic' boundaries or rituals or taboos at least as idiosyncratic. Looking toward the 'grand picture' would-be rationalists neglect important detail, and their own follies.

It is accordingly unsurprising that environmentalists are often very suspicious even of the 'ecologically educated' dictats authorised by Rio, the World Bank, Exxon or publically funded scientists. What sound to their originators like sound reasons may be only artfully disguised aggrandisement. If there were Platonic philosopher-kings to guide us, who would not follow them? It does not follow that good Platonists should follow anyone who thinks himself or herself such a ruler. If someone really knew how the world worked (or even this little bit of the one world, the Earth) then he or she might reasonably lay out a programme for world health, might be the 'geophysician' of Lovelock's dream. In the absence of any convincing reason to believe even that anyone who had such knowledge would make such decrees, and still less that anyone who claims it actually has it, we may 'reasonably' prefer more 'bioregional' approaches. Think globally, the saying goes: act locally[16]. Chesterton understood the Crusades as a defence of the mystery of locality, incarnation, art against 'a devouring giant out of the deserts to whom all places were the same', 'a quarrel between one man who wanted [Jerusalem] and another man who could not see why it was wanted' (1917, p. 64 f.). The charge against *Islam* is unjust, except that in those centuries it was the Muslim world (as it is now the Western) that was the most threatening of imperial, 'civilised' powers. Those Muslims who now denounce the Great Satan do precisely what European Christians did in denouncing 'Mahound', and perhaps with as good a cause.

Can such attachments to localities, and even such neglect of global strategies proposed by would-be global agencies, be part of a properly Platonic programme? Why not? 'The land is our ancestral home and we must cherish it even more than children cherish their mother; furthermore, the Earth is a goddess and mistress of mortal men, and the gods and spirits already established in the locality must be treated with the same respect.' Or as another Platonist insisted: 'When Jacob woke out of his dream, he said, "God is here, and I wist it not. How dreadful is this place! This is none other than the House of God, and the Gate of Heaven"' (Traherne I.31: 1960, p. 15).

Abbot Suger, speaking of the rebuilt abbey of St Denis in the early thirteenth century, said that in it he saw himself 'dwelling in some strange region of the universe which neither exists entirely in the slime of the earth nor entirely in the purity of heaven' – a place between (Panofsky 1946, p. 65). In this he echoed common responses to the Church of Hagia Sophia in Byzantium, and added another 'holy place' to the list.

> There is a geography of the holy places, the places where the saints have dwelt, Oxford and Athos, Canterbury and Cernica, St David's and Zagorsk; places whose beauty has been revealed by lives which have been open to God in such a way as to show that this world is not a system closed upon itself. (Allchin 1978, p. 20 ff.; see Clark 1986, MacCormack 1990)

The fully opened eye may detect that beauty anywhere. Even those still half asleep can recognise a beauty that must not be desecrated in such places, and in the whole Earth seen from far away.

IMAGINING THE REAL WORLD

'For Platonism, the world is valuable because it can remind us of higher realities. In the sufism of Kemani and Iraqi, the world is valuable because it can be irradiated by the divine oneness' (Wilson 1988, p. 119). But this too is to misinterpret Plato. The divine oneness, the Good, irradiates the world: the world, in all its manifold types, is the expression of that Good, not some other real thing from which we turn away. Travelling toward the One is not, as Plotinus taught us, 'a journey for the feet', but an alteration of our attitude. Nor is that alteration a matter of intellectualising, mathematising, abstracting a mere diagram, as Blake supposed was meant: we see the world most truly when we see it like Traherne: 'It is the place of Angels and the Gate of Heaven.'

Plato's Socrates declares (*Phaedrus* 230) that he has no interest in the land outside the city walls because 'the people in the city have something to teach [him], but the fields and the trees won't teach [him] anything'. It is perhaps surprising that readers take this for the truth: Plato's Socrates is always telling lies (or speaking with Socratic irony), especially about his wish to learn something from the people he talks to. So far from being unacquainted with the country, and dependent, as he mockingly insists, on Phaedrus as a guide (*Phaedrus* 230), Socrates has already corrected him on the exact location of a legendary abduction (*Phaedrus* 229). In the dialogue that follows Socrates claims quite the opposite, that it is from 'the stream and shrine of the Nymphs' that he has received an important message (*Phaedrus* 278). 'The priests in the sanctuary of Zeus at Dodona declared that the earliest oracles came from an oak tree, and the men of their time, who lacked [Phaedrus's] modern sophistication, were simple-minded enough to be quite satisfied with messages from an oak or a rock if only they were true' (*Phaedrus* 275). It is not from carefully composed speeches that we learn the truth, but from the silent inspiration of nature (see *Phaedrus* 238), from the hieratic shapes that arise in our imaginative reason[17].

The question is, of course: what nature? The nature that Socrates encounters in this dialogue is one suffused with stories: there Boreas abducted Oreithyia; here the cicadas are the Muses' messengers. Pundits may 'rationalise' the legends, interpreting them as laboured metaphors for 'natural' events: the north wind (Boreas) blew Oreithyia off the rocks. 'But though I find such explanations very attractive, they are too ingenious and laboured' (*Phaedrus* 229). Socrates declares that he has no time for this, because he can find 'more complicated and puffed-up sort[s] of animal than Typho' (*Phaedrus* 230) in his soul. We have been writing our stories into the world of natural events for as long as we have been human, and those stories – often enough – are about our characters and motives. The landscape we inhabit is one constructed by the human imagination: literally so in that no part of the globe is unaffected by our actions, and metaphorically in that the land embodies historical and personal memories (see Schama 1995), ghosts and fancies.

The Enlightenment endeavour has, of course, been to exclude all figments from our picture of the 'real world'. So Thomas Sprat:[18]

> The poets of old to make all things look more venerable than they were, devised a thousand false Chimaeras; on every Field, River, Grove and Cave they bestowed a Fantasm of their own making: With these they amazed the world . . . And in the modern Ages these Fantastical Forms were reviv'd and possessed Christendom . . . All which abuses if those acute Philosophers did not promote, yet they were never able to overcome; nay, not even so much as King Oberon and his invisible Army.
>
> But from the time in which the Real Philosophy has appear'd there is scarce any whisper remaining of such horrors . . . The cours of things goes quietly along, in its own true channel of Natural Causes and Effects. For this we are beholden to Experiments; which though they have not yet completed the discovery of the true world, yet they have already vanquished those wild inhabitants of the false world, that us'd to astonish the minds of men.

It is this endeavour that has ended by convincing some enquirers[19] that the mind itself is a figment: true causes are to be discovered only among the so-called 'primary qualities' of matter. But such qualities, by hypothesis, cannot explain the real existence of the 'secondary qualities', still less such aspects of the really experienced world as values, identities or subjective feelings. Either such things don't exist – and the words that seem to represent this thought are themselves mere phantoms – or they are uncaused and ineffective epiphenomena.

But though the Enlightenment project is on the verge of self-destruction it remains a noble one: to put aside our prejudice, cut the world at its true joints and stop pretending that we know exactly what 'the purpose' of the world might be. It would be sheer romanticism to imagine that those who spoke of Naiads, Dryads, Oreads and the army of King Oberon were kinder to the natural world than those who abjured them. Spinoza regards anthropocentrism (the belief that everything was made for our welfare) as completely ridiculous (see *Ethics*, Part I Appendix)). Once again, this has been a consistent message from later Platonists as well.[20] Descartes is devoted to a God wholly beyond his comprehension, whose acts and motives are similarly incomprehensible. Though it was 'a good and pious thought', he said, 'to believe that God created all things for us' it is in no way likely that God had no other purpose in creating them (*Principles of Philosophy* Part 3.3). 'We shall entirely reject from our

Philosophy the search for final causes; because we ought not to presume so much of ourselves as to think we are the confidants of His intentions' (*Principles* Part 1.28). In that sense, Plato was indeed an 'enlightenment philosopher', because he desired Truth rather than Appearance, Nature rather than Artifice, and denied that we could easily identify the Good which was the final explanation of the world's existence simply with *our* good. Where he differed from the later effort founded on the Democritean suggestion that there was nothing real but 'atoms and the void' was in believing that it was Beauty which should be uncovered.

Democritus proposed, apparently, that there was nothing real but atoms and the void, and that the truth lay hidden in the depths. But he also acknowledged the absurdity of rejecting the appearances on which our rational grasp of any hidden truth was founded. Truth may, paradoxically, be hidden, but it can also be disclosed: 'paradoxically', because the word for 'truth' (*aletheia*) is punningly related to 'what does not stay unnoticed' (*a-lanthanei*).[21] It is sometimes important to practise an intellectual discipline which attends only to a world of 'primary qualities', unaffected by our own sensual markers, sentiments and self-serving understandings. That discipline should leave us free to acknowledge the independent value of the world we see with the eyes of intellect. The unfortunate effect has sometimes been, instead, to deny all value to that 'objective world', and hence make it available for any use at all. But the very point of seeing past our senses, past our sentiments and easy egotism was to discover something of far greater value. If the objective world is not worth admiring it is not worth knowing either.

But we need not suppose that there is quite so great a contrast between the 'real world' and the world of story. What matters is that we distinguish what we do seriously, and what we do as diversion: 'Would a sensible farmer take seed which he valued and wishes to produce a crop, and sow it in sober earnest in gardens of Adonis at midsummer, and take pleasure in seeing it reach its full perfection in eight days?' (*Phaedrus* 276)[22]. The stories which animate the world of our experience (and which now include, of course, the results of several centuries of scientific thought) have often revealed, exactly, that that world is not ours alone. Even the landscape around Athens where Phaedrus goes for walks is not wholly tame: the wind from nowhere can sweep people far away; the sound of the cicadas reaches out into a world of story having nothing much to do with fashionable plans. When Wittgenstein demanded that we 'remember that the spirit of the snake, of the lion, is [our] spirit' (Wittgenstein 1961: 20 October 1916), he spoke from within a long, unduly romantic tradition. The actual spirit of the snake and lion is certainly not ours, but even the spirit of those creatures as it is revealed in story is not ours: on the contrary, the story snakes and lions are there to show us something not ourselves, and something well worth loving. 'In nothing is the modern German more modern, or more mad', said Chesterton, 'than in his dream of finding a German word for everything; eating his language, or in other words biting his tongue. And in nothing were the mediaevals more free and sane than in their acceptance of names and emblems from outside their most beloved limits' (1917, 59).[23]

The question still remains: how much of our immediate sensibility should we renounce? The world we at first encounter is one animated by human stories, built round human needs. The Enlightenment endeavour is not necessarily a bad one: to be aware instead that Things have their own principles, and that to understand them is also to appreciate them. The theoretician contemplates a truth, and – specifically – a truth that is worth contemplating, because it is beautiful. The theoretician, in brief, sees beauty, and may do so, Aristotle assured us, on the word of Heraclitus, in the most trivial-seeming circumstances (see Clark 1993b). The relevant passage, from his *Parts of Animals*, is regularly quoted by working scientists (almost, indeed, the only passage of Aristotle that some scientists seem to have read, though this does not stop them abusing him), and can stand another citation:

> We must avoid a childish distaste for examining the less valued animals. For in all natural things there is something wonderful. And just as Heraclitus is said to have spoken to the visitors, who were wanting to meet him but stopped as they were approaching when they saw him warming himself at the oven – he kept telling them to come in and not worry 'for there are gods here too' – so we should approach the inquiry about each animal without aversion, knowing that in all of them there is something natural and beautiful.[24]

There is an echo, doubtless deliberate, in Claude Bernard's more sinister observation about 'the science of life [as] a superb and dazzlingly lighted hall which may be reached only by passing through a long and ghastly kitchen'.[25] Bernard missed Aristotle's point, that there was a real, discoverable beauty in the most trivial or even immediately disgusting things: a beauty to be acknowledged, even worshipped, and not torn apart to add a little detailed 'knowledge' to the library. What matters to the kind of philosopher that Plato, Aristotle and many others praised is to fill her soul with the sight of beauty. There is another kind, whose aim is to master beauty, to remove its challenge by getting it in our power, by showing or pretending to show that it is nothing very special, by 'eating' it. Reductionist science of the kind that explains medium-sized objects and events by showing them to be the mathematical results of microscopic objects and events need not have that reductionist effect of eliminating beauty. In fact, the reduction usually depends for its plausibility on the amazing beauty of the microscopic universe revealed as underpinning the universe of our immediate experience.[26] But it may be that some such scientists really believe what is often said, that there is no 'real beauty' out there in the world, that it is only a projection of our aesthetic appetite upon a literally unmeaning realm of matter in directionless motion. What value there is in discovering such a 'truth' is more than I have ever seen, unless it is the familiar effort of the tailless fox to persuade his fellows that they would be better off de-tailed.

If there were no beauty to be discerned in nature it would not be worth discovering this. 'The scientist does not study nature because it is useful; he studies it because he delights in it, and he delights in it because it is beautiful. If nature were not beautiful, it would not be worth knowing, and if nature were not worth knowing, life would not be worth living'.[27] If nature were not beautiful, it would not even be possible to know it: as I remarked above, scientific theories about the unseen structure or forgotten past depend on our recognition of the subtle beauty of the mechanism involved. If there is no real beauty it is absurd to think one theory is more veridical because it is more beautiful. But the truth to which great scientists have testified is that Beauty is their firmest guide to truth: 'It is indeed an incredible fact that what the human mind, at its best and most profound, perceives as beautiful finds its realization in external nature' (Chandrasekhar 1987, 66).

This recognition is certainly not easy.

> We live in a world of unreality and dreams. To give up our imaginary position as the centre, to renounce it, not only intellectually but in the imaginative part of our soul, that means to awaken to what is real and eternal, to see the true light and hear the true silence. A transformation then takes place at the very roots of our sensibility, in our immediate reception of sense impressions and psychological impressions. It is a transformation analogous to that which takes place in the dusk of evening on a road, where we suddenly discern as a tree what we had at first seen as a stooping man; or where we suddenly recognise as a rustling of leaves what we thought at first was whispering voices. We see the same colours, we hear the same sounds, but not in the same way. To empty ourselves of our false divinity, to deny ourselves, to give up being the centre of the world in imagination, to discern that all points in the world are equally centres and that the true centre is outside the world, this is to consent to the rule of mechanical necessity in matter and of free choice at the centre of each soul. Such consent is love. The face of this love which is turned towards thinking persons is the love of our neighbour: the face turned towards matter is love of the order of the world, or of the beauty of the world which is the same thing. (Weil 1959, 115).

Weil's account, and Plato's, is an improvement on an undiluted Stoicism. For the Stoic sage there is nothing to be regretted or repented: all happens exactly as divine providence requires, even our most serious-seeming errors. There is no ideal to fall away from: the actual facts are the only and unique ideal. But for that very reason, so their opponents reasonably said, they can have no grounds for criticising anything.

> Let us suppose we are confronted with a desperate thing – say Pimlico. If we think what is really best for Pimlico we shall find the thread of thought that leads to the throne of the mystic and the arbitrary. It is not enough for a man to disapprove of Pimlico: in that case he will merely cut his throat or move to Chelsea. Nor, certainly, is it enough for a man to approve of Pimlico: for then it will remain Pimlico, which would be awful. The only way out of it seems to be for somebody to love Pimlico: to love it with a transcendental tie and without any earthly reason. If there arose a man who loved Pimlico, then Pimlico would rise into ivory towers and golden pinnacles; Pimlico would attire herself as a woman does when she is loved. (Chesterton 1961, 66).[28]

What is required, in fact, is Platonism: we know a thing best when we love it best, and (loving it) desire it to be that perfect thing, itself, the thing that it shall be. Whether we should also accept the epistemological implications of the Platonic or the Hermetic tradition is another story.[29]

NOTES

1. As Chief Seattle almost certainly did *not* say: see Callicott (1989, p. 204).
2. A term characteristically adopted by those who wish to feel superior to old-style exploiters but do not wish to make any radical changes in their way of life: 'stewards' are apparently licensed to cull, imprison and discipline quite as vigorously as despots.
3. Gore is certainly not the only writer to make this charge: see Ruether (1992), LaChapelle (1988).
4. The translation in Trevor Saunders (1970, p. 208): it could be argued that the goddess in question is not strictly Earth, but rather the land in which Plato's Stranger has, in imagination, placed his new city. It is difficult to see how one could seriously respect such a land and not respect the geological processes that sustain it alongside other, neighbouring lands. Conversely, respecting 'the Earth' may well involve us in loving our locality: 'God gave all men all earth to love,/ but since our hearts are small,/ ordained for each one spot should prove/ belovèd over all' (Kipling 1927, p. 211).
5. *Asclepius* (25): Copenhaver (1992, p. 82). Compare the speech attributed to Chief Seattle 'by one Ted Parry as a film script for a movie called "Home" produced by the Southern Baptist Convention in 1971–2' (Callicott 1989, p. 204).
6. Gore (1992, p. 385) suggests that his information comes from conversations between scientists and religious leaders, together with the works of Paul O. Kristeller.
7. See Cicero, *On Ends* (3.6 ff.): Long and Sedley (1987, Vol. 1, pp. 348 ff. (57F)). The remark regularly cited from Aristotle (*Politics* 1.1256b 15 ff.), that plants are 'for' animals, and animals 'for' human beings, also misrepresents Aristotle's view (which is that there is beauty to be admired in every living thing, however 'base' it seems (*De Partibus Animalium* 1.645a 15 ff.: see below), and that human beings are certainly not the best or most important creatures in the world).
8. Plato, *Laws* (903cd): Saunders (1970, p. 437).
9. Which casts grave doubt on Johnson's claim that Plato or his followers believed that 'the natural function of animals was to be ruled by rational beings, humans, and to serve their interests' (Johnson 1991, p. 13). On the contrary, true rulers, by Plato's account, always look to the interests of those they rule, and 'animals' are not, as a class, our subjects.
10. Cicero, *On the Nature of the Gods* (2.16); see Aristotle, *Nicomachean Ethics* (6.1141a 20 ff.).
11. 'Those who delight in the sexual charms of boys in bloom' should resist the attraction, so Xenophon (*Memorabilia* 2.6.22) says Socrates declared, 'in order to cause no distress to those who should be spared it'. *Pace* Vlastos (1991, pp. 38 ff. I do not see that Plato and Socrates disagreed on this, even if Plato's text seems to allow more physical intimacy with boys than Xenophon's, and to be more sceptical of the claims of any sexual pleasure.
12. Berkeley (1948, 7, p. 207). T. Traherne made a similar point (*Centuries* 1.31: 1960, p. 15).
13. 'Dialogues': Berkeley (1948, 2, p. 171).
14. Augustine, *Confessions* (7.17.23): see Clark, G. (1996).
15. Which is why we need a *religious* revolution: see Clark (1993a, pp. 4 ff.).
16. The saying was René Dubos': it has been regularly cited since, for example by Ruether (1992, p. 272).
17. See Plotinus, *Enneads* (V.8.6) on the wisdom of the Egyptians in using pictures more than words. The Hermetic Corpus went still further: 'The very quality of the speech and the sound of Egyptian words have in themselves the energy of the objects they speak of' (Copenhaver 1992, p. 58). The Egyptians, that is, had the 'true speech' which scientists and mystics seek.
18. *History of the Royal Society* (1702, p. 340), cited by Wiley (1940,: p. 213). Sprat was Bishop of Rochester, and one of the many who, oddly, associated a belief in fairies with Catholicism, and the Reformed Church with a reformed epistemology, 'the true science'. Catholicism was actually just as hostile to King Oberon and other such imaginative forms.
19. The Churchlands, for example: see 'The Reality of Shared Emotion' (Clark 1990), now reprinted in my *Animals and their Moral Standing* (Routledge, 1997).
20. See, for example, Porphyry, *On Abstinence from Flesh* (3.20.4–6).

21. A point I explore in Clark (1991, pp. 48 ff.).
22. See Detienne (1977) for an account of these gardens; Baudy suggests, contra Plato, that they were not merely ornamental, but germination tests to assess the quality of the seed corn (1995, p. 285). This may provide another useful metaphor for philosophical thought experiments.
23. There are several self-consciously 'postmodern' thinkers nowadays who reproduce the irrationalism against which Chesterton declaimed. It is fashionable to say that there is no truth, or that we cannot find it out, or that the laws of non-contradiction and excluded middle have been (simultaneously) disproved by physicists and revealed as bourgeois or patriarchal plots. It is even fashionable to adopt Siger of Brabant's Two Truth theory, that the provinces of scientific knowledge and religion are so far distinct that what is false in science may be true in religion. It was this, by Chesterton's account, that roused Aquinas to a last great burst of fury (1933, pp. 106 ff.). Speaking as a rational realist, even if not a Thomist, I applaud Aquinas's and Chesterton's intransigence in this. Those who say there is no truth are liars; those who say we cannot find it out admit they have no reason for what they say.
24. Aristotle, *De Partibus Animalium* (1.645a 15 ff.: Balme (1972, p. 18 – see p. 123: 'possibly a polite euphemism for "visiting the lavatory"' – which is also a euphemism).
25. Claude Bernard (1927, p. 15); Bernard was the father of modern physiology, and an unrepentant vivisector who conducted many of his brutal experiments on dogs immobilized with curare.
26. Aristotle elsewhere suggests that beauty depends on magnitude and order, and animals too small to see (or to see clearly) hence cannot be beautiful (*Poetics* 1450b): microscopes reveal a beauty that was real, and intelligible, beforehand.
27. H. Poincaré, cited by Weber (1986, p. xix). On the possible corruption of this ideal, see O'Neill (1993).
28. This too has its corruptions: what is required is *letting* Pimlico – or whatever other thing – adorn itself, not making it over into something it is not, on the specious plea of 'love'.
29. On which see Clark (1995a, 1996).

REFERENCES

Allchin, A. M. (1978) *The World is a Wedding* (London: Darton, Longman & Todd).
Balme, D. F. (ed.) (1972) *Aristotle, Parts of Animals I & Generation of Animals I* (Oxford: Clarendon Press).
Baudy, G. (1995) 'Cereal diet and the origins of man', in J. Wilkins, D. Harvey and M. Dobson (eds), *Food in Antiquity* (Exeter: Exeter University Press), pp. 177–95.
Bernard, C. (1927) *Introduction to the Study of Experimental Medicine*, trans. H. C. Greene (New York: Macmillan).
Burnet, T. (1965) *The Sacred Theory of the Earth*, intr. B. Wiley (Fontwell: Centaur Press; first published 1691).
Callicott, J. B. (1989) *In Defense of the Land Ethic* (New York: suny Press).
Cardenal, E. (1974) *Love*, trans. D. Livingstone (London: Search Press).
Chandrasekhar, S. (1987) *Truth and Beauty* (Chicago: University of Chicago Press).
Chesterton, G. K. (1917) *Short History of England* (London: Chatto & Windus).
Chesterton, G. K. (1933) *St Thomas Aquinas* (London: Hodder & Stoughton).
Chesterton, G. K. (1961) *Orthodoxy* (London: Fontana; first edn 1908).
Clark, G. (1996) 'Cosmic sympathies: nature as microcosm and as message from God', in G. Shipley and J, Salmon (eds), *Human Landscape in Classical Antiquity*, Leicester-Nottingham Studies in Ancient Society 6 (London: Routledge), pp. 31–29.
Clark, S. R. L. (1986) 'Icons, sacred relics, obsolescent plant', *Journal of Applied Philosophy* 3: 201–10.
Clark, S. R. L. (1990) 'The reality of shared emotion', in M. Bekoff and D. Jamieson (eds), *Interpretation and Explanation in the Study of Behavior* (Boulder, CO: (Westview Press), Vol. I, pp. 449–72.
Clark, S. R. L. (1991) *God's World and the Great Awakening* (Oxford: Clarendon Press).
Clark, S. R. L. (1992) 'Orwell and the limits of language', *Philosophy* 67: 141–54.
Clark, S. R. L. (1993a) *How to Think about the Earth* (London: Mowbray).
Clark, S. R. L. (1993b) 'The better part', in A. Phillips Griffiths (ed.', *Ethics* (Cambridge: Cambridge University Press).
Clark, S. R. L. (1995a) 'Objective values, final causes', *Electronic Journal of Analytical Philosophy* 3: 65–78 (http:www.phil.indiana.edu/ejap/).

Clark, S. R. L. (1995b) 'Nations and empires', *European Journal of Philosophy* 3: 63–80
Clark, S. R. L. (1995c) 'Herds of free bipeds', in C. Rowe (ed.), *Plato's Stateman*. (Sankt Augustin: Academia Verlag), pp. 236–52.
Clark, S. R. L. (1996) 'Understanding animals', in M. Tobius (ed.), *Intimate Relationships* (forthcoming).
Copenhaver, B. P. (trans) (1992) *Hermetica* (Cambridge: Cambridge University Press).
Descartes, R. (1970) *Philosophical Letters*, ed. A. Kenny (Oxford: Clarendon Press).
Descartes, R. (1983) *Principles of Philosophy*, trans. R. P. and V. R. Miller (Dordrecht: Reidel).
Detienne, M. (1977) *The Garden of Adonis*, trans. J. Lloyd (Brighton: Harvester).
Drels and Krantz (1959) *Die Fragmente der Vorsokratiker*, 5th edn (Berlin: Weidmannsche Verlagsbuchhandlung).
Gore, A. (1992) *Earth in the Balance* (London: Earthscan).
Johnson, L. E. (1991) *A Morally Deep World* (Cambridge: Cambridge University Press).
Kipling, R. (1927) *Verse 1885–1926* (London: Hodder & Stoughton).
LaChappelle, D. (1988) *Sacred Land, Sacred Sea* (Divangu, CO).
Long, A. A. and Sedley, D. (eds) (1987) *The Hellenistic Philosophers* (Cambridge: Cambridge University Press).
Lovelock, J. (1979) *Gaia: A New Look at the Earth* (New York: Oxford University Press).
Lovelock, J. (1988) *The Ages of Gaia* (Oxford: Oxford University Press).
MacCormack, S. (1990) '*Loca Sancta*: the organisation of sacred topography in late antiquity' in R. Ousterhout (ed.), *The Blessings of Pilgrimage* (Chicago: University of Illinois Press).
O'Neill, J. (1993) 'Science, wonder and the lust of the eyes', *Journal of Applied Philosophy* 10: 139–46.
Orwell, G. (1954) *Nineteen Eighty-Four* (Harmondsworth: Penguin; first published 1949).
Panofsky, E. (ed.) (1946) *Abbot Suger on the Abbey Church of St.-Denis* (Princeton, NJ: Princeton University Press).
Robinson, K. S. (1993) *Red Mars* (London: HarperCollins).
Ruether, R. R. (1992) *Gaia and God: An Ecofeminist Theology of Earth Healing* (London: SCM).
Saunders, T. J. (1970) *Plato's Laws* (Harmondsworth: Penguin).
Schama, S. (1995) *Landscape and Memory* (London: HarperCollins).
Traherne, T. (1960) *Centuries* (Oxford: Clarendon Press).
Weber, R. (1986) *Dialogues with Scientists and Sages* (London: RKP and New York: Methuen).
Weil, S. (1959) *Waiting on God*, trans. E. Crawford (London: Fontana; first published 1951).
Wheatley, P. (1971) *The Pivot of the Four Quarters* (Edinburgh: University Press of Edinburgh).
Wiley, B. (1940) *The Eighteenth Century Background* (London: Chatto & Windus).
Wilson, P. L. (1988) *Scandal: Essays in Islamic Heresy* (New York: Autonomedia Inc.).
Wittgenstein, L. (1961) *Notebooks: 1914–1916* (Oxford: Blackwell).

2

NATURE FOR REAL:
IS NATURE A SOCIAL CONSTRUCT?

Holmes Rolston III

Six words are especially significant in our world-view; they model the world we view: (1) 'Nature'; (2) 'Environment'; (3) 'Wilderness'; (4) 'Science'; (5) 'Earth' and (6) 'Value' as found in nature. But how far are these words for real? Have they extensions to which their intensions successfully refer? 'The world' is variously 'constituted' by diverse cultures, as we are lately reminded, and there is much doubt about what, if anything, is 'privileged' about the prevailing Western concepts. All words have been made up historically by people in their multifarious coping strategies; these six now have a modernist colour to them, and the make-up of the words colours up what we see.

More radically, all human knowing colours whatever people see, through our percepts and concepts. Trees are not really green after we have learned about electromagnetic radiation and the optics of our eyes, though we all view the world that way. Indeed, the scepticism runs deeper. Many question whether humans know nature at all, in any ultimate or objective sense (the pejorative word here is 'absolute' comparable to 'privileged' as revealing our bias in 'right' or 'true'). Rather we know nature only provisionally or operationally ('pragmatically' is the favoured word). We will first look in overview at the tangle of problems in which these words are caught up, then turn to each word in more detail.

Natural science seems a primary place where humans know nature for real; that couples the first and the fourth of these signifying words, with epistemic success. No, some reply, humans know nature through socially-constructed science. Catherine Larrère claims that nature *per se* 'does not exist . . . Nature is only the name given to a certain contemporary state of science.'[1] Science exists – no one doubts that – but science knows nature conditionally, perhaps phenomenally; science is an interaction activity between humans and a nature out there that we know only through the lenses, theories and equipment that we humans have constructed. Science does not know an unconditioned nature objectively, or noumenally, certainly not absolutely. Alexander Wilson claims: 'We should by no means exempt science from social discussions of nature . . . In fact, the whole idea of nature as something separate from human existence is a lie. Humans and nature construct one another.'[2]

Turn then to the more modest word 'environment'. Surely humans know a local external environment; that, after all, is what environmentalists are trying to save. Be careful, though, warns Arnold Berleant:

> I do not ordinarily speak of 'the' environment. While this is the usual locution, it embodies a hidden meaning that is the source of much of our difficulty. For 'the' environment objectifies environment; it turns it into an entity that we can think of and deal with as if it were outside and independent of ourselves . . . 'The' environment [is] one of the last survivors of the mind–body dualism . . . For there is no outside world. There is no outside . . . Person and environment are continuous.[3]

Environments are horizons that we carry about and reconstitute as we move here and there. Objectively, there are no horizons in nature.

Try again. 'A wilderness, in contrast with those areas where man and his works dominate the landscape, is hereby recognized as an area where the earth and its community of life are untrammeled by man, where man himself is a visitor who does not remain.'[4] That seems to take people out of the picture. Alas, once more – so the self-conscious humanists will protest – we are still very much in the picture. Roderick Nash, tracing the history of *Wilderness and the American Mind*, reaches a startling conclusion: 'Wilderness does not exist. It never has. It is a feeling about a place . . . Wilderness is a state of mind.'[5]

That seems extreme; still, wilderness does have to be designated, as it has been by the US, Congress. A society has to decide what wilderness means and where they will have it. Wilderness is another one of Berleant's human environments, even though one about which we have made atypical designations, resolving to leave such areas untrammelled. 'Wilderness' is a foil we have constituted in contrast to late twentieth-century, Western, technological culture. Nash concludes: 'Civilization created wilderness.'[6]

Apparently, then, we are going to have to look all over the world, the Earth, to find nature for real. No, the search is impossible – the objectors continue – because the problem is not what we are looking at, some world-Earth, it is what we are looking with, a world-view: our reason, our culture and its words. We must not think, warns Richard Rorty, that 'Reason' offers 'a transcultural human ability to correspond to reality'; the best that reason can do is ask 'about what self-image society should have of itself.'[7] The big mistake is 'to think that the point of language is to represent a hidden reality which lies outside us.'[8] Jacques Derrida's remark, 'There is no outside-the-text,' by this account, forbids any correspondence theory of truth.[9] We can hardly have descriptions, much less valuations, of nature as it lies outside of us. That is 'the world well lost'.[10]

Philosophers have perennially found themselves in an epistemic prison, as every freshman discovers early in the introductory course. There is no human knowing that is not looking out from where we are, using our senses and our brains, from an anthropocentric perspective. That is the lesson of Plato's myth of the cave from ancient Greece, or the tale of the blind men and the elephant from India. These fables, all over again (so they say), enshrine the deepest truth of all: all knowledge is relative; there is no 'mirror of nature'.[11] Viewing one's world, the realist hopes 'to detach oneself from any particular community and look down at it from a more universal standpoint.'[12] This can't be done. Hilary Putnam explains to us 'why there isn't a ready-made world.'[13]

Yes, but at least there are those magnificent pictures of Earth taken from space, and the conviction returns that we humans can look over the globe at least, and find a world that had 'already made' itself. We ourselves are part of its making, whatever making up we do after we arrive and turn to view it. Using our 'reason', somewhat transculturally it would seem,[14] perhaps we can couple the question what self-image our society wishes to make of itself with what to make of this planet we find on our hands, imaged in those photographs.

So there is an epistemic crisis in our philosophical culture, which, on some readings, can seem to have reached consummate sophistication and, the next moment, can reveal debilitating failure of nerve. We need to ask, in theory, whether nature is for real to know, in practice, whether and how we ought to conserve it. Mirrors or not, the self-image question is entwined with the image of nature.

Environmental ethics is said to be 'applied philosophy' (sometimes with a bit of condescension), yet it often probes important theoretical issues about nature, which (we add with matching condescension) has been rather mistreated in twentieth-century philosophy, overmuch concerned with the human self-image. Is environmental philosophy another of those para-professional 'philosophy and . . . ' spinoffs, not really philosophy *per se*, only philosophy '*ad hoc*'? Yes, but philosophy is always philosophy of X: and if the object, X, is 'nature' described and evaluated, is not such enquiry axial philosophy, right at the centre?

Now we reach the sixth, and most loaded, of our appraisal words. Surely, comes the retort 'value' is something we humans impose on the world. Nature may be objects there without us. There may be a ready-made world, but human values are not found ready-made in it. We make up our values. But not so fast: perhaps we humans do find some non-human values, or some of our values already made up, in the evolutionary history of our Earth, or our ecology. We ought not to beg that question.

After all, the less we really know about nature, the less we can or ought to save nature for what it is in itself, intrinsically. Indeed, if we know that little, it may be hard properly to value nature even instrumentally. We cannot correctly value what we do not to some degree correctly know. Even if we somehow manage to value wild nature *per se* without making any utilitarian use of it, perhaps this valuing project will prove to be a human interactive construction. Such value will have been projected onto nature, constituted by us and our set of social forces; other peoples in other cultures might not share our views. They too will project greenness onto trees; they might, nevertheless, value them in other ways, perhaps as natural classics, perhaps as the abode of spirits, perhaps as cellulose for technology. But then, if none of us knows nature for real, who is to say that any of these valuations is privileged? The conservation project falls to the whims of these ambiguous social projections – different strokes for different folks. The epistemic crisis is as troubling as the environmental crisis, and one must be fixed before the other can.

NATURE

'Nature' is a grand word; the root lies in the Latin *natus* or *gnatus*, 'being born' or 'produced', related to the Greek, *gignomai*, 'to be born', roots that survive in 'pregnant', 'genesis' and 'native'. Nature is whatever has been generated and come to be.[15] The reference is more or less to all that there is; the contrast classes are perhaps the supernatural, also, on some meanings, the cultural, the artifacted world as this has remade the spontaneously wild. For metaphysical naturalists, the non-natural or unnatural is an empty set. Whatever is, is natural.

The scope is just the problem. One cannot refer to everything and get any meaningful work done with words. What 'nature' means takes on the particulars of the occasions of reference, and these are, the linguists will speedily remind us, as much generated in the mind of the speaker for the uses at hand as found in the external world. One cannot encounter (see, hear, taste, touch or feel) nature-as-a-whole, only more or less specific processes or products that come to focus out of the whole, such as a lion or the rain. These natural 'objects' always show up when we are in some relation to them, constituting these relationships. We have names for these particulars within grand nature, and these names figure into a bigger picture. Lions will mean one thing to an ecologist, something else to a tourist, still something else to tribal Africans who see their totem animal. Rain on the Serengeti is a hydrological phenomenon to a meteorologist; rain is an answered prayer to the Islamic herdsmen troubled with drought and starving cattle.

'Nature' has to be abstracted out of this blooming, buzzing confusion of myriads of encounters with whatever is actually out there, which nobody fully, 'absolutely' knows. 'Nature,' the one word, singularises the variety of phenomena, and soon metaphysics comes trailing in. Metaphysically, there are, of course, differing conceptions of nature. Materialists have one, Christians another, Buddhists still another; the Druid concept of nature is *this* way; Einstein's is *that* way, seen quite differently. Nature is a loaded word, as is revealed by the metaphors that have been used to describe it: the creation of God, the Great Chain of Being, a clockwork machine, chaos, an evolutionary ecosystem, Mother Nature, Gaia, a cosmic egg, *maya* (appearance, illusion) spun over *Brahman*, or *samsara* (a flow, a turning) which is also *sunyata*, the great Emptiness, or *yang* and *yin* ever recomposing the *Tao*. 'Nature' is not so much anything out there as a category we have invented into which to put things; and we reinvent the category with our shifting models that describe this collection called 'nature', depending on the mindset of the beholder.

Neil Evernden concludes, 'What we know as nature is what we have *constituted* as *nature*'; that is 'the social creation of nature'.[16] He elaborates:

> It is fair to say that before the word was invented, there was no nature. That is not, of course, to suggest that there were not the entities and phenomena we now attribute to nature, but rather to say that people were not conscious of there being any such entity as 'nature.' For nature is, before all else, a category, a conceptual container that permits the user to conceive of a single, discernible 'thing.'[17]

'It is our habit, and perhaps an inevitable one,' he continues, 'to subsequently construe nature as the *source itself.* Yet nature is not the well, but the bucket, and a leaky one at that.'[18]

Yes, but 'nature' is a category we invent and put things we meet into, because there is a realm out there, labelled nature, into which things have been put before we arrive. Leaks or not, we do catch things in our buckets that come from some source out there. Nature is what is *not* constructed by the human mind. We can, through various constructs of the human mind, find out things that are not created in the human mind. Anyone who thinks that there is any knowledge of the material world believes that; no one can survive without considerable success in knowing what is out there in the world he or she must move through. All those persons who did not think that 'lion' refers to a real predator lurking in the grass are extinct. 'Nature' is a generic word for these objects encountered and the forces and processes that produce them.

Well, yes, perhaps 'lions' are out there, but 'nature' is not. The word 'lion' has reference but what is the reference of 'nature'? Many will think that of these concepts of 'nature' some are better, some worse: almost nobody any more is a convinced Druid; botany books are pretty standard the world over; Einstein is universally praised for his insights deep into the nature of reality. So we in the West have what concepts we now have as a result of the testing and sifting of the ideas generated in human experience encountering nature over the millennia and around the world; therefore the prevailing ones are true, or at least truer to the world than the concepts they have replaced.

That claim, metaphysically, is hard to press, however, because there is little or no consensus on what nature ultimately is. Here the seeming successes of science, in botany for instance, seem to run out at the bottom of physics. Nature is quarks, or gluons, or the bottomless energy pit out of which all comes, or the outflow of the Big Bang, and the ultimate questions are left as open as ever. Metaphysicians, so far as these still remain, construct diverse meanings of 'nature', and all we really have for sure is these human relations with 'nature', including the scientific ones. 'Nature' is something out there behind the sensations, never nakedly, wordlessly known.

An environmentalist, however, need not be quite so metaphysical, at least not so cosmological. A global view will do; maybe zoology, botany, geology, meteorology and ecology, if we can get these evaluated. This seems an order of magnitude away from astronomy and astrophysics above us, with the atomic and subatomic yet another order of magnitude below us, and we earthlings might be better at epistemology and get the ontology right at these native ranges. On Earth, nature is natural history, and no one has any real doubt that there are lions and trees, mountains and rivers, fauna and flora.

If we set aside the deep metaphysics, can we not be local realists enough to speak of nature not just here with us but also out there, or, more accurately, since the world is a plural place, of various natures out there? This knowing of various things in nature, and their natures, will be relational, for, after all, we humans too live here on Earth, are among its residents, and we have to cope. Are these not relations with others, genuine others, whom we can know as being there in themselves? Further, these others are together in ecosystems, in which they have evolved and are maintained; and can we not place these others in a self-organising system out there for which 'nature' is a rather good word?

The word 'nature' arises in our language, constructed by humans, because we need a container matching this world that contains all these myriads of creatures and phenomena we encounter, lions and five million other species, and mountains, rivers and ecosystems. There may be something to be said for giving up ultimates and absolutes, noumena and essences, or even quarks and superstrings, and certainly the vocabulary we use is one we humans have constructed. But do we really want to give up discovering how nature, at least at the scales we inhabit on Earth, does things on its own, did so before we arrived, and continues to do so when our enquiry is leaving them alone?

We cannot think about anything without language, and in language we can only use meanings that the wordsmiths of our past have forged for us. Yes. We need to think about language, about the concept of 'nature'. But this does not mean that we cannot think with such words about the world. There is always some sort of cognitive framework within which nature makes its appearance, but that does not mean that what appears is only the framework. Maps map the world; they selectively represent some of it, and 'nature' refers to this world-making activity out there. 'Nature', if a category ('bucket') we have constructed, has real members, that is, things that got there on their own in this world-container, and remain there independently of our vocabulary. That idea of 'source' is, after all, the fundamental connotation of the word 'nature', and the word successfully denotes a spontaneously generated world that we encounter, producing a conviction that it precedes and surrounds us.

ENVIRONMENT

Coming more local, or earthy, as we have just done, limiting the scope of our claims about 'nature', perhaps we need to shift to a less grand word, and such a word is ready at hand in 'environment'. 'Environment' is not nature, for nature is all there is anywhere anything is. An 'environment' must surround someone; in that sense 'environment' is quite similar to 'ecology', the logic of a home. Various organisms have their various homes, and at least we humans can know the logic of these homes, both ours and that of others around us. Only solipsists doubt that humans have environments both social and also natural. Humanist pragmatists realise that they live in such environments.

Yes, and now the pragmatists are quick to claim that 'environment' is obviously a relational word. Somebody, some organism has got to be in dialectical relationship with it or it isn't an environment. Maybe we can get beyond the word in our language, but not beyond relation to our environment. For humans, Berleant puts is this way: 'Environment arises out of the reciprocal interchange between my self as the source and generator of perception and the physical and social conditions of my sensation and actions . . . For environments are not physical places but perceptual ones that we collaborate in making, and it is perceptually that we determine their identity and extent.'[19] The environment is as much of nature as gets caught in one's perspective, as comes within one's horizon. 'Environment is no region separate from us. It is not only the very condition of our being but a continuous part of that being.'[20] He continues: 'This is what environment *means*: a fusion of organic awareness, of meanings both conscious and unaware, of geographical location, of physical presence, personal time, pervasive movement . . . There are no surroundings separate from my presence in that place.'[21]

We need to clear up some confusion in this 'fusion' by the use of modifiers. *My* environment is my inhabited landscape, where I work and reside; *our* human landscape is where we have placed our culture. Landscapes are more public and stable than horizons; we coinhabit them with neighbours. So *my* environment, though it is a perspective that is true in shortest scope, is rather too private a term. My environment when encountered as a landscape is a commons shared, your environment too, *our* environment. That fosters social solidarity, fortunately. It also demands another, fuller sense in which *the* environment is objectively out there, and this is not only our social world, but the natural world that we move through, there before we arrive, and there after we are gone. We can put a definite article before the word. We have our environments, plural, because there is a world out there, *the* environment, in which all these horizons are sustained. Environment is not my creation; it is the creation. I do not constitute it; it has constituted me; and now it seems arrogant and myopic to speak of foreground and background, of what I frame on *my* horizons. Environment is *the* ground of my being, and we can remove the 'my' because 'the' environment is the common ground of all being.

David Cooper demurs. The problem with environmentalists is that

> their notion of environment is of something much too big . . . Let us take our lead from those terms – 'milieu', 'ambience', 'neighbourhood' even – which, until recently at least, were close relatives of 'environment'. Those terms denote what a creature knows its way about . . . An environment as milieu is not something a creature is merely *in*, it is something it *has* . . . An environment, that is, is something *for* a creature, a field of meanings and significance.[22]

That seems solidly relational; but, on pain of solipsism again, these creatures come in the plural, other humans in their environments, but also non-human others in their environments.

As we find ourselves in this webwork of environments the definite article points to this common environment shared by us all, including non-humans, or we can even say the whole: 'The Environment'. Perhaps there is no such singular thing as 'the environment' out there – as with the word 'nature', we are again inventing a category into which we can put things. We invent, however, because, as we move through our environment, we find others in their environments. There are ecosystemic causes and effects, relating these others in biological and geomorphological nature; the whole milieu is a shared commons we tag 'the environment'. This notion can perhaps get too big; still, it does need to be big enough to include non-human neighbours and their relations. We are 'in' this environment, though what an organism 'has' is the niche it occupies in this larger environment; and humans, unlike the other creatures, can take some overview of this larger Environment.

Rorty deplores 'the impossible attempt to step outside our skins – the traditions, linguistic and other, within which we do our thinking and self-criticism – and compare ourselves with something absolute.' He urges philosophers to suppress the 'urge to escape from the finitude of one's time and place.'[23] Yes and no; no creature can get outside its skin, that is a biological impossibility. Analogously for humans to escape language is a linguistic impossibility. But the central idea of ecology is that skins are semipermeable membranes. Life is a skin-out affair as much as a skin-in affair. Life is impossible without transactions across skins, mediated for the fauna by their senses, by limbs with which they step around in the world, by mouths with which they take in the world. Ecology is all about the interactions of real organisms located in their real worlds.

For humans, such ecological exchanges are facilitated by our traditions, our language; we are not so much prisoners inside our skins as persons incarnate in the world. We do not want to escape the finitude of time and place, rather to establish the reality of time and place, and then to evaluate life in its historical, earthy finitude. We perhaps cannot compare our percepts and concepts with something absolute, but we can compare them with a world on the other side of our skins, which we move through, forming a self-image co-responding with this world image.

Any speaker's field of immediate significance is, of course, 'me and my ecology', yet, if there are listeners, that soon enough means 'us and our ecology'. Rorty wants that much solidarity with the significances that surround other persons; that makes ethics possible. The solidarity, or community, that environmental ethics requires finds significances in others in their ecologies too. We discover the webwork of connections as objective fact, outside our language, an 'environment' that we need for environmental ethics. How can we care for others if we cannot see outside our skins enough to know both that they exist in their different modes of being and that they have their own fields of significances? We will do this, of course, from within our skins and languages, and these things will come to have significance *for us*. Still, the environment, the biotic community, cannot be reduced to *our* field of significance, any more than can the cultural community be reduced to *my* field of significance.

Wendell Berry continues these doubts about 'environment', again fearing a kind of dualism that might let us separate our human selves from these surroundings external to us.

> The concept of country, homeland, dwelling place, becomes simplified as 'the environment' – that is, what surrounds us. Once we see our place, our part of the world, as *surrounding* us, we have already made a profound division between it and ourselves. We have given up the understanding – dropped it out of our language and so out of our thought – that we and our country create one another, depend on one another, are literally part of one another . . . Our culture and our place are images of each other and inseparable from each other.[24]

Berry is a combination English teacher and farmer, and that leads him to combine what language does to the world with what farmers do to the world. True, Kentucky farmers and their countryside 'create' (shape) each other, and they need a language that incorporates them sustainably into their rural world. Every culture interacts with the natural place in which it is situated. Meanwhile there is also 'the' world that does surround us, that we did not create, and we do not want this world to drop out of our language, but to use 'the environment' as a word enabling us successfully to refer to it. We may even wish to separate out parts of that environment, in Kentucky and elsewhere, to conserve it free of our culture.

WILDERNESS

'Wilderness' is not so cosmic a word as 'nature' but it does suggest that we put the significant prefix 'wild' before nature; and nature with this modifier, 'wild nature', should make it abundantly clear that we are using words to refer to a world outside the human sector, in this case to nature unmodified by humans. The reference, it would seem, is not just to us and our environment, and that will avoid the confusion we had with the word 'environment'. Not so, say the grammarians; notice that 'wilderness' is a modern word we have made up. Non-Western peoples typically do not have the word in their vocabulary, and even some Western languages (like Spanish) do not have such a word. In English, the word has multiple meanings, shifting over the centuries. Wilderness was once untamed, uncivil nature, nature cursed after the fall of Adam, savage nature beyond the 'frontier' which it was the American/European manifest destiny to conquer. Only with the Romantic movement, and still more recently with the modern wilderness movement, did the current concept of wilderness arise, a pristine realm unspoiled by humans.

Such a state is not something humans have ever really known; 'wilderness' so imagined is a foil for their culture, a romanticised Garden of Eden. The word gets made up when there is very little of wild nature left, as in Europe, when explorers leave for exotic places, or in the United States, when the frontier is closed, and wild places are threatened by the success of civilisation. Thereby hangs much of its fascination, for wilderness enthusiasts have a kind of archetypal longing for, or archaic vision of, a world with no people in it. David Lowenthal says, 'The wilderness is not, in fact, a type of landscape at all, but a congeries of feelings about man and nature of varying import to different epochs, cultures, and individuals.'[25]

David Graber explains:

> Wilderness has taken on connotations, and mythology, that specifically reflect latter-twentieth-century values of a distinctive Anglo-American bent. It now functions to provide solitude and counterpoint to technological society in a landscape that is *managed* to reveal as few traces of the passage of other humans as possible . . . This wilderness is a social construct.[26]

'Wilderness' is a myth of the urbane, mostly urban mind. Wilderness is another one of those filter-words with which we colour the nature we see. The truth is, say the reconstructionists, that we, being people, cannot know any such people-less world; that is only pretence.

Seemingly at the risk of doublespeak, but in fact clarifying our language, we have to say that in the wilderness there is no wilderness, just as there is no date or time of day. 'Wilderness' is a region that the US Congress (or other national statutory authority) has 'designated' as such, placed boundaries around and made laws about. By intersubjective agreement, we define it in relation to ourselves; it is 'untrammelled by man', no people live there; it is a place where we moderns, with so much technological power, resolve to restrain ourselves. We have mapped it, managed it, studied it. All this defining and resolving 'constitutes' a wilderness-lens through which we modern Westerners see nature; 'wild' is as much construct as 'West', and postmoderns see this.

The trouble is that the postmoderns see so much language-lens that they can no longer see nature. It cannot count against 'wilderness' having a successful reference that some earlier peoples did not have the word. Yes, 'wilderness' is, in one sense, a twentieth-century construct, as also is 'the Krebs cycle' and 'DNA' and the 'Permian/Cretaceous extinction'; none of these terms were in prescientific vocabularies. Nevertheless, these constructs of the mind enable us to detect what is not in the human mind. We must not confuse what we see with how we see it, even though how we see does shape what we can see. There are no doubt many things going on in the wilderness that we yet fail to see, because we do not have the constructs with which to see them. That does not mean, however, that there is no wilderness there, nor that these things are not going on.

Civilisation creates wilderness? Lately yes, originally no. Civilisation designates wilderness; more specifically, the US Congress acting for its citizens designates wilderness, and other legislative bodies can and ought do so as well. That is a legislative meaning of 'create', not the biological meaning. Wilderness created itself, long before civilisation; everybody knows that, Nash included, and it is only setting up conundrums to exclaim, 'Civilisation created wilderness.' Historians of ideas are permitted such language; analytic philosophers and natural historians must disentangle what they mean. It ought not be that difficult for Lowenthal, a geographer, to distinguish between the wilderness idea, which has its vicissitudes in human minds, and wilderness out there, wild nature in the absence of humans – unless one really has been hypnotised by the erudite withdrawal into a windowless web of words, symbols without referents. A 'congeries of feelings of varying import to various individuals in various epochs' is not wilderness worth saving. With more denotation with the connotations, there is plenty of surviving objective reference in the word, outside not only the twentieth century, but also all civilisation. Reference can remain constant through changes in meaning, as has happened with 'water', or 'gold', and 'wilderness'.[27]

Pre-Darwinian peoples had an immediacy of encounter with nature that scientists today may lack, and among them there are forgotten truths. They too had places in nature that they only visited, not to remain. But they had only groping access to the depths of historical time and change that have characterised Earth over the millennia. They had neither evolution nor ecology as sciences on the one hand (nor microbiology nor astronomy), and their cultural developments, on the other hand, did not (not so evidently to them, at least) threaten the health and integrity of their ecosystems. Even we Westerners have re-educated ourselves in this century about these matters. We have increased access to non-human phases of nature; we increasingly threaten such nature.

This is why we have constituted the word 'wilderness' as a filter with which the better to see these foundational forces, not earlier so well known, and to care appropriately for them, resolving in our high-tech cultures that there will always be places where humans only visit and do not remain. Wilderness is, if you like, a new 'idea(l)' ('myth') we have recently set up, but we did so because we discovered wilderness for 'real'. We want to conserve this realm for what it is in itself, naturally there; we also want it because it can help us dispel these myths of humans imprisoned in their own ideas, giving us new idea(l)s that make humanism too still more real. The rescue attempt is recent; the reality is primordial.

No, comes the reply, such rescue of ideal wilderness is a bad myth because we use it to suppose a pristine nature separate from humans, when the better view is a world with which humans are always in some interactive encounter. Listen to David Rothenberg:

> It is the idea of nature independent of humanity which is fading, which needs to be replaced by a nature that includes us, which we can only understand to the extent that we can find a home in the enveloping flow of forces which is only ever partially in our control . . . There is no such thing as a pure, wild nature, empty of human conception. . . . Wilderness is a consequence only of a civilization that sees itself as detached from nature . . . This a romantic, exclusive and only-human concept of a nature pure and untrammeled by human presence. It is *this* idea of nature which is reaching the end of its useful life.[28]

Wade Sikorski continues:

> The wilderness is not the opposite of civilization, as it has long been characterized in the Western tradition, virginal, unhandled, inhuman, untouched, but rather a building that we dwell in . . . In going into the wilderness, which is as easily found in the city as in the vast rain forest, we are going home because wilderness is the place where we recover the things that are most ourselves, but that we have denied, repressed, forgotten. Building wilderness is a lot like

interpreting dreams. In doing it, we encounter . . . an otherness that is not really so other because it is our own Being.[29]

Well, if that is true, if wilderness is as readily had in New York City as in the Bob Marshall Wilderness in Montana, if – something like interpreting dreams – we are only plumbing depths of our own subconscious to find our earthy connections, then the US Congress has wasted a lot of time with its wilderness designations, finding and protecting the untrammelled places where there are no human beings. We can timber the wilderness, because wilderness can be built by clever people going home to find their earthy selves. But surely that is a travesty on what wilderness objectively is; wilderness is not built by our states of mind, despite Sikorski's poetic licence. The literati can play with words as they please; analytic philosophers say, more carefully, that we need to build 'wilderness' sensitivity in the human mind because wilderness is discovered as what is there before us and without us.

Henry David Thoreau seems almost to agree with Sikorski:

> It is vain to dream of a wildness distant from ourselves. There is none such. It is the bog in our brains and bowels, the primitive vigor of Nature in us, that inspires that dream. I shall never find in the wilds of Labrador any greater wildness than in some recess in Concord, *i.e.* than I import into it.[30]

But restore that passage to its context: Thoreau had gone cranberrying nearby in an infrequented bog and he discovered, unexpectedly, a small, northern cranberry, *Vaccinium Oxycoccos*, which was known previously no closer than Labrador. He delights that this bit of wildness remains in the nooks and crannies of the Concord landscape. 'I see that there are some square rods within twenty miles of Boston just as wild and primitive and unfrequented as a square rod in Labrador, as unaltered by man.'[31] That does not deny objective wildness; it affirms it.

Finding this wildness unexpectedly near brings Thoreau to the further thought, expressed rather exuberantly, that there is wildness nearer still, even wildness within us, a primitive vigour of nature in our bowels. Nature lies in, with and under culture. He himself, returning to the bog, imports that inner wildness carried along in his body. We also wish to discover our continuing rootedness in wild nature; spontaneous nature is still there in our brains and bowels, our biochemistries and our evolutionary legacy. But none of this means that we 'build wilderness' in Sikorski's phrase.

When we know anything, we are there; wilderness unexperienced by humans is wilderness unknown by humans. But these subjective experiences are *of* nature objective to us (as well as of nature in our bowels); and if we lose that conviction, and see wilderness as nothing but modern myth, we can forget wilderness preservation. Contrary to Nash, wilderness is not a state of mind; it is what existed before there were states of mind. We may not have noumenal access to absolutes; we do have access to some remarkable phenomena that have taken place and continue to take place outside our minds, outside our cultures. Some of such nature ought to continue to exist, wild ecosystems, over and beyond whatever of nature (what 'wildness') we humans embody within ourselves or need for ourselves.

SCIENCE

'Environment' plunges us into surroundings in which we reside; 'wilderness' dreams of a world that humans only visit; both are emotively charged words. The word we need is 'science'. Natural science can take a disinterested approach. Alas, however, not even science is beyond these epistemic doubts.

Don Cupitt puts this quite bluntly:

> Science is at no point privileged. It is itself just another cultural activity. Interpretation reaches all the way down, and we have no 'pure' and extra-historical access to Nature. We have no basis for distinguishing between Nature itself and our own changing historically-produced representations of nature . . . Nature is a cultural product.[32]

David Pepper, urging a postmodern science, insists:

> Above all, a historical and ideological perspective teaches us that there is no one, objective, monolithic truth about society-nature/environment relationships, as some [scientists] might have us believe. There are different truths for different groups of people and with different ideologies . . . Each myth functions as a cultural filter, so that adherents are predisposed to learn different things about the environment and to construct different knowledges about it.[33]

Pepper could be right if he only means that different societies will put their knowledges of nature to different uses, but he wants also to argue, with Cupitt, that there is nothing privileged about Western science; it is only another 'cultural filter'. Cupitt is right that there is no '"pure" and extra-historical access to nature'; but does it follow that nothing in our 'changing historically-produced representations of nature' represents what is actually there in 'Nature itself'?

Yes, so the humanists claim, joined by some philosophers of science. Look right at the fundamental claim of science. The alleged disinterested objectivity is a myth. Nature-as-mere-object-for-science is a distorting lens that views nature badly, although it does give us a knowledge capable of manipulating nature. The alleged disinterest is a veil for Western, rationalistic, world-conquering, analysing, technological interest, a secular power position. C. S. Lewis claims, 'We reduce things to mere Nature *in order that* we may "conquer" them . . . "Nature" is the name for what we have, to some extent, conquered.'[34]

Yes, but many scientists take considerable interest in describing natural history, not nature-as-conquerable-thing but nature-as-actually-there, encountered and independent of the human presence. Our interest is whether environmental science can describe objects in nature *in order that* we may conserve them. Is that only another myth, which happens to be our currently fashionable cultural filter?

'Science describes a world already there!' No, says Rorty, 'we must resist the temptation to think that the redescriptions of reality offered by contemporary physical or biological science are somehow closer to "the things themselves" . . .'[35] We do not encounter, for instance, ready-made lions out there in natural history. True, those who did not take 'lion' to refer to a predator lurking in the bush are extinct. Still, surviving people do not have any naked percepts of lions; people believe in lions in diverse, culturally constructed ways, through the traditions of their rearing. Science is one more such schooling. Everyone 'sees' lions; a zoologist will 'see that' lion behaviour is 'territorial defence', and some particular lioness is the 'dominant matriarch' in the pride. Richard Dawkins sees that lions are full of 'selfish genes', a powerful symbol of nature as a whole. 'I think "nature red in tooth and claw" sums up our modern understanding of natural selection admirably.' Winning organisms are always 'like successful Chicago gangsters.'[36]

That could be more of the conquest mentality. Paul Keddy, finishing the leading book on *Competition*, notices that mutualism is rarely mentioned in ecology textbooks, while competition and predation are everywhere featured. He puzzles over this, since mutualism is everywhere in nature; the explanation, he finds, is 'that scientists are heavily influenced by their culture (consciously and subconsciously) when they . . . select models to describe nature . . . With respect to research in ecology, we may be projecting our own cultural biases upon nature rather than studying forces in relative proportion to their importance in nature itself.'[37]

A decade hence the theories could be different, emphasizing perhaps the pride's cooperation, the harmonious balances between predator and prey, or the comparative unimportance of predators, or population control by parasites, or how the fate of the lions, at the top of the food chains, is more an accident of rainfall and grass for wildebeest to eat than of successful selfish genes or red teeth and claws. A scientific account today is as culturally constructed, 'like Chicago gangsters', as was seeing the lion as 'the king of beasts' yesterday, taken as the lordly power symbol of the British empire or as the totem of some African tribe. Science is really transitory because it is framed by passing scientific fashions.

Rorty concludes:

> 'We may have no more than conformity to the norms of the day . . . this century's "superstition" was last century's triumph of reason . . . the latest vocabulary, borrowed from the latest scientific achievement, may not express privileged representations of essences, but be just another of the potential infinity of vocabularies in which the world can be described.'[38]

Science only provides makeshift sketches that we will replace, after more explorations, with a new round of cartoons. Today's science is just another passing metaphor.

This is bothersome. Without entering the larger debate about realism in science, we do need to settle whether science describes fauna, flora and states of affairs at the ranges where environmentalists are concerned about saving nature. In earth science and ecology, much of what is observed is on this side of Bas van Fraassen's observability divide: those lions, for example.[39] We *see* and we *see that* there are natural kinds to which our words refer. The Kalam of New Guinea recognise 174 kinds of vertebrates; all except four correspond to species, genera, and subspecies recognised by Western systematists today, and such parallels are often true with aboriginal peoples.[40] That suggests considerable objective reference in taxonomical science.

Scientists can go further than such peoples, who have a limited range of experience and no microscopes, in the naming of invertebrates – ants, for instance – or in comparisons with plants around the world, using a herbarium to place a plant in its family. Given an unknown plant, a good botanist can take out floras, which are full of words and a few sketches, and key it out to one species among the 300,000 named species of plants. Another botanist using those books will get the same result (without denying that there are judgement calls and borderline disputes). Maybe the correspondence theory of truth is not philosophically respectable, but it seems as if these botanists have put down in words some descriptions of what is objectively there in the world.

One cannot, however, by direct observation locate a species in its phylogenetic lineage. The hyrax (*Procavia*), a primitive African and Middle Eastern ungulate, though small and resembling a rabbit, and even once placed by systematists with the rodents or lagomorphs, is now considered to be more nearly related to the elephant or rhinoceros, the largest of animals. This discovery is the result of fossil and anatomical evidence, the finding that there were much larger hyraxes in the paleontological past, also the finding that dentition, morphology such as the structure of the feet, and physiology relates them to primitive ungulates.[41] Such science certainly seems to be describing what is the case in phylogenetic lineages.

The truth in such a claim is not to be dismissed by noting that systematists 'came up with' this classification in the twentieth century, and used eyes to see the fossils and the anatomy, and brains to interpret what the evidence meant. Reason does offer, contra Rorty, 'a transcultural human ability to correspond to reality.'[42] Maybe what we should resist is not the temptation to think that evolutionary and anatomical science have indeed brought us closer to the hyraxes themselves, but rather this claim from the academic left that it has finally got it right and that nobody is objectively right about anything. To be sure, claims about hyraxes are not metaphysical claims, not ultimate claims, not, in that sense, transcendent. But they are claims that humans know something about surrounding phenomena, transcending culture, claims about events past and present that are true because they describe the phenomena as these exist in themselves.

There are plenty of features of mid-scale Earth to which our human senses are not attuned – cold fronts, El Niño currents, ultrasonic insect calls, low-frequency elephant communication, or phenotypes coded in genotypes, or natural selection. Biological theory and practice can alert us to these events. Often, the problem of scale becomes that of time, which makes much invisible to our myopic eyes. We cannot see mountains move, or the hydrological cycle, or species evolve, though sometimes one scale zooms into another. Water flows, mountains quake, rarely; and we can see incremental differences between parents and offspring. We can see occasions of mutualism and of competition, though we have to estimate their force. We can examine the fossil record and conclude that there was the Permian Period and a catastrophic extinction at the end of it.

Often the problem of scale is that of size, and cellular biology and biochemistry have revealed microscopic nature. The sporophyte generation of mosses is haploid. Malaria is carried by *Plasmodium* in mosquitoes. Neither of those facts is likely to change with a new cultural filter. Golgi apparatus and mitochondria are here to stay. There is no feasible theory by which life on Earth is not carbon-based and energised by photosynthesis, nor by which water is not composed of hydrogen and oxygen, whose properties depend on its being a polar molecule. Glycolysis and the Krebs cycle, APT and ADP, will be taught in biology textbooks centuries hence, as well as lipid bilayers and immunoglobulin molecules. Oxygen will be carried by haemoglobin. Although no one can 'see' any of these things, and although biologists constructed these ideas using lots of theories and instruments, they are right that CO_2 is released in oxidative phosphorylation and that this cycles through photosynthesis II and photosynthesis I, so that in the world there is a symbiotic relationship between plants and animals and that this is a vital ecosystemic interdependence.

There is no unmediated nature; therefore we know nothing of nature as it is in itself? But this assumes that media cannot, reliably, descriptively, transmit truths about what is there. Biologists do abstract, and this can result in falling to see what is left out of the abstractions. They invent the theories with which they see, and these may blind them to other things. But inventions can also help us see. Science can regularly check its constructs against causal sequences in nature. Does not Keddy move to correct the prevailing bias toward competition, because he is constrained by what is encountered, rather than just introduce a new fashion? Better theories will come as a result.

These are only relative, local truths, a critic will protest. Yes, but they are settled, final truths locally. Or, for the purist who insists that we know nothing empirically with apodictic certainty, they are far more certain than are beliefs about the cultural relativism of science. Even if some of these claims should be revised, as they will be, the general cluster of discoveries is not going to fail. True, the mirroring of nature is only partial; we see through a glass darkly. One doesn't have to know it all to know something. These claims are modest, specific, earthbound, even, if one insists, fragmented. They only catch up a part of a scene in which much else is going on of which we are as yet unaware. They are mixed with error. They are not arrogant, universal (true in all worlds), total, grand, absolute. But they are still significantly true in that they describe what is going on here on Earth, objectively and specifically in Earthbound organisms and ecosystems.

But all this is so naive! – the sophisticated will now claim. Though our epistemological prison may not have mind or skin as walls, we cannot escape the local world. Neither scientists nor anybody else has any access to unconceptualized reality to check such intellectual representations against the way nature is built; we can only get at the world through concepts and these models are human-built. Hilary Putnam insists, 'There is a real world *but* we can only describe it in terms of our own conceptual schemes.'[43] Everything has been 'conceptually contaminated'[44] when we see it. He continues, '"Objects" do not exist independently of conceptual schemes. *We* cut up the world into objects when we introduce one or another scheme of description.'[45]

Lions? Yes, because kinds of objects do not exist until we construct them conceptually, such as the lion-kind. 'We must observe that "of the same kind" makes no sense apart from a categorial system which says what properties do and what properties do not count as similarities. In *some* ways, after all, anything is "of the same kind" as anything else.'[46] Consider the species *Panthera leo* (lion). Confronting a lion, what's out there is in fact "of the same kind" as the species *Panthera tigris* (tiger) – if one is choosing the category of genus, or of mammal, or vertebrate, or heterotroph, or four-legged critter. Or of quarks, since all lions and tigers are all of these things. Confronting a lion some systematists see the same thing (genus) as many other cats, and put *Panthera* in the genus *Felis*; the question is what weight one gives to the hyoid bones, developed from the second visceral arch and which support the tongue. So there are judgements of our choice that decide whether things are of the same kind.

But why not say, more precisely, that we can choose various sets – buckets in which to collect things – but that some of these sets are registering natural forms? Our construction of some sets is constrained by what has been constructed by nature. There are, sometimes, judgements of our choice about which labels to use for these different natural kinds of things (different cats) that we find. Sort our labels as we may, the question is not, fundamentally, our categories of choice, but whether we confront, at the native range level, a natural kind in lions, one that all peoples of all cultures must recognise because this kind is found ready-made in nature.

Surely we do not think that lion-objects come into being when we humans arrive and cut up the world into such objects. Lion-objects are instances of organismic individuals; each individual exists instantiating a natural lion-kind, a historical lineage of ancestral-descendant populations propagated dynamically over generations for millions of years on the plains of the Serengeti. This lineage, could it be traced further back, would find ancestors whose lines branched into the various vertebrates and mammals, with subbranches of this speciating being the cats. Lions being 'of the same kind' makes sense because, apart from any human categorial system, lions – members of the lion species – reproduce themselves over again and again, their genetically encoded information determining what properties count as the similarities needed to make another lion. Humans, in their categorial systems, get lions right when they describe such objects and events. Humans cannot cut up the world any way they please; they have to 'carve nature at the joints.'[47]

We cut up the world into objects? Is there then only some undifferentiated flux before we cut? No, Putnam backs off a bit, we should not describe the view of the anti-realist as one 'in which the mind *makes up* the world ... If one must use metaphorical language, then let the metaphor be this: the mind and the world jointly make up the mind and the world.'[48] But now what is getting contaminated conceptually is *epistemological* making up the world with *ontological* making up the world, the order of knowing with the order of being. True, we humans make up our categories as we know the world; that is epistemology. But it is also true that the world made up these natural kinds once upon a time; that is ontology. These are two very different makings-up, and it only confuses them to telescope them into a joint metaphor.

The problem with the joint making-up aphorism is that the Earth-world was quite made up with objects in it long before we humans arrived with our minds; the Earth-world made our minds over several billion years of evolutionary history, as it also made up our hands and our feet. True, our minds are unfinished, and we make up our metaphors in this construction, but joint make-up is another half truth, which becomes false in the whole. Our mind, with our words, is made to reach for objects as much as our hands, with our fingers. What the realist wishes to claim is that human-made epistemology can, and often does, track world-made lions in their African savanna ecosystems. Ontologically, we should begin with an account of the world out there, and, at or near the end of this account, move inside to the mind 'in here' and how it knows what is out there. Epistemologically, we do have to start within and move out. We may find sometimes that objects in the world are conceptually illuminated as much as conceptually contaminated by our linguistic conceptions.

Still, replies Putnam, we can have only a limited objectivity, realism with a human face:

> Our conceptions of coherence and acceptability are . . . deeply interwoven with our psychology. They depend on our biology and our culture; they are by no means 'value free'. But they *are* our conceptions, and they are conceptions of something real. They define a kind of objectivity, *objectivity for us*, even if it is not the metaphysical objectivity of the God's Eye view. Objectivity and rationality humanly speaking are what we have; they are better than nothing.[49]

Are the lions then only objective *for us*, and not for the Thomson's gazelles, who have a different psychology, biology, and no culture at all? Are the lions differently objective for gazelles because gazelles have evolved with defences against lions, keen eyes and quick limbs? The smell of a lion probably figures large for a gazelle. But does that mean lions are not objects for us both? Or that we cannot know the relations between gazelles and their lion-objects? Are the hyraxes related to the elephants and rhinoceros only *for us*? If intelligence had appeared in some other phylogenetic line (the elephants or gorillas perhaps), might something else be true for them? God might have still a third opinion?

But – the critic continues – we must know whatever we know in some humanised way. 'We can't get out of our skin to reach what's really there. We can't get out of our culture for culture-free comparisons. It is impossible to get beyond the sense experience of consciousness; all we can do is analyze events, their regularities and particularities, within the sensorium of conscious experience.' It may seem as though this is obviously true, something like we can't think somebody else's thoughts or feel their pain. But realists ought not to accept such arguments too easily. On a more ecological view humans do not have to get out of their skins to reach what's really there; there are windows out and in – they are called eyes, ears, noses, hands. Life is a matter of transactions across semipermeable membranes.

The can't-get-out-of-our-skins argument seems so persuasive. It is trivially true, and this gives it its rhetorical appeal. For those who take an ecological view, however, the skin-out world is as vital as the skin-in world. Those who live within the skin, without ecological exchange, are soon dead. Perception is not unintelligible as contact with something out there; perception is only intelligible if it is contact with objects and events out there. Likewise with the conceptions that humans in their cultures use to describe, in human language, a web of experience that is continually contacting what is out there, presenting, representing it. All study of nature takes place from within some culture or other; but it does not follow that scientific study is not constrained by the objects it studies external to culture.

Now the objection takes another form. These are only truths about the phenomena. True, but the objection is curious. From the perspective of deep metaphysics (the energy pit below the quarks, or behind the Big Bang, the mystic's *maya*, the Kantian noumena) this may be only the surface of things. But biological claims do not try to get underneath to some noumenal realm; biology claims that these phenomena are given in themselves. Photosynthesis is going on whether or not humans are experiencing it or capturing photosynthetic energy for some human utility. If other investigators, unlike ourselves, were to visit Earth from space, they would find out these same things, although, of course, they would have a different vocabulary for tagging these events, and even though they might be colour-blind and not see trees as green. They would have parallel experiences, because this is the way the world is.

EARTH

Philosophers are fond of talking about 'the world', about world-view and the way we humans see or cut up the world. Environmentalists incline to think of an Earth-world. Maybe there is no mirror of nature, but there are photographs of Earth. These are artifacts of a technological culture, and only of the surfaces of Earth. Still, we see Earth, the big environment. Nowadays, everyone in any culture, if reasonably well educated, is convinced that there is a planet Earth, this 'world' which preceded and continues to support all cultures, including the technological ones. 'Earth' certainly seems to have objective reference, a proper name for a particular planet. Contrary to Rorty's 'world well lost', environmentalists want a world well saved, and he likely agrees that we ought to save the Earth.

There is an Earth, reply the constructivists, but still these Earth-pictures become texts; they help people reconstruct nature again: now not so much as selfish genes, or nature red in tooth and claw, or *maya* or *samsara*, but as the global village, the small, fragile planet. The round planet merely observed has no content, no overview of nature comes ready made with it. The photograph of this Earth-world goes into a larger world-view; it becomes an icon. The photograph, which in itself doesn't say anything, becomes an argument for a way of viewing Earth. Look at the photographers and the social forces that put them into space. Here are men 'with the right stuff', the right know-how and expertise, all the technology making the picture possible. Look at how the global images are used in the media, how differently when put on the covers of *Science* or *Scientific American* (a planet to be managed with GIS systems), or on *The Whole Earth Review* (the biospheric whole) or as Buckminster Fuller's Spaceship Earth, or on the dustjacket of James Lovelock's *Gaia*. Environmentalists see an ecumenical Earth, the habitable Earth, longed for in contemporary, Western social vision.

The astronauts were earthstruck. Viewing Earthrise from the moon, Edgar Mitchell was entranced, 'Suddenly from behind the rim of the moon, in long slow-motion moments of immense majesty, there emerges a sparkling blue and white jewel, a light, delicate sky-blue sphere laced with slowly swirling veils of white, rising gradually like a small pearl in a thick sea of black mystery. It takes more than a moment to fully realize this is Earth . . . home.'[50] That is quite a text accompanying the picture, a world-view attached to this view of the world. The home planet! That is not some noumenal, essentialist nature in the absence of humans. Maybe the cosmos surrounding Earth is a deep black void, but Earth is an actual reality. Is there not an overwhelming sort of objectivity in, with and under the astronaut's subjective feelings?

The camera does have an object in focus. There Earth is, out there in space, an object to which these varied interpretations make reference. And the confrontations demand response. Here is a notable mixture of humans standing apart, overseeing, and being grasped by their encounter. This is seeing the whole, yet not with detachment and uncaring, rather with attachment and caring. Humans make objective reference outside themselves to the biosphere in which they live and move and have their being. Fred Hoyle wrote, 'Once a photograph of the Earth taken from *the outside* is available . . . a new idea as powerful as any in history will be let loose.'[51] Here is an outside view that convinces us how much we are insiders, Earth seen from above, the views convincing the viewers how much they are earthlings, though not the only earthlings. The distance lends enchantment, a new image of nature – so the myth-makers will say.

Yes, but is not this a special-kind of new image, one that brings us home again? The distance helps us to get real. We get put in our place. Metaphysically and epistemologically we are cautioned: 'There is no big picture.' All that anyone can do is tell his or her local story. Avoid totalising discourses. There is no 'grand narrative', not even in science; the definition of 'postmodern' is 'incredulity toward metanarratives'.[52] There is no philosophy-in-the-round, no nature-in-the-whole. Well, maybe, if one is speaking cosmologically or metaphysically. Meanwhile, there is this Earth-in-the round, Earth-as-a whole, and that is big picture enough, a rather grand narrative – even before we humans, much less modern or postmodern humans, arrived. If anyone were to try to tell his or her local story forgetful of the larger story taking place on this Earth location, that would be too individualistic, too isolationist, for the human and the Earth stories have entwined destinies. We cannot know who we are without knowing where we are.

'Man only deceives himself when he regards his own linguistic constructs as embodying some trans-anthropological truth. Escape to a purer, strictly representational language is not even possible; at most one can revel in the fact that man, like the spider, spins out of himself the world which he inhabits.'[53] But this is only partially true, whether of spiders or of humans, and if taken for the whole it becomes false. Spiders spin their webs, located in a larger ecology. The linguist slips from: We can never speak of the world without human concepts and percepts, to: We can never speak of the world without speaking of ourselves, to: We can never speak of the world, only of ourselves. We cannot escape virtual reality.

Though spiders make a web in the nearby few inches they inhabit, they live in an enormously larger world, of which they are enormously unaware. Humans build their cultural worlds and live in those webs. Spiders may take an arachnocentric, humans an anthropocentric view. But even spider webs catch objects from the outside world. We humans know how much the world exceeds the cultural webs we have made up, not despite how linguistically entrapping these webs are, but because of their linguistic power enabling focus, reference and analysis. Language wraps around many things that our senses bump into, these 'objects' on which we were before insisting, and now this 'Earth-world' on which we find ourselves. We construct, and continually reconstruct, our language to make sense of what constrains our senses. We have not just spun some babel of words; we have successfully coped because words copy enough of a world that lies on the other side of language for us to survive and flourish. Webs, like other constructed nets, catch what they do not create. Continuing the metaphor, epistemologists who fail to get their world in some objective focus are too much like spiders; they threaten to capture us in a web of words from which we are powerless to escape. Disabled so, we fail to understand the world that has spun out both spiders and humans.

At this point, perhaps the planetary photographs can trigger a privileged symbol. You do think Earth is real, do you not? Is it only or simply some web we have spun? The word 'Earth' successfully refers, no matter that there are differences in the accompanying texts, and the photographs could be successfully taken, because humans now know a round planet, orbiting the sun; we know something of its circulations, evolutionary origins, ecosystemic connections, fauna and flora. There is no more flat Earth, no turtle island cosmology, no more Earth created in 4004 BC with a garden planted in Eden in the Middle East, no Izanagi and Izanami stirring up the Japanese islands, or Amaterasu bringing order to them. There is no more enchanted world, populated with fairies and demons, though perhaps there remains, as much as ever, a sacred or numinous world, as the astronauts often discovered in their interactions with the whole. Any truth in these pre-scientific views, other cultural filters, will have to be demythologised, and if one insists that this is remythologising, then know that the right world-views, the 'true myths', must be trans-scientific, trans-humanist, transcultural, that is, science, humans and culture must take reference points outside themselves in these planetary events.

The planetary view eliminates boundaries between nations and cultures; this is 'the home planet'. It also eliminates boundaries between humans and nature, but as much by containing humans within an objective nature as by constituting nature within human cultural intersubjectivities. Earth is the commonwealth of living beings sustained and generated by Earth. In their knowledge about Earth, people on the planet have reached a certain threshold of maturity in synoptic, extra-cultural knowledge from which there is no turning back. We have become overseers, over-seers. This objective truth is not naked truth. It lays commands on us, just because it is for real. We have enough truth to be 'true to' an understanding and a vision of values in nature and an environmental ethic.

VALUE

In these ultra-sophisticated circles, if describing nature is an illusion, prescribing duties toward nature is illusion on illusion, nonsense on stilts. Humans are unable to discover natural forms, and, a *fortiori*, natural norms. We ought not pretend to value nature outside our cultural frameworks. Do not try, warns Eugene Hargrove, to develop a non-humanist argument that 'such values exist independently in nature . . . The best way . . . to deal with this concern is actively to defend these values as part of our cultural heritage, not to try to develop a metaphysical/epistemological theory of objective nonanthropocentric intrinsic values that constitutively trumps individual judgment and culturally evolved values.'[54] We concede that this might be a better tactic for pressing wilderness legislation on the floor of Congress, or for political ecologists writing a green party platform, but what about this retreat philosophically?

The retreat is wise, it is insisted, because knowing non-anthropogenic intrinsic value requires humans to do what they cannot, get out of their skins, languages, minds, and to value nature independently of human perceptions and preferences. Hargrove continues: 'The search for a nonanthropocentric intrinsic value seems to me to be comparable to a Kantian search for actual objects in the noumenal world. To succeed, the nonanthropocentrists apparently need to go beyond valuing based on the human perspective – which seems impossible.'[55]

Is it so impossible? Will not actual objects in the *phenomenal* world serve to take us beyond? Think of the animals, which – so we all believe – are out there, independently of humans. Listen to Rorty:

> The idea that we all have an overriding obligation to diminish cruelty . . . seems to take for granted that there is something within human beings which deserves respect and protection quite independently of the language they speak. It suggests that a nonlinguistic ability, the ability to feel pain, is what is important . . . [56]

Rorty takes continues: 'Pain is nonlinguistic: It is what we human beings have that ties us to the nonlanguage-using beasts.'[57] Amen, but this is precisely the first evidence we need of autonomous value and disvalue in these beasts, empathetically but transculturally known, to which we successfully refer with our word 'pain', sometimes in contexts in which we threaten value in their lives, which we ought to respect. Or, if the word 'value' is too European, then speak of 'goods' and it will be difficult to find a culture or a language without some such term, difficult to think some goods are not extra-culturally common to humans and animals. So we can see outside our sector, this far at least.

Rorty has been insisting 'that the world does not provide us with any criterion of choice between alternative metaphors, that we can only compare languages or metaphors with one another, not with something beyond language called "fact".'[58]

So if one says that chimpanzees are only 'dumb machines', but another replies that they are 'living flesh and blood' suffering similarly to ourselves, and hence we ought not to perform experiments on them, are we stuck comparing metaphors with each other, without recourse to checking metaphors against facts of chimpanzee biology or behaviour? That is incredible. Such checking will be reported in language, but the behaviour is beyond our language. Chimpanzee 'pain' is unintelligible without reference to a non-human experience; 'increased pain' must report a state of affairs in which value is at stake.

Rorty wants to 'set aside the idea that both the self and reality have intrinsic natures, natures which are out there waiting to be known'.[59] So the two trading off their metaphors are really just choosing their self-images. But how about the idea that there is a chimpanzee self out there which can be known, not entirely, not 'absolutely', but sufficiently so that we find that the intrinsic chimpanzee self-integrity ought not to be lightly sacrificed? Such reference is forbidden by the epistemology of radical pragmatism, but just that reference is required for an adequate axiology of conservation. 'Intrinsic' is another word much frowned upon these days, but if there is no value held by the chimpanzee in itself, why should a human bother to save it?

Even if there is reference, is this not done from our perspective? Bernard Williams replies: 'A concern for nonhuman animals is indeed a proper part of human life, but we can acquire it, cultivate it, and teach it only in terms of our understanding of ourselves.'[60] Well, yes and no. The concern has to be ours, and our relation to animals will affect our self-understanding, especially with pets and domestic animals. But we also need to understand animals in their wild, non-cultural settings. Environmental ethics is not ethics by extension, not just humane moralism toward our cousins in fur and feathers.

We treat animals and humans differently, for instance not interfering in the pain of wild animals in distress, letting nature take its course, which would be monstrously cruel should we treat humans this way. Pain in a medically skilled culture is one thing; pain in wild nature, where animals have their integrity under the forces of natural selection, is another. 'Our ethical relations to each other must always be different from our relations to other animals.'[61] But just such valuing requires extra-cultural objectivity, a window outside our self-understanding. We have in common with animals the capacity for pain, but they live in wild nature, we live in culture superimposed on nature. In environmental ethics, one has to be discriminating about these differences.

It is not just the beasts with whom we have such ties. We share sentience with higher animals, we share vitality with the invertebrates, the plants, the protozoans. The net is valuable to the spider because the spider is able to value itself, valuable on its own. If we think not, we will have to ask, as an open question, 'Well, the spider has a good of its own, but is there anything of value to it?' We can know what the spiders eat, what they instrumentally value. Why is it so impossible to conclude that these spiders are valuing themselves? The world is full of eyes, legs, wings, antennae, mouths, webs and eggs, all being used in the defence of life. Is it consistent to say that animals defend lives that they do not value?

Nor need we suppose that this depends on minimal sentience in animals. Consider plants. Though things do not matter *to* plants, things matter *for* them. We ask, of a failing plant, what's the matter *with* that plant? Arranging for sunshine and fertiliser, can we ask, as an open question: 'The plant is benefiting from the sun and the nutrients, but are those valuable to it?' That hardly seems coherent. *Benefit* is, everywhere else we encounter it, a value word. 'This tree was injured when the elk rubbed its velvet off its antlers, and the tannin secreted there is killing the invading bacteria. But is this valuable to the tree?' Biologists regularly speak of the 'survival value' of such things as thorns, stickseeds or nectar that attracts pollinators.

Every organism is a spontaneous, self-maintaining system, sustaining and reproducing itself, making a way through the world, checking against performance by means of responsive capacities with which to measure success. Its genetic set is a *normative set* in the sense that by such coding the organism distinguishes between what *is* and what *ought to be*. The organism is an axiological, though not a moral, system. So the tree grows, reproduces, repairs its wounds and resists death. A life is defended for what it is in itself, without necessary further contributory reference. Every organism has a *good-of-its-kind*; it defends its own kind as a *good kind*. In this sense, the genome is a set of conservation molecules.

These are observations of values which are at the same time biological facts. It is also true that science, just because of its desire for objectivity, is inadequate to teach us all we need to know about valuing nature. Yet value in nature, like value in human life, is something we can see and experience, and biology can help elucidate what these values are. Such values are biological facts – spiders value their nets and their lives – even if it remains true that such a value-laden world confronts us with further evaluative questions beyond science.

Yes, comes the reply, but the shapes these phenomenal values take reflect our constituting framework, whether it is the 'board-feet-of-timber' of the technologists, the 'intrinsic value' claims of environmental philosophers, or the 'caring' of ecofeminism, the 'enchanted worlds' of indigenous peoples or the 'creation' of biblical Judaism and Christianity. Reinterpreted pragmatically, the idea of 'intrinsic value' reveals that we are concerned with maintaining our human relations with these plants and animals, and that, in forming our self-understandings, we enjoy these experiences of nature and want to sustain them because they are intrinsically valuable *to us*. All these values come through with a human face; they have to be enjoyed by humans in their cultural places, as flesh-and-blood subjects incarnate in the world. So we are warned: Do not try to go beyond and fall into the mistake of thinking that you know anything objective about either nature or values there.

But that seems incomplete and unreal. Here is an account offered in the name of pragmatism, or neo-pragmatism, that seems most impractical in this denial that we humans can know anything outside our society, while we all know very well that we are residents on a planet where there is nature that transcends humans, and that various organisms pursue their own lives independently of our culture. This is as evident as that we are humans who live in culture. To fall back into conserving nature as, and only as, important in 'our cultural heritage' is to slip into another of these anthropocentric illusions that have long plagued philosophy, the mind turned in on itself, once again, in a self-reflexive trap, unable to test either its facts or its values against an external world. The objectivity myth, so alleged, is replaced by a subjectivity (or inter-subjectivity) myth.

Environmental ethics is a lived ethics on a geographical landscape. This ethics must be inhabited; it takes narrative form and needs personal backing, interacting with nature. So why not accept that in such an encounter, nature always wears a human face?[62] Why all this insistence on otherness out there? Because the appropriate behaviour for humans, faced with ethical decisions here, often involves knowing what good there is in other lives, and remains there when humans face in other directions. Environmental ethics is about being native to a place, so why not think of it as choosing our human story? Because there is more story to consider, solidarity with a larger biotic community with whom we share this place, about whom we must gain truth enough to know something of their places before we can rightly choose ours. Nature may not be as given as the naive realists suppose; but, upon finding this out, we make an equally naive mistake to think that nature is not given at all. Moral agents are not found outside society; but it does not follow that morality, arising within society, cannot or need not find value in the natural world. This finding of value is going to have to be intellectually credible before it can be morally imperative.

We humans are a peculiar Earth-species. Social construction is necessary but not sufficient for our being. Some values on Earth are not species-specific to *Homo sapiens*. If other investigators from space – having found out about DNA and photosynthesis, or food webs involving lions and gazelles, or hyraxes and elephants – were to evaluate these phenomena, they would (or ought to) respond with admiring respect to these worthwhile achievements and conserve them, even though they themselves were not dependent for their energy sources on photosynthesis, nor had they themselves any DNA, nor eyes and ears like ours, even though they had no entwined destinies with the planet on which they were visiting and therefore no 'place' to establish for themselves in residence here. An extraterrestrial scientist ought not to experiment with chimpanzees if this causes great suffering; this is because of what chimpanzees are in themselves, even if these space visitors have no evolutionary kinship with the chimpanzees.

It is true that, on Earth, humans are the only evaluators who can reflect about what is going on on these global scales, who can deliberate about what they ought to do to conserve it. When humans do this, they must set up the scales; humans are the measurers of things. Animals, organisms, species, ecosystems or the Earth cannot teach us how to do this evaluating. But they can display what goods are to be valued. The axiological scales we construct do not constitute all the value, any more than the scientific scales we erect create all that we thereby measure. There is value wherever there is positive creativity.

Too much lingering in the Kantian conviction that we humans cannot escape our subjectivity makes us liable to commit a fallacy of misplaced values. We must release some realms of value from our subject-minds and locate these instead out there in the world, at the same time that we are involved enough to feel the bite that registers values, getting past mere science to residence in a biotic community. If we cannot have that much truth, we have not only lost a world, we have become lost ourselves. Socrates claimed that the unexamined life is not worth living; that truth perhaps remains even if nature is not for real. Environmental philosophers also insist that life in an unexamined world is not worth living either. Humans miss too much of value, and for that we must have nature for real.

NOTES

1. Catherine Larrère, 'Ethics, politics, science, and the environment: concerning the natural contract', in J. Baird Callicott and Fernando J. R. da Rocha (eds), *Earth Summit Ethics: Toward a Reconstructive Postmodern Philosophy of Environmental Education* (Albany, NY: SUNY Press, 1996), p. 122.
2. Alexander Wilson, *The Culture of Nature: North American Landscape from Disney to the Exxon Valdez* (Cambridge, MA: Blackwell Publishers, 1992), p. 13.
3. Arnold Berleant, *The Aesthetics of Environment* (Philadelphia: Temple University Press, 1992), pp. 3–4.
4. US Congress, *The Wilderness Act of 1964*, s. 2(c). 78 Stat. 891.
5. Roderick Nash, *Wilderness and the American Mind*, 3rd edn. (New Haven, CT: Yale University Press, 1982), and summary conclusion, 'Wilderness is all in your mind', *Backpacker* 7 1, 1979: 39–41, 70–5 (Issue no. 31).
6. Nash, *Wilderness*, p. xiii.
7. Richard Rorty, *Objectivity, Relativism, and Truth: Philosophical Papers, Volume 1* (New York: Cambridge University Press, 1991), p. 28.
8. Richard Rorty, *Contingency, Irony, and Solidarity* (New York: Cambridge University Press, 1989), p. 19.
9. Richard Rorty, *Consequences of Pragmatism* (Minneapolis: University of Minnesota Press, 1982), pp. 96–7.
10. Rorty, *Consequences*, 'The world well lost', pp. 3–18.
11. Richard Rorty, *Philosophy and the Mirror of Nature* (Princeton, NJ: Princeton University Press, 1979).
12. Rorty, *Objectivity*, p. 30.
13. Hilary Putnam, 'Why there isn't a ready-made world', in *Realism and Reason, Philosophical Papers*, Vol. 3 (Cambridge: Cambridge University Press, 1983), pp. 205–28.
14. Tens of thousands of Earth photographs have been taken by over 200 men and women from 18 nations, from virtually every continent, though they all took some Western education to become astronauts. Kevin W. Kelley (ed.), *The Home Planet* (Reading, MS: Addison-Wesley, 1988).
15. A similar Greek root is *physis*, whatever has sprung up, the originated physical, biological world. 'Nature' has multiple, overlapping meanings; Lovejoy gives thirty-nine. The commonest is 'what a thing really is', what is 'innate', inborn; things have their various natures. Our interest is the 'world out there' that has generated such things. See 'Some meanings of nature' in Arthur O. Lovejoy and George Boas, *Primitivism and Related Ideas in Antiquity* (Baltimore, MD: The Johns Hopkins Press, 1933), pp. 447–56; C. S. Lewis, 'Nature', in *Studies in Words*, 2nd edn (Cambridge: Cambridge University Press, 1967), pp. 24–74.
16. Neil Evernden, *The Social Creation of Nature* (Baltimore, MD: The Johns Hopkins University Press, 1992), p. 30.
17. Ibid., p. 89.
18. Ibid., p. 110.
19. Berleant, *Aesthetics*, pp. 132–5.
20. Ibid., p. 131.
21. Ibid., p. 34.
22. David E. Cooper, 'The idea of environment', in David E. Cooper and Joy A. Palmer (eds), *The Environment in Question* (London: Routledge, 1992), pp. 165–80, on pp. 167–9.
23. Rorty, *Consequences*, p. xix.
24. Wendell Berry, *The Unsettling of America* (San Francisco: Sierra Club Books, 1977), p. 22.

25. David Lowenthal, 'Is wilderness "Paradise Enow"? Images of nature in America', *Columbia University Forum* 7 (2), 1964: 34–40, on p. 35.
26. David M. Graber, 'Resolute biocentrism: the dilemma of wilderness in national parks', in Michael E. Soulé and Gary Lease (eds), *Reinventing Nature? Responses to Postmodern Deconstruction* (Washington, DC: Island Press, 1995), pp. 123–35, on pp. 123–4.
27. Saul A. Kripke, *Naming and Necessity* (Cambridge, MA: Harvard University Press, 1980), p. 115ff.
28. David Rothenberg, 'The greenhouse from down deep: what can philosophy do for ecology?' *Pan Ecology* 7(2), Spring, 1992: 1–3.
29. Wade Sikorski, 'Building wilderness', in Jane Bennett and William Chaloupka (eds), *In the Nature of Things: Language, Politics, and the Environment* (Minneapolis: University of Minnesota Press, 1993), pp. 24–43, on p. 29.
30. Henry David Thoreau, *Journal*, 30 August 1856.
31. Ibid.
32. Don Cupitt, 'Nature and culture', in Neil Spurway (ed.), *Humanity, Environment and God* (Oxford: Blackwell Publishers, 1993), pp. 33–45, on p. 35.
33. David Pepper, *Modern Environmentalism: An Introduction* (London: Routledge, 1996), pp. 3–4.
34. C. S. Lewis, *The Abolition of Man* (New York: Macmillan, 1950), p. 44.
35. Rorty, *Contingency*, p. 16.
36. Richard Dawkins, *The Selfish Gene*, new edn, (New York: Oxford University Press, 1989), p. 2.
37. Paul A. Keddy, *Competition* (London: Chapman & Hall, 1989). The quotation is from his 'Is mutualism really irrelevant to ecology?' *Bulletin of the Ecological Society of America* 71, 1990: 101–2.
38. Rorty, *Mirror of Nature*, p. 367.
39. Bas C. van Fraassen, *The Scientific Image* (Oxford: Clarendon Press, 1980), p. 72.
40. Ralph N. H. Bulmer, 'Folk biology in the New Guinea highlands', *Social Science Information* 13(4/5), 1974: 9–28. Cecil H. Brown, *Language and Living Things: Uniformities in Folk Classification and Naming* (New Brunswick, NJ: Rutgers University Press, 1984).
41. David Macdonald (ed.), *The Encyclopedia of Mammals* (London: Unwin Hyman, 1989), pp. 462–5; Ronald M. Nowak, *Walker's Mammals of the World*, 5th edn (Baltimore, MD: Johns Hopkins University Press, 1991), pp. 1287–90.
42. Rorty, *Objectivity*, p. 28.
43. Hilary Putnam, *Meaning and the Moral Sciences* (London: Routledge & Kegan Paul, 1978), p. 32.
44. Hilary Putnam, *Reason, Truth, and History* (Cambridge: Cambridge University Press, 1981), p. 54.
45. Ibid., p. 52, emphasis in original. Notice that 'objects' is in quotes in the first half of the sentence but not the last.
46. Ibid., pp. 52–3.
47. Recalling Plato, *Phaedrus*, 265e.
48. Putnam, *Reason*, p. xi.
49. Ibid., p. 55.
50. Edgar Mitchell, in Kelley, *The Home Planet*, at photographs 42–5.
51. Fred Hoyle, in Kelley, *The Home Planet*, inside front cover.
52. Jean-François Lyotard, *The Postmodern Condition: A Report on Knowledge* (Minneapolis: University of Minnesota Press, 1984), pp. xxii–xxiv.
53. Janet Martin Soskice, *Metaphor and Religious Language* (Oxford: Clarendon Press, 1985), p. 80, summarising Derrida, Nietzsche and linguistic views she critiques.
54. Eugene Hargrove, 'Weak anthropocentric intrinsic value', *The Monist* 75, 1992: 183–207, on p. 186.
55. Ibid., p. 192.
56. Rorty, *Contingency*, p. 88.
57. Ibid., p. 94.
58. Ibid., p. 20.
59. Ibid., p. 11.
60. Bernard Williams, *Ethics and the Limits of Philosophy* (Cambridge, MA: Harvard University Press, 1985), p. 118.
61. Ibid., p. 118.
62. Elizabeth M. Harlow, 'The human face of nature: environmental values and the limits of nonanthropocentrism', *Environmental Ethics* 14, 1992: 27–42.

3

TRIVIAL AND SERIOUS IN AESTHETIC APPRECIATION OF NATURE

Ronald W. Hepburn

The aesthetic appreciation of both art and nature is often, in fact, judged to be more – and less – serious. For instance, both natural objects and art objects can be hastily and unthinkingly perceived, and they can be perceived with full and thoughtful attention. In the case of art, we are better equipped to sift the trivial from the serious appreciation: for the existence of a corpus, and a continuing practice, of criticism (and philosophical study) of the arts – for all their internal disputatiousness – furnishes us with relevant criteria. In the case of nature, we have far less guidance. Yet it must matter, there too, to distinguish trivial from serious encounters. When we seek to defend areas of 'outstanding natural beauty' against depredations, it matters greatly what account we can give of the appreciation of that beauty: how its value can be set alongside competing and vociferously promoted values involved in industry, commerce and urban expansion. If we wish to attach very high value to the appreciation of natural beauty, we must be able to show that more is involved in such appreciation than the pleasant, unfocused enjoyment of a picnic place, or a fleeting and distanced impression of countryside through a touring-coach window, or obligatory visits to standard viewpoints or (should I say) snapshot-points.

That there is much work to be done on this subject is of course due to the comparative neglect of natural beauty in recent and fairly recent aesthetics. Although it was the very centre of concern for a great deal of eighteenth-century aesthetics and for many of the greatest Romantic poets and painters, subsequent movements such as Symbolism and Modernism tended to see the natural world in a very different light. Darwinian ideas of nature were problematic and disturbing compared with theistic and pantheistic perspectives. Some later aesthetic theories made sense when applied to art, but little or none applied to natural beauty. Formalist theories require a determinate, bounded and shaped artifact; expression theories presuppose an artist behind an art-work.

What, first of all, do we mean by 'aesthetic appreciation of nature'? By 'nature' we must mean not just gentle pastoral landscape, but also tropical forest, tundra, ice floes, deserts and objects (and events) made perceptible only by way of microscope or telescope. If nature's materials are vast, so too is the freedom of the percipient. We have endless choice of scale, freedom to choose the boundary of attention, choice between the *moving* – whether natural objects or the spectator or both – and the *static*. Our choice of viewpoint can range from that of the underwater diver to the view of the upper surface of clouds from an aircraft or an astronaut's view of the planet as a sphere.

What sort of aesthetic responses and judgements occur in our encounter with nature? We may speak of 'beautiful' objects in nature, where 'beauty' is used in a narrower sense, when we respond with delight, with love and with wonderment to objects before us. In that sense we may see beauty in the gradations of sky- and cloud-colours, yellow-orange evening light transfiguring a summer landscape, early morning sunrays seen through mist in woodland, water calm in a lake, or turbulent or cascading in the mountain stream that emerges from the lake. The *feel* of moss or rock. Sounds – curlew, oyster-catcher, lark – and where a single bird's cry makes the surrounding silence the more vividly apprehensible. We may see beauty in formal qualities: flower-patterns, snow- and wind-shapes, the balancing of masses at the sides of a valley: in animal forms and in the grace of animal movement.

'Beauty' is, however, also used more widely. It may cover the aesthetically arresting, the rewarding-to-contemplate, a great range of emotional qualities, without necessarily being pleasurable or lovable or suggestive of some ideal. Tree branches twisted with age or by wind, a towering thundercloud, black water beneath a steep rocky hillside.

We need to acknowledge a duality in much aesthetic appreciation of nature, a *sensuous component* and a *thought-component*. First, sensuous immediacy: in the purest cases one is taken aback by, for instance, a sky-colour effect, or by the rolling away of cloud or mist from a landscape. Most often, however, an element of thought is present, as we implicitly compare and contrast *here* with *elsewhere*, *actual* with *possible*, *present* with *past*. I say, 'implicit'; there may be no verbalising or self-conscious complexity in the experience.

We cannot deny the thought element, and it cannot reasonably be held (as such and in general) to fight with the aesthetic character of an experience. Consider that paradigm case of aesthetic experience of nature – the fall of an autumn leaf.[1] If we simply watch it fall, without any thought, it may or may not be a moving or exciting aesthetic object, but it must be robbed of its poignancy, its mute message of summer gone, its symbolising *all* falling, our own included. Leaf veins suggest blood-vessel veins – symbolising continuity in the forms of life, and maybe a shared vulnerability. Thus the thought element may bring analogies to bear on the concrete particulars: this fall with other falls; and temporal links – this autumn with innumerable other autumns, the deep carpet of leaves in forests, the cycle of the seasons.

Or we watch the flight of swifts, wheeling, screaming; and to our present perception is added the thought of their having, in early summer, just returned from Africa – the thought (schematically) of that huge journey, their seeming frailness, their frantic, restless, frightening burning up of energy in their nearly ceaseless motion. All that is directed to (and fused with the perception of) the tiny, never still bird forms themselves. Maybe we think of a wider context still, in relation to the particular animal form (or rock form) under our gaze – awareness of the wide evolutionary procession of forms: or one may even be aware of the broadest metaphysical or religious background of all – the world as divinely created – or as uncreated, enigmatically *there*. Not even in the latter sort of case is the thought extraneously or externally juxtaposed to the perception of the natural object or scene. The union, or fusion, is much closer. There is an overall modification of awareness, in which the feeling and thought elements and the perception all interact.

Although analogies with art suggest themselves often enough about how to 'frame' the objects of our aesthetic interest, where to establish the momentary bounds of our attention, on other occasions the objects we attend to seem to repudiate any such bounding – to present themselves as essentially illimitable, unframable, or to be in a way surrogates for the unbounded. This is particularly the domain of elemental experience, of the awesome and the sublime. There is an essential, though contested and variable, thought element here again: it is particularly obvious in the Kantian versions of sublimity, where imagination aspires, but is unable, to cope with a great magnitude or energy of nature. It recoils, but its defeat is compensated for by the realisation of moral and intellectual capabilities which are not daunted at all, but whose supreme worth is vividly brought home to the subject. Coleridge descending Sca Fell enacted that Kantian reflective content of sublime experience:

> The sight of the Crags above me on each side, and the tempestuous clouds just over them . . . overawed me. I lay in a state of . . . Trance and Delight and blessed God aloud for the powers of Reason and the Will, which remaining, no danger can overpower us.[2]

Other theories, Schopenhauer's, for instance, saw the moment of ascendancy in our proving able to take a contemplative attitude towards hostile nature.[3]

Without an adequate thought element, particularly self-image, counterbalancing the daunting external powers, the experience of the sublime may shrivel, or never establish itself in a subject. To some – Mikel Dufrenne, for one – it remains the chief moment in the aesthetic experience of nature, whereas others, for instance Adorno, see the sublime as a historically ephemeral and by now faded mode of sensibility.[4]

To chronicle the effects rather than the components of aesthetic experience of nature would require a much longer story than can be attempted here. Among the most general of these, clichéd though it is, must be the 'life-enhancing' effect of beauty, release from the stress and anxiety of practical, manipulatory, causally engaged relations with nature into the calmly contemplative. These work together, I suggest, in the case of natural beauty with a lasting, or always renewable, sense of mystery or wonder that it should be there at all.

Can we then make any reasoned case for distinguishing trivial from serious in this field? If it is a form of perception-and-reflection that we are considering, then as I said at the start, we know that perception (taking that first) can be attentive or inattentive, can be discriminating or undiscriminating, lively or lazy: that the doors of perception can need cleansing, the conventions and the simplifications of popular perception can need resisting. The reflective component, likewise, can be feeble or stereotyped, individual, original or exploratory. It can be immature or confused. And indeed we may secretly be anxious that the thought which sustains our valued experience of nature is in the end metaphysically untenable. To *discard* these issues, to narrow down on a minimally reflective, passive perception, would seem to trivialise in another way. Adorno suspected that our very concept of nature is 'idyllic, provincial, insular'.[5] I would argue that it is not always so; but it can be, and from comfortable selectivity comes trivialisation by another route.

Some of these points, then, suggest the following first approximation: that an aesthetic approach to nature is trivial to the extent that it distorts, ignores, suppresses truth about its objects, feels and thinks about them in ways that falsify how nature really is. All this may be coupled with a fear that if there is to be some agreeable aesthetic encounter with nature, call it trivial if you will, one had better not look too attentively nor think too hard about the presuppositions (the thought components) on which one's experience rests. To break open the parcel might dissipate the aesthetic delight and set one an over-arduous task to regain at some deeper, more serious level what one had possessed at a more superficial one.

If it trivialises to see nature in terms of ready-made, standard 'views', so does it also to see oneself merely as the detached viewer – or indeed as a noumenally free and rational ego. There is a deepening of seriousness when I realise that I am myself one with, part of, the nature over against me. So, I want to say, an aesthetic appreciation of nature, if serious, is necessarily a self-exploration also; for the energies, regularities, contingencies of nature are the energies, principles and contingencies that sustain my own embodied life and my own awareness. Nature may be 'other' to us, but we are no less connatural with it. We do not simply look out upon nature as we look at the sea's drama from a safe shore: the shore is no less nature, and so too is the one who looks.

On a superficial reading of nature, objects tend to have an invariable, univocal expressive quality. Fused, however, with less conventional thoughts, considered in wider or less standard contexts, these qualities admit of endless modification. It is reasonable, then, to include among the trivialising factors bland unawareness of that potential variability, and among factors making for serious aesthetic appreciation of nature must be a background realisation of it.

Anticipating later discussion, I need to say here that 'seriousness' or 'depth' in aesthetic experience of nature cannot be correlated in any simple way with intensity or fullness of thought content. Some thoughts (perhaps of causal explanation of the phenomena at the level of particle physics) might not enrich but neutralise the experience, or at least fight and fail to fuse with its perceptual content. Or they might trivialise. Other thought contents again, and in contrast, relate to quite fundamental features of the lived human state, and bear directly upon the perceptual, phenomenal dimension, which their presence cannot fail to solemnise and deepen. Think, for instance, of that realisation (thought and sense experience in fusion) of the whole earth's motion, in Wordsworth's skating episode in *The Prelude*, as he suddenly stopped in his tracks while skating in the dark:

> So through the darkness and the cold we flew,
> And not a voice was idle; with the din
> Smitten, the precipices rang aloud;
> The leafless trees and every icy crag
> Tinkled like iron; while far distant hills
> Into the tumult sent an alien sound
> Of melancholy not unnoticed, while the stars
> Eastward were sparkling clear, and in the west
> The orange sky of evening died away.
> Not seldom from the uproar I retired
> Into a silent bay, or sportively
> Glanced sideway, leaving the tumultuous throng,
> To cut across the reflex of a star
> That fled, and, flying still before me, gleamed
> Upon the glassy plain; and oftentimes,
> When we had given our bodies to the wind,
> And all the shadowy banks on either side
> Came sweeping through the darkness, spinning still
> The rapid line of motion, then at once
> Have I, reclining back upon my heels,
> Stopped short; yet still the solitary cliffs
> Wheeled by me – even as if the earth had rolled
> With visible motion her diurnal round![6]

A second important duality characterises an aesthetic concern with nature. On the one hand, it is nature, nature's own forms, structures, sequences, that we seek to contemplate; and the more serious our engagement, the more earnest will be our regard for, and our respect for, the integrity and the proper modes of being of the objects in nature themselves, inanimate and animate. We see sentimentality, for instance, as trivialising in its tendency, because it may falsely posit human feelings and human attitudes in the non-human – or more likely posit *failed* human life and human attitudes instead of *successfully* attained non-human life. To put it very schematically, a serious aesthetic approach to nature is close to a Spinozistic intellectual love of God-or-Nature in its totality. It rejects Kant's invitation to accord unconditional value only to the bearers of freedom and reason, and to downgrade phenomenal nature save as it hints at a supersensible, an earnest of which is furnished in nature's amenability to be perceived, its purposiveness without purpose. It rejects, likewise, Hegel's downplaying of natural beauty in favour of the spirit-manifesting practice of art.

But there is another side: even when we discard the excesses of anthropomorphism, to admit no more than this other-respecting concern is to exclude too much. The human inner life has been nourished by images from the natural world: its self-articulation and development could hardly proceed without annexing or appropriating forms from the phenomenal world. They are annexed not in a systematic, calculating, craftsmanlike fashion, but rather through our being imaginatively seized by them, and coming to cherish their expressive aptness, and to rely upon them in our efforts to understand ourselves. Not all of this can be categorized as strictly *aesthetic* encounter or *aesthetic* contemplation: some of it can, and the lines of connection are obvious and important.

That may serve us as a sketch of the duality within our commerce with nature – a respect for its own structures and the celebrating of those, and the annexation of natural forms. Though divergent, those approaches are not opposed: nature need not be misperceived in order to furnish symbols for our inwardness. But their focus and their intention are distinct. Each presents some problems in relation to the spectrum between trivial and serious.

First then we are to consider and contemplate nature in its own terms. This is an aim that sets one serious goal for aesthetic appreciation. What *problems* come with it?

One interpretation of the phrase 'in its own terms' would prompt us towards supplying a scientific thought component. Now, it may well enrich our perception of a U-valley to 'think in' its readily imaginable glacial origins. But, as I claimed earlier, one could not have an obligation to think in *perception transcending* ideas or explanations. These might be explanations in physical theory of transformations at the molecular and atomic level that produced the rock of which the valley is made. We cannot oblige ourselves to think in what must fragment or overwhelm or dissolve the aesthetic perception instead of enriching it. Aesthetic experience must be human experience – episodic, phenomenal. To destroy it can hardly be to *deepen* it!

We spoke of 'respect' for natural objects, and particularly for living beings. But a further and different problem arises when we recall that nature itself shows only a very limited respect for its individuals. For me to respect something is to perceive it as intrinsically valuable. I affirm, even rejoice in, its being and in its manner of being. Suppose, however, I do that with (say) a zebra or a brilliantly coloured butterfly newly emerged from its chrysalis. I am going to be hurt and saddened when a lion tears the zebra to pieces, and a bird snaps up the butterfly when it has scarcely tried out its wings. That bleak thought of the vulnerability and brevity of individual life can easily attach itself also to perceptions of *flourishing* living beings, and there is no doubt that to perceive them so is to be closer to the truth of things than not to. Does it follow that in the interest of 'depth' one must cancel or at least qualify every response of simple delight at beast or bird? There is conflict here. On the one hand, to seek depth or seriousness seems to rule out optimistic falsifications: but on the other hand, since we are *also* trying to attend in a differentiating and appreciative mode, we surely cannot claim that an undifferentiated consciousness of nature's dysteleology must always predominate in any aesthetic experience.

There is poignancy, too, in the thought that some of the most animated, zestful and aesthetically arresting movements of living beings are directed at the destruction of other living beings – the ballet of swifts feeding on the wing, lithe and rapid movements of panthers or leopards. If we are tempted to abstract from, or attenuate or mute the disturbing thought content in any such case, is that not to move some way towards the trivial end of our scale? Nature, that is, can be made aesthetically contemplatable only by a sentimentalising, falsifying selectivity, that turns away from the real work of beak, tooth and claw. That would indeed be to move, and very significantly, in the trivialising direction, and to shirk the challenge to the would-be appreciator's own creativity.

In some situations at least aesthetic appreciation of nature may be made sustainable – without falsification – through fashioning less simplistic (and less inappropriately moralised) concepts of nature's processes and energies. If, for instance, we can celebrate nature's overall animation, vitality – *creative and destructive* in indissoluble unity – we may reach a reflective or contemplative equilibrium that is neither unqualified by melancholy nor disillusioned and repelled.

Rather than follow that strenuous route, we may be tempted, as some aestheticians have been, once more to deny that we are properly concerned, in aesthetic experience, with how things actually are, but we should be concerned only with their immediately given perceptual qualities, the sensuous surface. To accept such a limitation, however, though it would lead us thankfully past a great many puzzles and problems, would leave us with a quite unacceptably *thin* version of aesthetic experience of nature. The falling autumn leaf becomes a small, fluttering, reddish-brown material object – and no more, the swifts only rapidly flitting shapes. The extreme here is to purify away, regressively and evasively, all but the merest sensuous show: nature dissolving, fragmenting to kaleidoscopic splinters.

We are working here, implicitly, with a scale. Near one end of it aesthetic experience attenuates towards the perception-transcending substructure of its objects. We do not have an obligation to place ourselves there: with the aesthetic, it is on the phenomenal, the *Lebenswelt*, concrete and abstract both, that we must focus attention. At the other end of the scale, as we have just noted, we exclude all thought, and leave sensuous immediacy only. At both extremes we lose what John Findlay singled out as aesthetic essentials, the poignant and the perspicuous in combination. These opposite dangers are run only when the ready-made stereotyped snapshot appreciatings of nature are transcended, and the subject is actively seeking his or her own synthesis – maximally poignant and perspicuous – with nature's materials perceived and pondered. *Between* the extremes, we might find an acceptable ideal for serious aesthetic perception in encouraging ourselves to enhance the thought-load *almost* to the point, but not *beyond* the point, at which it begins to overwhelm the vivacity of the particular perception.

In my second approach to nature the forms of nature are annexed in imagination, interiorised, the external made internal. Is there in this, in contrast with the previous theme, a suggestion of the solipsistic or at least the narcissistic? Not necessarily: since if we share a common environment, the annexed forms can range from the universally inter-subjective, through the shareable though not universal, to the highly individual and personal. *Basic* natural forms are interiorized for the articulating of a common structure of the mind. Through these, the elusively non-spatial is made more readily graspable and communicable. We speak of depths and heights – in relation to moods or feelings or hopes or fears: of soarings and of glooms. We are lifted and dashed, chilled, spiritually frozen and thawed. We drown, we surface; we suffer dark nights of the soul. Again, there is no simple one-to-one correlation between mental state and natural item. I may interiorise the desert – as bleak emptiness, *néant*: or I may interiorise it as unscripted openness, potentiality . . .

As already suggested, metaphor is of the essence in such appropriations. No aestheticising of natural objects can occur in these ways unless we have discovered metaphor. And that gives us the clue we need in order to apply the distinction between trivial and serious to this area. Many metaphors we use constantly to articulate conscious life are dead metaphors: some are at any time capable of reanimation. But on occasion (and we can let Wordsworth mark for us the extreme point in metaphorical appropriation), a person catches from events in the natural world 'a tone, / An image, and a character' so deeply and individually apt that they reorganise or recentre his or her life. But these too need not be incommunicably private; they may be 'fit to be transmitted and made visible / To other eyes.' Wordsworth, for instance, saw in the workings and self-transformings of nature on the grand scale (as he narrated in *The Prelude* XIII, on the effects of mist and moonlight on Snowdon) metaphors for the poet's understanding and evaluating of his own imaginative transforming activity, in the fashioning of his own poetry. He explicitly acknowledges the co-presence of perception and thought. 'By sensible impressions not enthrall'd, / But quicken'd, rouz'd, and made thereby more fit / To hold communion with the invisible world.'

The 'invisible world' is the world of spirit, of mind, the spiritual being precisely articulated and modified by its imaginative annexing of the outer world – that is, the sensible impressions derived from it, but also imbued with thought. Our topic is not simply the search for the descriptively apt metaphors from nature for the structure and the ongoings of human inwardness, structures and ongoings that would exist or occur identically and independently whether or not the search is successful, but the annexing is also a moulding and making of that inwardness, reflectively or perfunc-torily achieved. No doubt some of this can be done by images drawn from domestic or urban life, but there is more than a little suggestion of anxious self-protectiveness in such restriction to the man-made environment. The gain would be that we screen ourselves from the natural immensities that daunt us; the loss that we cut ourselves off from that 'renewal of our inner being' which the Romantics saw as derived from meditating on the great permanencies of nature.

A person may find it hard not to take certain natural sequences as generalisable and significant, though enigmatic, 'messages' of nature. For instance, the natural sequence of events in a sunrise or the clearing of weather after a storm may seem to carry an optimistic message. Adorno, in *Aesthetic Theory*, writes of the 'yearning for what is promised but never unveiled by beauty . . . a message seems to be inscribed' on some aspect of nature, 'not all is lost yet.' But, he adds, 'the statement that this is how nature speaks is meaningless, nature's language is not propositional.'[7] Analogously, on listening to a particular piece of music, I may swing between saying (1) What I am enjoying is simply the emotional quality – a cheering, happy quality – of *this* sequence of tones and rhythms; and (2) this expresses a generalisable cheering, a justified hopefulness. Perhaps in both nature and music, to go to the stronger claim must be to risk illusion. To be safe, I would have to keep to the cautious, and certainly valid inference: because this state is actual, this state is at least a human possibility, and (I may add, still fairly cautiously) a renewable one.

What would trivialising be, here? I think it would be either to be 'fundamentalist', literalist about 'messages of nature', or to reject the whole topic, again in a literalist spirit – that or nothing. More adequate, and with a claim to seriousness, is to be aware of the metaphoricality and the enigmatic quality, and to allow that awareness to characterise the thought side of the experiences.

The combination of distanced and yet intimate or enigmatically meaningful is nowhere more intensely realised than in *dreams*. Indeed it has been claimed that in any strikingly beautiful landscape there is an element of the dreamlike. The interiorisation seems half-completed in nature itself, imparting an almost mythological character to any figures such a scene contains. All are apprehended with a mysterious sense that the components (or some of them) deeply *matter* to us, though one cannot say how: the shape of a hill, the precise placing of a stand of trees or a solitary rock. To decide that there is no readable significance is not necessarily to discredit such an experience or to show it up as illusion. Any discrediting is again the work of literalism. Naively serious, and *thus* trivial. We seem invited to 'transcend the sheer sensible impressions': we do transcend them, but only into our state of perplexity and wonder. But no demythologisable message could be more memorable than these half-perceived, half-dreamed visionary scenes.

Another respect must be noted in which there occur large individual differences in the aesthetic appreciation of nature. This is in the degree to which imagination is active in connecting diverse separated natural forms. I am thinking of the relating of object with object, structure with structure, searching out analogies between features of otherwise very remote phenomena. We may see the hills as 'lifting themselves in ridges like the waves of a tumultuous sea,' or we see 'high cirrus cloud' as 'exactly resembling sea sand ribbed by the tide' (Wordsworth and Ruskin, respectively).

To be imaginatively alert to such common structures has an obvious unifying, integrating effect – enhancing the sense that we are dealing with a single nature, intelligible in its forms. In at least two ways, however, pursuit of resemblances and analogies can become absurd or one-sided, and so can trivialise aesthetic perception of nature. Some wholly fortuitous, fanciful likeness may be made the object of an excessive wonderment, as when the guide to a system of limestone caves introduces a stalagmite as the Virgin Mary. Again there can result a falsely comforting simplification and idealisation of nature. For not *all* is intelligible structure or perspicuous geometry. The veining of rocks, wind-shaping of clouds, undulating of hills – all of these have (as well as their undoubted symmetries) their elements of arbitrariness and opacity, at the phenomenal level. To Kant's important claim that nature looks as if made for our cognitive faculty, we have surely to add the equally important antithetical claim, that in some respects it looks *not at all* as if it were made for us to perceive and to know.

Nature's otherness is as real and as aesthetically significant, if we are 'serious', as is its readily perceptible chiming forms.

This combination, in our aesthetic perception of nature, of the readily graspable and the opaque, sheerly contingent and alien, merits more than a sentence. The realisation that the combination characterises our aesthetic dealings with nature in general must again count as a mark of seriousness. It is a distinction vital, for instance, to a monotheistic view of nature. If the world of nature were itself divine, then one would expect intelligibility to prevail throughout. If the created world were distinct from God, though the product of his all-rational mind, one would expect a nature with a magnificently intelligible structure, but with signs of the insertion of divine *will* – the contingent, the might-have-been-different. Even if we do not hold a theistic belief system, there can be a parabolic application of this duality, indicating truthfully enough that the distinction runs very deep in our experience of nature.

What is more, we are able to make aesthetic use, to make a topic of appreciation, of that dichotomy. There would be an aesthetic thinness or emptiness, if the perceptible forms of nature, its skylines and contours and living beings, could all be generated by mathematicians' equations of relatively simple kinds. Perhaps wind-formed sand-dunes and wave-patterns come near, though even there the complexity soon defies our perception of intelligible form. Realising the duality is one main element in our perceiving of a natural configuration such as one may see on many shores: strata in a rock-face tilted to an arch, but crumbling and weathered, supporting grasses and the nests of seagulls on its ledges and shelves.

So far, the aspects of aesthetic appreciation of nature which we have considered have sustained our intuition that appreciation can be more or less superficial, more or less serious. It is possible, however, to be moved by sceptical thoughts which suggest that the *whole* of this area of experience is nothing other than trivial, that aesthetic experience of nature – being founded on a variety of illusions – can never really be serious.

Aesthetic experiences of nature, it may be said, are fugitive and unstable, wholly dependent upon anthropocentric factors such as scale, viewpoint, perspective. The mountain that we appreciate for its majesty and stability is, on a different time-scale, as fluid as the ripples on the lake at its foot. Set any distinctive natural object in its wider context in the environment of which it is a part, and the particular aesthetic quality you are enjoying is likely to vanish. You shudder with awe at the base of your cliff towering above you. But look at the cliff again (if you can identify it in time) from an aircraft at thirty thousand feet, and does not the awe strike you as having been misplaced, as somewhat theatrical and exaggerated, childish even? Can an experience be serious if it can so readily be undermined?

First of all, something not very different can be true of art experience as well. A too remote viewpoint or a too distant listening point can ruin the impact of a picture or performed music, and without a sympathetically and elaborately prepared mental set, and the appropriate context of attitudes and ideas, many works of high art can strike one as grotesque, fatuous, bathetic or comically solemn. Yet these familiar facts about the conditions of satisfactory art experience do *not* seem to undermine its worth when the conditions are in fact happily fulfilled.

It is not quite the same with art as with nature. The appreciators of nature have in one way more to do than the art appreciators; they play a larger creative role in fashioning their aesthetic object. They have to find their viewpoint, decide on boundaries of attention, generate the thought content. The experience is more of a cooperative product of natural object and contemplator. But what lurks behind the more comprehensively dismissive and sceptical movements of mind with regard to *nature* is an assumption about what we might call 'authority'. The view from an aircraft allegedly shows you what the cliff *really* is like and shows that your awe was misplaced. Likewise, in the case of the 'majestic' and 'stable' mountain, a sceptical critic may appeal to the facts of the oneness, the connectedness of the items of the natural world, and of the universality of change and flux; and these are taken to annul or destroy our serious appreciation of the perceptual qualities of a self-selected fragment, our perceptual snapshot or 'still' – artificially isolated (as these qualities are) from the whole and the 'becoming' of the whole.

To occupy the discrediting perspective is being understood as entitling the critic to say: 'I know (or I see) something you are not aware of! From my distance – or from my height – your awe is shown up as misplaced.' Or is there something deeply amiss in that comment? And could not I (at the foot of my cliff) say something very similar? 'You in your aircraft, though you can see a great deal, are simply unable to perceive and respond to the perceptual qualities that generate the awe *I* feel. Your viewpoint has its limitations too.' What happens very often, I think, is that the ironical, anti-Romantic, belittling, levelling reaction tends uncritically to be favoured today as the authoritative reaction ('You won't put anything over on me'). Why this should be so for many people in our society would need study in the sociology of religious, moral and aesthetic values in their interconnections. What I should certainly want to say myself is that a readiness to conform to such a social trend can be a factor on the side of trivialisation, not the side of seriousness, in aesthetic appreciation. Our aesthetic experience of nature is thoroughly dependent on scale and on individual viewpoint. To fail to realise *how* deeply would surely trivialise. Coming to realise and to think in to one's aesthetic experience the fact of that perspectivity is certainly a factor in the maturing of this experience. But what is highly contestable is the implicit claim that *one* perspective, *one* view, *one* set of resultant perceived qualities takes precedence over another, and so can discredit or undermine another – or even all the others: that one of them has, in an aesthetic context, greater authority than another. It is easy enough to deal with the art examples. Generally speaking, the painting we can assume to have been *made* to be viewed from the distance at which its significant detail can be discriminated and its overall structure seen as a unity, and the music to be heard closely enough to occupy our auditory attention with all *its* detail.

But the analogy with art may be developed in a further way, one that carries important implications. In the subject-matter of art there is no 'authoritatively appropriate' and 'inappropriate'. Equally fitting objects of attention are substances, relations, events, the abstract as well as the concrete, the momentary, the minute, the everlasting, the insubstantial, even the perceptually illusory. Any of these may be the subject of, say, a poet's celebration and scrutiny. (A study which argues vigorously for this 'ontological parity', as its author calls it, is Justus Buchler's *The Main of Light* – particularly Chapter 6 (New York: Oxford University Press, 1974)). Is there any reason why this principle should apply any less plausibly to the aesthetic appreciation of nature? It would legitimise any viewpoint on any subject-matter – substance or shadow, any perceptual qualities, physical materials, mica, quartz, sand, or more elusive perspective-dependent qualities like the blueness of the sky, the colours of the rainbow, the enhancement of distance perception on an atmospherically clear day, or the merging of objects in mist. It would of course follow that if I denied special authority to any perspective whatever, I would have to deny it to the perspective which I (still at the foot of my cliff) would very willingly judge to have some preferred status. That it could not have.

The reader will have been aware, as I have been aware, that two recurrent elements in the account I have been giving exert pressures in different directions, or (if you like) remain in stressful relation with one another. On the one side, one way to seriousness in our aesthetic dealings with nature involved a respect for truth – more accurately, for the objective truth such as the sciences pursue – so long as that path does not carry us beyond what can be incorporated in still essentially *perceptual* experience. The terminus in that direction, then, would be the thinking-in to our perceptual experience of what we know to be objectively the case. Remember the examples of glaciation as once shaping the now green valley, and anxiety colouring our response to sighting the wild animal whose predator is seldom far off. There is a correcting or guiding of our episodic experience through an objectivising movement of mind.

Nevertheless, we have also felt the attraction of a radically anti-hierarchical, in some respects anti-objectivising movement, towards acceptance of 'ontological parity'. And according to *that*, the perceptually 'corrected' and veridical has no stronger or more serious claim to aesthetic attention than has the illusory.

Is there any way, then, of dealing rationally with these conflicting pressures? Should we say: all this is, ultimately, about a *game* we play with nature, for enjoyment and the enriching of our lives? In any particular situation follow whichever option promises more reward. We are free to respect, or to ignore, the objectivising option. To feel bound always to pursue it is not really to show commitment to so-called seriousness, but rather to show a profound misunderstanding of the aesthetic. Or would that be simply and shockingly, at the very end, to capitulate to the trivialisers?

NOTES

1. For a treatment different from my own, see Pepita Haezrahi, *The Contemplative Activity* (Allen & Unwin, 1954), ch. 2.
2. *Tour in the Lake Country*, 1802, cf. also, David Craig, *Native Stones: A Book about Climbing* (London: Secker & Warburg, 1987), p. 132.
3. A. Schopenhauer, *The World as Will and Representation*, trans. E. F. J. Payne (New York: Dover Books, 1969), I, paragraph 39.

4. M. Dufrenne, *Esthétique et philosophie*, I, 'Expérience esthétique de la nature,' p. 45. T. W. Adorno, *Aesthetic Theory* (London: Routledge & Kegan Paul, 1984, first published 1970), p. 103.
5. Adorno, *Aesthetic Theory*, p. 100.
6. W. Wordsworth, *The Prelude*, Bk. I, lines 438–60.
7. Adorno, *Aesthetic Theory*, pp. 108–9.
8. Versions of this essay were given as lectures at Lancaster and Boston Universities.

4

'ADMIRING THE HIGH MOUNTAINS': THE AESTHETICS OF ENVIRONMENT

John Haldane

EXPERIENCES OF LANDSCAPE AND ENVIRONMENT AESTHETICS

My title is drawn from a passage in St Augustine's *Confessions* (X. 8.15) as quoted by Petrarch in a famous letter addressed to Francesco Dionigi da Borgo San Sepolcro, an Augustinean professor of theology. Dated 26 April 1336, it recounts an ascent of Mont Ventoux (the 'Windy Peak') made that same day by Petrarch, his brother and two servants. After describing his preparations for the climb and its early stages he turns to religious matters drawing parallels between the difficulties of the physical ascent and the process of spiritual formation. Having reached the highest summit he reflects on his recent past and then, as the sun begins to set, he looks around again in all directions:

> I admired every detail, now relishing earthly enjoyment, now lifting up my mind to higher spheres after the example of my body, and I thought it fit to look into the volume of Augustine's *Confessions* . . . Where I fixed my eyes first it was written: 'And men go to admire the high mountains, the vast floods of the sea, the huge streams of the rivers, the circumference of the ocean, and the revolutions of the stars – and desert themselves.' I was stunned, I confess. I bade my brother, who wanted to hear more, not to molest me, and closed the book, angry with myself that I still admired earthly things. Long since I ought to have learned, even from pagan philosophers, that 'nothing is admirable besides the mind; compared to its greatness nothing is great.' [Seneca, *Epistle* 8.5] I was completely satisfied with what I had seen of the mountain and turned my inner eye toward myself. From this hour nobody heard me say a word until we arrived at the bottom.[1]

This is an interesting passage and for more than one reason. It belongs within a corpus that bears the marks of the emerging Renaissance humanism, and the letter itself has often been referred to as anticipating later European mountaineering interests; but what I think we should be struck by is the unironic willingness with which Petrarch sets aside his aesthetic delight as unworthy of the human mind. We have become accustomed to praising natural beauty and to thinking of its appreciation precisely as a mark of a refined sensibility and as something to be approved of and cultivated. Thus the implicit opposition of aesthetic and spiritual concerns is hard for us to accommodate. Consider how unexceptional (and congenial to modern environmentalism) seem the ideas, if not the form, of Hopkins' sonnet 'God's Grandeur':[2]

> The world is charged with the Grandeur of God.
> It will flame out, like shining from shook foil;
> It gathers to a greatness, like the ooze of oil
> Crushed. Why do men then not now reck his rod?
> Generations have trod, have trod, have trod;
> And all is seared with trade; bleared, smeared with toil;
> And wears man's smudge and shares man's smell: the soil
> Is bare now, nor can foot feel, being shod.
>
> And for all this, nature is never spent;
> There lives the dearest freshness deep down things;
> And though the last lights off the black West went
> Oh, morning, at the brown brink eastward, springs –
> Because the Holy Ghost over the bent
> World broods with warm breast and with ah! bright wings.

Of course Petrarch was writing over 650 years ago, long before Romantic quasi-panentheism, and addressing a theologian with whom he shared an admiration for Augustine. This large historical and intellectual gap helps to explain the otherwise puzzling deprecation of the aesthetic appreciation of nature. Yet even in more recent times sensitive and thoughtful authors have dismissed what are now canonised land-scapes in terms which are at least striking and which some will regard as blasphemous. Consider, for example, the following description from the pen of Dr Johnson writing of Scottish scenery:

> [The hills] exhibit very little variety; being almost wholly covered with dark heath, and even that seems to be checked in its growth. What is not heath is nakedness, a little diversified by now and then a stream rushing down the steep. An eye accustomed to flowery pastures and waving harvests is astonished and repelled by this wide extent of hopeless sterility. The appearance is that of matter incapable of form or usefulness, dismissed by nature from her care and disinherited of her favours, left in its original elemental state, or quickened only with one sullen power of useless vegetation.
>
> It will very readily occur, that this uniformity of barrenness can afford little amusement to the traveller; that it is easy to sit at home and conceive rocks and

heath, and waterfalls; and that these journeys are useless labours, which neither impregnate the imagination, nor enlarge the understanding.[3]

This text and Petrarch's letter should serve as reminders that there is nothing perennially obvious about the present-day reverence for nature and the elevation of its appreciation to the higher categories of human consciousness. The 'aesthetics of the environment' is like the 'politics of the home' – a term of art invented to label a set of concerns and an associated field of academic study each developed over time and out of particular cultural histories. In what follows I sketch something of the relevant philosophical background and consider some aspects of the growing interest in environmental aesthetics.

Recent years have seen the rapid rise to prominence of a range of studies, policy directives and initiatives concerned with the environment. These are some-times unphilosophical, pragmatic responses to perceived threats arising from, for example, heavy industrialisation and increasing levels of human activity. Very often, however, they are presented through patterns of judgement and justification that are avowedly moral, not to say moralistic. Those involved in such presentations are then liable to speak in terms of 'environmental *ethics*', or more likely of 'an environmental *ethic*'. Although there are reasons for doubting whether values can be thought of in compartmentalised isolation I want for present purposes, and so far as is possible, to place ethical concerns on one side and to focus on *aesthetic* considerations.[4] More precisely my interest is in whether, and if so how, philo-sophical aesthetics might be brought into contemporary thinking about the natural environment.

In advance one might suppose that the effect of introducing any kind of objective aesthetic element into the discussion of environmental values would be to strengthen the case for 'deep' ecology. It is, after all, a common plea made by those concerned with protecting the natural environment from the effects of industry, say, that these deface the landscape, transforming what is naturally beautiful into something ugly. How then could an interest in the aesthetic qualities of nature be other than an instance of respect for the environment considered as something valuable in and of itself? To answer that question I need to say something about the general character of aesthetic theory.

SOME ELEMENTS OF AESTHETIC EXPERIENCE

From antiquity through the Middle Ages, the Renaissance and the Enlightenment to the present day, there has been a movement in philosophical discussions of beauty and other aesthetic values (such as the sublime – and in later periods the picturesque) from attention to the *objects* of aesthetic experience to the character of the *experience* itself, and of the modes of attention or *attitudes* it involves. Although there is no agreed inventory of the elements or aspects of aesthetic experience, and certainly there is no agreement on their interrelationships, Table 4.1 sets out something of the broad range of favoured possibilities.

Again considered historically, the focus of interest has moved from left to right in

Table 4.1 The elements of aesthetic experience

Aesthetic object		Aesthetic value		Aesthetic response	Aesthetic attitude
Anything at all	Specific things	Intrinsic values	Extrinsic values		
	Reality	Content	Satisfaction	Pleasure	Detachment
	Emotion	Form	Release	Interest	Disinterest
	Form etc.	Sensuous	Understanding	Universal validity	Contemplation
		qualities etc.	etc.	Satisfaction	Isolation
				Understanding etc.	Psychical distance
					Interpretation etc.

the table. Thus in *pre-modern aesthetics* (to the extent that one can reasonably speak in these terms of a subject that is often thought to have originated only in the eighteenth century)[5] aesthetic objects and values are generally taken to be prior, with aesthetic responses and attitudes being held to be posterior to and explicable in terms of these. So, for example, it might be argued that the 'objects' of aesthetic experience are the forms of natural entities, and that aesthetic value consists in the harmonious organisation of parts realised in such forms. An aesthetic experience will then be any experience in which these forms and values are attended to and appreciated, and an aesthetic attitude will be an (or perhaps *the*) attitude induced by such experiences.

Clearly any view of this sort, if it is to avoid explanatory circularity, must postulate certain objective features that are the basis for our experiences of beauty. The task of doing so is a challenging one and though there are still efforts to complete it many have come to think it is impossible. Such scepticism together with other factors led, in the *modern* and *Enlightenment* periods, to the development of broadly subjectivist accounts of aesthetics. By 'subjectivist', here, I do not mean arbitrary or idiosyncratic. Rather, the unifying feature of such accounts is that the direction of explanation runs from the attitude or experience to the value or object. One might, for example, identify the aesthetic attitude as one of detachment from theoretical and practical concerns or of disinterested contemplation, thereby specifying the character of aesthetic experience as being that of expressing or being conditioned by such an attitude. Following this one might then say that an aesthetic object is any object attended to in that kind of experience, and an aesthetic value is any feature singled out in such an experience as rewarding of attention, or, and more likely, any feature of the experience itself which is found to be pleasant or beneficial. Once again explanatory circularity will only be avoided so long as one does not at this point appeal to aesthetic objects in order to specify the relevant class of attitudes and experiences.

Even if that can be done, however, it is tempting to suppose that a consequence of a subjectivist approach is that there can then be no question of correct or incorrect aesthetic judgements, or relatedly of better and worse judges; for without autonomous aesthetic objects surely there can be no aesthetic objectivity. One familiar reaction to this thought is to welcome it, arguing that one of the main reasons for favouring subject-based approaches is precisely that aesthetic judgements lack criteria by which to be assessed. However, a subtler response recognises that in giving explanatory priority to the aesthetic attitude and aesthetic experience one is not wholly precluded from having external criteria of greater or lesser, coarser and more refined aesthetic sensibility; for one may hold that there are *inter-subjective* standards.[6]

Consider the case of table manners. At the level of serious reflection we should not be tempted to suppose that there are objectively offensive modes of eating. Rather we should say that manners are a function of culturally shared interests. A mode of eating is offensive for a given community if in normal circumstances it would be judged offensive by a competent member of that community, competence here being explained not in terms of an ability to discern objectively offensive eating practices but by reference to mastery of certain social conventions governing public eating. Although these norms are *subjective*, in the sense of being rooted in the dispositions of *subjects*, nonetheless their existence allows for the idea that some member of that community can go wrong in his or her style of eating, and thereby correctly be described as ill-mannered.

It should be clear then that the resources of certain 'subjectivist' aesthetic theories are more considerable than might initially be supposed. Moreover, as Table 4.1 indicates, there are many different elements and combinations that might be included in an aesthetic theory of either objectivist or subjectivist orientations. Rather than pursue these possibilities in detail, however, I want to consider next how the aesthetics of the environment is likely to fare when considered from these perspectives. An objectivist approach will look for certain features of environments which will serve as the basis for aesthetic experience and evaluation. Immediately, however, various difficulties suggest themselves. To the extent that we think of artworks as the paradigm class of objects involved in aesthetic experience we will see a problem in seeking for beauty in nature. If, like Hopkins, one were a creationist, holding that the universe is an artifact fashioned by God, then of course one could treat it formally in just the same way. But traditional theists are likely to be cautious of aestheticising Divine creation, and others will find the theistic assumption at least unwarranted and perhaps incoherent.

However, while denying that the natural world is the product of deliberate design one might nevertheless regard it *as if* designed, and maybe even speak of 'Nature' itself as the source of aesthetic order. This move, however, generates problems of its own. Consider the question how many pictures there are in a given art gallery, or performances in a particular concert hall. Notwithstanding elements of the avant-garde this would, in principle, be a relatively easy matter to settle by reference to the form, content, matter and source of the works. However, if one eschews any claim of literal creation it seems in principle impossible to say where one work of nature begins and another ends. The category of the scenic view, for example, is all too obviously one of our own fashioning. If there is any element of art-making in nature it is surely present through the selective attention of spectators to aspects of a continuous realm. Furthermore, in deciding where to locate the boundaries of one scene our designs are influenced by the experience of actual art-works. In short, the effort to identify aesthetic objects in nature tends quickly to return one in the direction of the subject of experience and of his or her interests, cultural presuppositions and classifications.

Whether for these or other reasons, an objectivist might not choose to employ the art-work model but try instead the sort of approach I described as being characteristic of premodern thinking. That is to say, he or she might hold that the objects of environmental aesthetic experience are natural forms, by which I mean, primarily, the forms of organisms and derivatively those of non-organic entities. Something of this view is suggested by the fragmentary but very interesting remarks made by Aquinas in his discussions of beauty. He explicitly denies the claim that something is beautiful simply because we like it, insisting by contrast that our appreciation is directed towards the beauty of things, and that a thing is beautiful to the extent that it manifests its proper form or natural structure. He writes:

> Three things are required for beauty. First integrity or perfection (*integritas sive perfectio*), for what is defective is thereby ugly; second, proper proportion or consonance (*proportio sive consonantia*); and third clarity (*claritas*).[7]

The background assumption is that each substance or individual is possessed of a nature which, in the case of living things, is at once a principle of organic structure and a determinant of its characteristic activities. Integrity and proper proportion are directly related to this nature or form (*forma rei*) and the issue of clarity arises from them. *Integrity* consists in the possession of all that is required by the nature of the thing, such and such limbs and organs, active capacities and so on, while *proportion* includes both the compatibility of these elements and their being well-ordered. These two factors are then presupposed in the idea of *clarity*, for that concerns the way in which the form of a thing is manifest or unambiguously presented.

This neo-Aristotelian account has certain merits from the point of view of those interested in developing an objectivist environmental aesthetic. Forms are real, mind-independent entities, there to be discovered and contemplated. Thus the question of whether one member of a natural kind better realises the species' common nature is one that it makes sense to ask and one which informed attention can hope to answer. Also values and policies seem to be implicit or rootable in such facts. A 'good' specimen is *ontologically* better than a 'poor' one, that is to say it is a better instance of a being of that kind, and it is clear enough how industrial practices can be detrimental to these natural values by causing harm to individual organisms and injuring the species. Thus, unlikely as it might have been supposed given the tone of Petrarch's fourteenth-century reflections, it may seem that in the thirteenth-century writings of Aquinas there is a promising source for a deep ecological aesthetic, i.e. one in which the relevant values owe nothing to man's interests – save of course where the forms in questions are human ones.

However, this conclusion would be a mistake and it is important to see why that is so. First, although Aquinas is insistent that beauty is not simply a function of subjective preference, his account of its conditions indicates that there is a subtle form of subjectivity, in the sense of relativity-to-a-subject, in its very constitution. Recall that beauty requires perfection, proportion and clarity. The last of these I glossed as unambiguously presented or manifest form. The existence and character of a given form may be a wholly mind-independent affair, but to speak of its presentation implies actual or possible knowers. Furthermore, whether something is unambiguous or clear is in part a function of the cognitive powers and accomplishments of the actual or imagined subject. So to say that something is beautiful if the perfection of its form is clearly presented indicates that, of necessity, beauty is something which involves a spectator. It is also apparent both from what Aquinas says and from the logic of his position that the spectators in question require the sort of intellectual capacity which there is little reason to think is possessed by any other creature lower than man. In short, natural beauty is constitutively tied to human experience.

Second, on Aquinas's view there is an equivalence between goodness and beauty – known as the 'convertibility of the transcendentals'. What this means is that in thinking or speaking of these attributes one is referring to the same feature of reality, namely the condition of the natural form that constitutes an item's essential nature. Thus a thing is good and beautiful to the extent that its form is perfected. This is an interesting thesis, and on reflection a plausible one with relevance for environmental philosophy. But it has a corollary that moves aesthetics deeper into the territory of humanistic ecology, i.e. an account of environmental values that explains them in terms of human interests and well-being. If the referents of 'good' and 'beautiful' are one and the same how do the terms differ? Aquinas answers that each expresses a distinct kind of interest in, or concern with, the forms of things.

> The beautiful is the same as the good, and they differ in aspect only. For since good is what all seek, the notion of good is that which calms the desire; while the notion of the beautiful is that which calms the desire by being seen or known. Consequently those senses chiefly regard the beautiful which are the most cognitive, *viz.*, sight and hearing, as ministering to reason; for we speak of beautiful sights and beautiful sounds . . . Thus it is evident that beauty adds to goodness a relation to the cognitive faculty: so that *good* means that which simply pleases the appetite; while the *beautiful* is something pleasant to apprehend.[8]

Thus although Aquinas roots his account of beauty in objective fact, the existence of aesthetic objects and values involves human subjects taking delight in perceptually and intellectually discernible structures. His view should be congenial to those concerned with environmental axiology in general and with aesthetic values in particular. It accords a major role to natural forms and can accommodate within this classification entities more extensive than individual organisms, such as species and even ecosystems. Further, unlike the aesthetics of the scenic, it need not confine itself to the 'visible surface' of the world. It can, for example, allow the aesthetic relevance of ecological history and of the sorts of environmental structures to which Aldo Leopold's *A Sand County Almanac* did much to draw attention. In 'Marshland Elegy' Leopold writes:

> Our ability to perceive quality in nature begins, as in art, with the pretty. It expands through successive stages of the beautiful to values as yet uncaptured by language. The quality of cranes, lies, I think, in this higher gamut, as yet beyond the reach of words.

This much though can be said: our appreciation of the crane grows with the slow unravelling of earthly history. His tribe, we now know, stems out of the remote Ecocene. The other members of the fauna in which he originated are long since entombed within the hills. When we hear his call we hear no mere bird. We hear the trumpet in the orchestra of evolution. He is the symbol of our untameable past, of that incredible sweep of millennia which underlies and conditions the daily affairs of birds and men.[9]

It should be clear, however, that like the earlier attempt to conceive an aesthetics of the natural environment along the lines of a philosophy of art, an element of which is also present in Leopold's thinking, Aquinas's theory of natural beauty has an ineliminable subjective aspect. My general conclusion, then, is that whichever side of the table one starts from – focusing on the aesthetic attitude or the aesthetic object – one should be led to think that human experience plays a constitutive role in environmental aesthetics.

CONTEMPORARY ENVIRONMENTAL AESTHETICS

Let me round off this discussion by considering, and offering a critique of, some recent writings in environmental aesthetics. Much contemporary literature in the area belongs to the tradition of naturalistic humanism, and in the effort to understand the relationship between art and nature some of it entertains the possibility that appreciation of art derives from a more basic 'biological' attitude to landscape forms. In *The Experience of Landscape*, for example, Jay Appleton presents an account of our attitudes to natural environments which treats them as originating in a biological response to the need to survive and flourish in various habitats.[10] One objection to this proposal is that it risks committing a genetic fallacy, that of supposing one has given an exhaustive assessment of the content of experience by providing an account of its cause or source. It might well be that religious belief, for example, has a biological origin but that fact neither wholly explains the content of beliefs nor provides a criterion by which to assess their truth or plausibility. In a more recent work on *The Aesthetics of Landscape*, Stephen Bourassa does not mention this objection as such, but he is rightly troubled by the reductionist tendency of Appleton's theory.[11] Thus he looks for another way of integrating the biological dimension into a richer and more elaborately structured account of experiences of landscape. Likewise, while he accepts the thesis that experience is shaped by cultural presuppositions and values, he is concerned to transcend the further element of determinism that this might be thought to imply, in order to leave a place for individual responses. The upshot of these explorations is the conclusion that a threefold process of historical development leads to three modes of human existence – the natural, the social and the personal – which contribute related biological, cultural and personal aspects to experience, these in turn giving rise to certain aesthetic laws, rules and strategies.

Appleton's biological theory suggests that aesthetic satisfaction is related to the experience of environments as affording conditions for survival – in short, favourable habitats. This introduces the possibility of empirical confirmation and Bourassa reports work on the responses of individuals to different kinds of environment. A major element of this 'habitat theory' is focused on the appeal of locations from which one can see the surrounding terrain without oneself being seen: 'prospect-refuge' contexts. Interesting as this hypothesis and its empirical evidence may be, Bourassa is right to worry about the connections between the conditions of our ancestors in the wild and our own reflective experiences of landscape. After all we want, for example, some understanding of the appeal of certain 'compositional' elements of a natural environment in terms which answer to the sense of them *as* compositional, and for that the ideas of foreground, background, contrast, incident, interval, tone and texture seem more apt than any talk of the 'prospect-refuge' needs of ancestors whose physical and cultural conditions of existence and cognitive accomplishments were utterly different from our own. When discussing variants on the habitat hypothesis, Bourassa refers to a biologically based theory advanced by N. Humphrey according to which 'beautiful "structures" in nature or in art are those which facilitate the task of classification by presenting evidence of the "taxonomic" relations between things in a way which is informative and easy to grasp'. This suggests an interesting parallel with the *claritas* condition of the neo-Thomist account I sketched earlier.[12]

As against the 'scientific' tendency of Bourassa, Arnold Berleant complains in *The Aesthetics of Environment* that too much of our thinking is conditioned by objectifying assumptions.[13] We regard environment as a container, or as that which is opposed to self, or again as landscape scenery. Instead, we need an idea of it as the field or medium of human life. Likewise, nature should not be thought of as opposed to culture, or as an established setting existing apart from of and prior to our location within it. Rather we must develop a sense of an all-encompassing unity:

> This last sense of nature, which does not differentiate between the human and the natural and which interprets everything as part of a single, continuous whole, corresponds to the largest idea of environment. It is more than an ecosystem, for that important idea still objectifies the human environmental complex, regarding it as a whole, but a whole that is to be scientifically studied and analysed from without. Environment, as I want to speak of it, is the natural process as people live it, however they live it. Environment is nature experienced, nature lived. (p. 10).

Truistically, monism denies pluralism, but without a plurality of elements it is difficult to see how anything like our ordinary and philosophical understanding of life can be made sense of. No doubt there is a case for holding that if we are to do justice to aesthetic experiences of (and other modes of intelligent engagement with) the spaces, places, contexts and conditions within which we live, move and have our being, then we may need to overcome, or at least to rethink, various dualisms: of self and other; observer and scene; passive spectator and active nature; contemplation and action; surface and depth, etc. But we had also better be wary of running too rapidly towards contrary assumptions: of supposing that all dualisms are untenable; that there cannot be intimacy without unity; and in general of getting carried away and ending up saying things that sound deep but are in fact of doubtful coherence. With this possibility in mind consider the following series of claims:

> The human environment is, in the final account, a perceptual system and, as such, an order of experiences. (p. 20)
>
> Not surface, no longer surroundings, environment takes on the character of an integral whole. It becomes both the condition and content of experience in which the human participant is so absorbed into a situation as to become inseparable from and continuous with it . . . (p. 35)
>
> Environment is no region separate from us. It is not only the very condition of our being but a continuous part of that being. Appreciating environment requires a sensitivity to these undulating forces and currents of the world. (p. 131)

The proper starting point for any treatment of aesthetic experience is the recognition that perception involves modes of awareness of objects, properties and situations by means of the sensory and conceptual powers of subjects who are identifiable independently of those objects, properties and situations. That is a modest dualism but without it there are no relata for experience to relate.

CONCLUSION

In recent writings such as those by Appleton, Bourassa and Berleant, there is a tendency to oppose, or at least to query, modern disinterest conceptions of the aesthetic attitude such as I listed in Table 4.1 (column 4). That is all to the good, though as may now be apparent this represents something of a return to older views. Certainly, the neo-Aristotelian object-based account I derived from Aquinas has little place for detached, non-practical, non-theoretical attitudes, and regards the primary (but not the only) mode of beauty as being, in Kant's terminology, *dependent* rather than *free*, i.e. form or nature, rather than imagination, based.

The wise course in philosophy is to be wary of generalisation. We do not need to say that aesthetic experience is exclusively of such and such a character, and we should be wary of exaggerating the possible forms of the real, common nature of experience. Culturally and philosophically we have come a long way from Petrarch's Augustinean-inspired revulsion at his own delight, but even so we are far from having a clear and complete account of the nature and value of the aesthetics of environment. Further progress in that task demands a more adequate understanding of issues in the philosophies of mind and value, and I conjecture that this is likely to take discussion further in the direction of the non-reductive naturalism of Aristotle and Aquinas.[14]

NOTES

1. Petrarch, 'The Ascent of Mont Ventoux', in *The Renaissance Philosophy of Man*, eds E. Cassirer, P.O. Kristeller and J. H. Randall (Chicago: Chicago University Press, 1956), p. 44.
2. G. M. Hopkins, 'God's Grandeur', in *The Poems of Gerard Manley Hopkins*, eds W. H. Gardener and N. H. MacKenzie (Oxford: Oxford University Press, 1970), p. 66.

3. S. Johnson, *A Journey to the Western Islands* ed. R. W. Chapman (Oxford: Oxford University Press, 1944), pp. 34–5. It is interesting to compare these remarks with those of Thomas Gray: 'I am returned from Scotland, charmed with my expedition: it is of the Highlands I speak: the Lowlands are worth seeing once, but the mountains are ecstatic and ought to be visited in pilgrimage once a year. None but those monstrous creatures of God know how to join so much beauty with so much horror. A fig for your poets, painters, gardeners and clergymen, that have not been among them, their imagination can be made up of nothing but bowling greens, flowering shrubs, horse ponds, Fleet ditches, shell grottoes and Chinese rails. Then I had so beautiful an Autumn. Italy could hardly produce a nobler scene, and this so sweetly contrasted with that perfection of nastiness and total want of accommodation that only Scotland can supply.' Letter of 1765, in *The Correspondence of Thomas Gray*, eds P. Toynbee and L. Whibley (Oxford: Clarendon Press, 1935), Vol. II: 1756–65, p. 899. I am indebted to Christopher Smout for this quotation. He uses it to introduce a fascinating discussion of attitudes to Scottish landscape: see C. Smout, 'The Highlands and the roots of Green consciousness, 1750–1990', Raleigh Lecture, *Proceedings of the British Academy*, 1990.
4. For a discussion of the way in which ethical concerns may constrain aesthetic appreciation see C. Foster, 'Aesthetic disillusionment: environment, ethics, art', *Environmental Values* 1, 1992: 205–15.
5. The first philosophical use of the term 'aesthetics' to identify a (more or less) autonomous field of experience is in writings of Alexander Baumgarten published in 1734. See A. Baumgarten, *Reflections on Poetry*, trans. K. Aschenbrenner and W. Holther (Berkeley: University of California Press, 1974). Baumgarten claims that the subject is the science of sensitive knowledge, *scientia cognitionis sensitivae*.
6. This in effect is the position advanced by Hume in his classic essay 'Of the standard of taste': see D. Hume, *Of the Standard of Taste and other Essays*, ed. John W. Lenz (Indianapolis IN: Bobbs Merril, 1965), pp. 3–24.
7. Aquinas, *Summa Theologiae*, trans. Fathers of the English Dominican Province (London: Washbourne, 1914), Ia, q. 39, a. 8. For a brief account of Aquinas's view and of related ways of thinking see J. Haldane, 'Aquinas' and 'Medieval and Renaissance aesthetics', in D. Cooper (ed.), *A Companion to Aesthetics* (Oxford: Blackwell, 1993).
8. Aquinas, *Summa Theologiae*, Ia, IIae, q. 17, a. 1, ad. 3.
9. Aldo Leopold, *A Sand County Almanac* (New York: Oxford University Press, 1989), p. 96. For an account of the aesthetic dimension of Leopold's writings see J. Baird Callicott, 'Leopold's land aesthetic', *Journal of Soil and Water Conservation*, 1983; reprinted in J. Baird Callicott, *In Defense of the Land Ethic: Essays in Environmental Philosophy* (Albany, NY: SUNY Press, 1989).
10. Jay Appleton, *The Experience of Landscape* (London: John Wiley & Sons, 1975).
11. Stephen Bourassa, *The Aesthetics of Landscape* (London: Belhaven Press, 1992).
12. See N. Humphrey, 'Natural aesthetics', in B. Mikellides (ed.), *Architecture for People: Explorations in a New Humane Environment* (New York: Holt, Rinehart & Winston, 1980). For some further suggestions on this score see J. Haldane, 'Aesthetic naturalism and the decline of architecture, Part 1: Architecture and aesthetic perception', *International Journal of Moral and Social Studies* 2, 19: 210–24; and 'Philosophy and environmental issues', *International Journal of Moral and Social Studies* 5, 19: 79–91.
13. A. Berleant, *The Aesthetics of Environment* (Philadelphia: Temple University Press, 1992).
14. This essay is a revised version of material originally published in *Environmental Values* 3, 1994: 97–106 and 173–82.

5

SUSTAINABILITY AND MORAL PLURALISM

Mary Midgley

INTRODUCTION

Discussions of environmental ethics, and of applied ethics generally, easily produce a sense of unreality. But they are not a luxury. Faced with a new and monstrous predicament, we do need new thinking. Enlightenment morality, on which we still largely rely, has had enormous merits, but it strongly tends towards egoism and social atomism. This makes it hard for us to think, as we now must, about larger wholes.

The reductive notion of 'sustainability' as just the continued meeting of our present 'needs' grows out of this egoist tradition. It sees other species and larger wholes more or less as alien immigrants begging for a share of the limited private pie. This approach does represent an advance on previous official attitudes because it shows some awareness of danger. It has noticed that the pie is actually limited. But it is both practically and psychologically an inadequate response to that fact.

Practically, it is too easily satisfied with short-term solutions, producing fudges that are not ecologically sound. Psychologically, it depends on a supposed tendency for self-interest to become enlightened – that is, thoroughly far-sighted. But this does not easily happen unless wider ideals and more positive feelings of outrage supply a non-selfish background. Arne Naess and others have shown that direct valuing of the non-human world for its own sake is actually widely present today. People do think these things matter. It is thus perverse and artificial for official statements to insist on justifying action only on grounds of species egoism.

We cannot, however, sum up just why they matter in a single tidy universal formula, any more than we can do this for the other major concerns of our lives. There are many reasons, and the supposedly scientific habit of attempting such formulae and setting them in competition is foolish. It has been part of the moral philosophers' evidently mistaken search for a single all-purpose 'moral theory'. Spokespersons who have to make general declarations are therefore quite in order in using various expressions to supplement one another, explaining that the underlying ideas do not compete, and often need to be related, but all converge towards a larger truth. Different cultures have different elements to contribute to this enterprise, and we should all be prepared to learn from one another.

VERTIGO TROUBLE

A certain sense of unreality easily infests applied ethics. Thus the bookshop lady was surprised when I asked about books on business ethics. 'Business ethics?' she said. 'Well, business books are just over there, but I think ethics must be somewhere upstairs . . .' She could not easily relate facts and values. This problem is not uncommon. Practical dilemmas tend to look static, fixed and solid. Powerful contending parties posing different threats seem to dominate the scene, allowing no scope for changes of direction. We see only painful, unintelligible choices of evils. At best, the question is 'what's the least bad compromise available here?' By contrast, discussions of moral theory seem to look upwards and forwards, away from the facts, at remote ideals, calling for a flexibility and clarity which may well seem unattainable.

This sense of unreality – this impression that the two approaches can't be brought together – is particularly strong over our present environmental difficulties because the scale of the predicament is so new. The challenge is extremely surprising for the whole human race and especially so for our own recent traditions. Putting it crudely, for a couple of centuries we have been brought up to believe in progress – to expect that in principle things on earth were getting better under the guidance of our own civilisation. Though we knew that we, as a culture, had moral faults, we thought that even there we were improving, and physically we certainly did not expect any very serious trouble. We were brought up to think that lapses, however bad, would be local and temporary.

Until lately, general confidence in this prospect was not seriously shaken by the various kinds of scepticism which have eroded other aspects of our thought. Belief in God might be under attack, but for most Western people belief in Man, and in the works belonging to his local avatar, stood firm. Now, however, we are called on to accept the very different story that Man himself, under his present flags, is producing actual disaster. This calls on us, not just to give up many comforts, but also to change those flags, which mark and celebrate some of our habitual ideals.

That drastic reversal, coming on top of the other sceptical trends just mentioned, calls for vigorous new thinking about values. It does not, of course, demand a completely 'new ethic' in the sense of a new hat, which is a meaningless idea,[1] but it does call for a great shift in perspective. We must change a habitual priority system, one which seemed relatively coherent because we were used to it, but which is no longer workable. We have to rethink the relation between our various ideals, and the way in which they are geared to life.

This effort can produce a sense of unreality leading to scepticism, dizziness and vertigo, sometimes to nausea. Bewilderment already expresses itself in various confused forms of relativism and subjectivism which tell us to abandon all attempt at clarity[2] – prescriptions which are often summed up at present as 'postmodernism'. This name can, however, also cover more positive rearrangements of ideals, more workable forms of pluralism, which we must look at shortly. The name 'postmodernism' is actually a bad one, both because it is vague and because it centres on fashion. It needs always to be translated into words that are more specific and less time-bound. But the mixed batch of ideals which we have vaguely grouped together under names like 'modern' and 'advanced' is indeed central to our troubles.

FINDING THE MIDDLE GROUND

The way to deal constructively with this impression of a hopeless gap between ideals and reality is always, I think, to attend to the middle ground that connects them. We need to think about the standards that we use for compromise, and the alterations that each side must make to its demands when it understands what its opponent is driving at. At this middle level, we can see how the practical approach actually demands the idealistic one to complete it. The two levels of concern are not rivals or alternatives; they are complementary. The only hope of resolving serious conceptual clashes is to rethink them in relation to their context, noticing what can be done about the ideas involved. (There are of course simpler methods of resolution, such as combat or ordeal, which have often been tried. But they have never proved very satisfactory).

Looking back, we can see how this careful rethinking has often managed to resolve dilemmas which, in their time, looked quite as incurable as our present lot. Moral thinking is not really just a luxury; it has often proved extremely effective. Thus, the religious wars of the seventeenth century did not just die out from exhaustion. They were eventually seen to be unnecessary in the light of new conceptions of toleration and the complexity of truth. Again, better notions about the nature of honour similarly removed the need for duelling.

After this kind of change has been made, however, the original difficulties tend to be forgotten, which is why we have the impression that such thought is impossible. This rethinking does undoubtedly require considerable effort. We have to sort out the various ideals that each side stands for to see why they are clashing, and to look at their relation to our whole range of ideals so as to see a new, more workable pattern. We are forced to stand right back from our immediate problems and to get our bearings in a wider moral field. This shift is not a distraction from the real dilemmas. It is what we need if we are to take them seriously.

But of course it is always hard to do that because the facts to be faced tend to be alarming. At present, the notion that our treatment of nature involves serious, avoidable crimes and dangers is still only very gradually seeping into public consciousness. Most of us still accept it only intermittently, and with a considerable sense of unreality. This slowness of perception is not unusual. Reading the letters and diaries of our forebears – even of very perceptive people – who lived at earlier times of rapid change we see it constantly. We sometimes want to shout to the writers and call on them to wake up. Thick, solid layers of habit always protect our established ways of life against criticism. And, rather surprisingly, they do not just block moral criticism. They numb the sense of danger as well. People have always farmed contentedly on the slopes of volcanoes. Christians have not been stopped from sinning by the expectation of eternal damnation. The dangers of modern weapons have not made us give up war. Habit, in fact, has extraordinary force, a force greatly exceeding the wish for self-preservation.

THE APPEAL TO EGOISM

Enlightenment thought, which we still use, has largely ignored this remarkable insensibility. It has put great trust in enlightened self-interest as the source of reform. Hobbes supposed that rational people only needed to be warned of threats against their personal safety in order to change their political ways. A similar strategy, on a larger scale, is now being used by prophets who hope to change our attitudes to nature purely by pointing out the risks that we, as human beings, are now running. The sense of 'sustainability' which just means 'protection of human use' is geared to that intention. The interest of our own species is presented as the only possible rational and parsimonious approach. Thus, Messrs Pearce and Turner (official environmental advisers to Mrs Thatcher and her successors) raise their eyebrows to enquire:

> If inherent/intrinsic and not just instrumental value exists, what is it and how do we discover it? It seems reasonable to conclude that we either justify our acceptance of intrinsic value at an intuitive level only, or we look for support via appeals to 'expert judgment'. Both of these forms of justification seem problematic.[3]

These writers seem to find the notion that, by contrast, all values might be merely instrumental, leading to no particular end at all, quite straightforward . . . This might seem odd. But they are, of course, actually assuming that human aims, which the instruments exist to meet, are given and need no discussion.

This approach gives a quite simple answer to the question why uses of wild species should be 'sustainable'. Very obviously, human beings are dependent on many of the threatened species and cannot survive without them. The word 'sustainable', now appearing in many official documents since the publication of the Brundtland Report, does signal some faint, dawning recognition of this glaring fact even among those politicians and administrators who are most thickly protected from it by the veils of official habit. It shows that former delusions about the infinity of resources, the need for an all-out war against nature and the omnipotence of the technical fix are becoming slightly weaker.

That progress towards wakefulness is, so far, immensely welcome. Enlightened self-interest is indeed a necessary component in change. Fright can certainly wake people up, and it sometimes concentrates their minds amazingly. The question is, however, how far can we rely on fright? Will it give us all the motivation we need to alter our attitudes? Does it articulate the considerations that we need to build into our changed world-picture?

This species-egoist approach has two serious limitations, which are the main subject of this paper. One concerns the detailed policies it recommends, the other, which interests me more, concerns the human psychology that lies behind those policies. About the detailed policies, clashes are notoriously already emerging. Ingrained habits of economic thinking ensure that the idea of conserving natural resources, or 'natural capital', in quantities sufficient for human needs will be tied to a minimal level. Thus, if humans need wood, trees must be replanted, but they should always be the trees that will supply this need most quickly and economically. There is no reason to conserve existing species, and certainly none to aim at diversity as such. And after all there are a lot of kinds of trees about. So, what could possibly be wrong with universal monocultured eucalyptus?

Surgeons, Lifeboats and First-Class Passengers

This question is being constantly and repeatedly answered at present by a patient, determined squad of hard-working environmentalists. Jared Diamond does the job as well as anyone. People ask, he says:

> Could we not preserve only those particular species that we need, and let other species become extinct? Of course not, because the species that we need also depend on other species . . . Which ten tree species produce most of the world's paper pulp? For each of these ten tree species, which are the ten bird species that eat most of its insect pests, the ten insect species that pollinate most of its flowers, and the ten animal species that spread most of its seeds? Which other species do these ten birds, animals and insects depend on? . . . Consider the following analogy. Suppose someone offers you a million dollars for the privilege of painlessly cutting out two ounces of your valuable flesh. You figure that two ounces is only one-thousandth of your body-weight, so you will still have nine-hundred and ninety-nine thousandths of your body left . . . But what if the surgeon just hacks two ounces from any conveniently accessible part of your body, or does not know which parts are essential? . . . If you plan to sell off most of your body, as we now plan to sell off most of our planet's natural habitats, you are eventually to lose your urethra.[4]

What interests me is the difficulty that even very prudent people have in believing simple arguments of this kind. When Garrett Hardin said that privileged people today were the occupants of an overburdened lifeboat who, despite their compassion, really could not risk taking anyone else on board, he struck many readers as realistic. Somebody promptly replied that these privileged people were actually first-class passengers who had just got a warning from the people in steerage that their ship is sinking. The tendency to reply 'not at our end' does not then seem so sensible. But this image has not caught on half as readily.

The psychological quirk that blocks our imagination here has already been seen in political life with the disappointment of Hobbes's hopes. People turn out not to be anything like as prudent as Hobbes supposed. Human selfishness is indeed very powerful, but it is closely linked to human narrowness. It tends to concentrate vigorously on the present. It is not imaginative. It discounts absent scenes and remoter futures just as it discounts other people's feelings. It can be extraordinarily short-sighted. It tends to be competitive rather than cooperative, setting individual self against others, even in places where rationality urgently demands cooperation. In short, egoism is by its nature rather *un*enlightened and hard to enlighten. If it is to power real reform, it always needs a wider framework of other motives.

These other motives are, however, available. Selfishness does not actually dominate our emotional lives in quite the way that Hobbes thought. Human rationality is not a monoculture, a simple system with a single aim. It is the project of bringing together in some sort of harmony the many motives, many interests, that naturally form part of human life. Moral 'pluralism' is correct in the sense that we really do have many distinct ideals. But of course we cannot just pursue them all at random. In trying to bring them together harmoniously, we need to have some sort of comprehensive world-picture, some vision of the whole within which we live and of our own relation to it.

Hardly anybody actually manages to handle human social life on Hobbes's extreme egoistic model. People are social beings who normally feel themselves to be part of a group, indeed part of many concentric and overlapping groups, with aims that are directly important to them. They often identify strongly with their various groups, and mind intensely about changing or maintaining group habits and qualities. Often they willingly sacrifice their individual interests for their groups, or for other individuals. They sometimes even die for them.

WIDER HORIZONS

But above and beyond these groups, they almost inevitably have a further sense of a wider whole, a theatre within which all groups play their part. And most cultures have not attempted to conceive that whole as exclusively a human one. This wider whole may not be something that we often think about, but the way in which we conceive it is surely crucial for our moral attitude. When this larger imaginative vision changes, the light in which we see all our various concerns is altered. Priorities shift, carrying a corresponding change in duties.

Christian morality, for instance, has certainly not been primarily a prudential, egoistic device to help individuals gain Heaven and avoid Hell. (People who have used it in that way have misunderstood it, and have usually fallen into deep trouble.) It has been meant as a way of acting that is shaped by the vision of the world as created by a loving God and lit up by love of one's neighbour. Whatever the failures of the actual institutions involved, this way of looking at things made possible many moral insights – for instance about the wrongness of slavery and infanticide – which we now take for granted, but which were not easily grasped before. The size and nature of our world-picture determines the range of our moral horizon. By altering the light in which we see our role, it always has direct, practical effects on what we feel called on to do.

THE REDUCTIVE PROJECT

Since the Renaissance, however, sages and prophets in the West have worked hard to shape our imaginative vision in a way that systematically narrows it. There has been a deliberate effort to exclude from concern everything non-human, and many supposedly non-rational aspects of human life as well. Though this campaign was aimed chiefly against the dominance of the churches, and was rooted in the horror of religious wars, it has usually taken the form of a 'humanism' that excludes non-human nature too. This is still the unquestioned creed expressed in the ministries and offices from which our society is run. Often, too, it is narrowed yet further to the economists' formula, which still defines 'rationality' in Hobbesian terms of individual self-interest.

Now it is not actually impossible to state the case for strong environmental action even in this restricted language. Though an isolated egoistic individual could probably count on free-loading for his or her lifetime, any wider concern, even for one's own friends and descendants, does call for marked changes. And the kind of prudence that extends to the whole human race would, if really enlightened, demand very drastic changes indeed.

This is the voice that, since the Brundtland Report, we have been hearing in the very general declarations made by governments about the importance of sustainability. But we rightly have a sense of unreality about these declarations, because we know that self-interest on this immensely public, long-term scale is not usually very enlightened. At this range, enlightened calculations tend to be too indirect to have much force, and ordinary, unenlightened sectional selfishness usually works quietly in their shadow. If prudence on this scale is to be effective, it needs to be supplemented by a much more direct, spontaneous moral feeling – in fact, by a sense of outrage.

What ended the wars of religion, and the savage treatment of heretics that went with them, was not just the wish for self-preservation, though that certainly played its part. It was also direct horror at the atrocities involved. Voltaire, though he was a prophet of reason, sounded this note of profound indignation as a persistent bass to his campaigns on this matter, and it was central to his effectiveness. It is equally so in environmental campaigning today.

WHAT DO WE REALLY THINK?

Arne Naess, who wanted to discover ordinary people's views, conducted a series of systematic interviews with them on the rights and value of animals, plants and landscapes. He reported:

> In spite of what one would guess from the way they vote (and I am speaking as a Scandinavian), there is a substantial majority with quite far-reaching ideas about the rights and value of life-forms, and a conviction that *every life-form has its place in nature* which we must respect.[5]

In short, people are not orthodox individualists. They do not proceed atomistically outward from the demands of each separate human, demanding credentials sternly from each new suppliant who wants to be taken into the lifeboat. They do not feel like immigration officers, defending the human race against alien outsiders. Instead, they feel that they live within a vast whole – nature – which is in some sense the source of all value, and whose workings are quite generally entitled to respect. They do not see this whole as an extra item, or a set of items which they must appraise and evaluate one by one to make sure whether they need them. They see it as the original context which gives sense to their lives. It is the background they start from. From this angle, the burden of proof is not on someone who wants to preserve mahogany trees from extinction. It is on the person who proposes to destroy them.

Naess reported this work in a detailed personal letter to 110 people who were influential on national environmental policy, asking for their comments. One in three replied, and commented very favourably, suggesting that, at least at a personal level, they too were much in line with Naess's 'ordinary people'. Naess concluded that there was a considerable gap between public feeling and the principles governing official policy, a gap that should be exposed and sharply attended to. As he put it:

> What is needed is a methodology of persistently connecting basic value judgments and imperative premisses with decisions in concrete situations of interference or non-interference in nature. What I therefore suggest is that those who are thought to be experts and scientists repeatedly and persistently deepen their arguments with reference to basic value judgments and imperative premisses. That is, they should announce their normative philosophy of life and discuss environmental problems in their most comprehensive time and space frame of reference.[6]

Some recent researchers have followed up Naess's work by interviewing twenty-four senior policy advisors to four European governments active in global climate change negotiations and the UNCED process. They report:

> In response to our questions, a majority of these advisors articulated deeply held personal environmental values. *They told us that they normally keep these values separate from their environmental policy activities* . . . We suggest that environmental policy could be improved if widely held values were articulated, validated and admitted into the process of policy analysis and deliberation.[7]

LOOKING OUTWARDS

The present position, in fact, is rather like what we would find in a ministry charged with running prisons if all humane talk about what life was like for the prisoners was banned and proposals for reform had always to be couched in terms of efficiency in preventing crime. This sort of indirectness is obviously misleading and wasteful. Naess is surely right that, on environmental questions, we need to stop being embarrassed about admitting that we are not all petty-minded egoists. As the recent researchers put it, we need this clearer moral position if we are to avoid situations in which 'decisions based on short-term goals and narrow interests lead to longer-term outcomes desired by no one'.[8]

Of course prudential arguments are important and must be stated. But the attempt to reduce the whole of morality to them is simply silly. We are creatures whose very nature constantly points us outwards towards questions and ideals that lead far beyond our own lives. The crucialness of this outward leading is commonly taken for granted in discussing the value of science, of art and of exploration, particularly the exploration of space, and of an enterprising approach generally. It is also assumed to be natural in the extension of compassion to the borders of the human species.

People who ask, as Pearce and Turner do, how there can possibly be inherent or intrinsic value need to have their noses rubbed in such cases. When a doubt actually does arise about the value of a particular province such as science or art, we are not, as they suggest, left gaping helplessly. We look at the various aims of this activity in some detail, and see how they relate to those of other important human activities. Though there is never complete agreement on such matters, much sensible thinking is already available. There are adequate maps for finding our way around the topic. We note the place of this particular activity in human life and in a wider firmament of values. Of course the enquiry is a vast and complex one, but it is not a blank. In thinking about it, we shall not fall dumb in the way that they suggest unless we have decided in advance that all thought about values is vacuous – a view which the Logical Positivists did indeed suggest in a euphoric moment, but which doesn't really make much sense in a world where the relative value of different things continually needs to be discussed.

Asking about the value of the whole within which all other valuable things have their place does indeed raise rather different problems. But they are not problems which can be solved by ruling that this whole is valueless. What does seem to happen here is that the word 'value' is reaching its limits. This word is in any case somewhat polluted by its constant use in economic contexts and other cost-benefit calculations, where it reverts to its literal meaning of 'price'. G. E. Moore, solemnly discussing the comparative 'values' of various large-scale states of affairs, managed to give an uncomfortably condescending impression of a distinguished connoisseur pricing pictures in an exhibition.[9] He wrote as if he stood in a secure, neutral, outside position, evaluating these things as an expert. But that is not a human situation at all.

MORE WORDS ARE NEEDED

The trouble surely is that, as we speak of things further and further out from ourselves, it gets steadily more suitable to speak in terms of awe, reverence, respect, wonder or acceptance, and steadily less satisfactory to use a word like 'value' whose original use is in describing everyday objects we might buy and possess. (A 'valuer' is, in ordinary life, just a person whom the insurance company sends round to check on your claim.) I do not mean that this word cannot be used. In outspoken metaphors, like Jesus' story of the merchant seeking the 'pearl of great price', it can work well. No doubt today the word *value*, like *rights*, can be used without danger at the everyday level. It may well be quite an appropriate word for the kind of public statements that are often now needed. But the philosophers who are now getting each other into muddles about the 'intrinsic' or 'inherent value' of non-human items are trying to make this single word bear far more weight than it can stand.

Their real problem is not, as they think, just one of fitting a few familiar terms together to produce a smooth, simple surface within moral philosophy. It is the big metaphysical and moral problem of what attitude creatures like ourselves ought to take towards the cosmos within which we are so small a part. It is an open-ended problem, where the most we can usually do is to get rid of certain pernicious elements that have crept in and infested our attitudes. The word 'value' has been used, by moral theorists as well as economists, to do a reductive job here, to simplify our status by exalting it. Thus used, it suggests that we have only to think about the satisfaction of certain selected human 'needs', which we shall, of course, define in terms that suit our current culture. That is why theorists like Pearce and Turner are so mystified by talk of 'values' which are not clearly reducible to such needs.

Moore, and many other moral theorists, have used the word 'value' as a central weapon in the campaign to assert the self-sufficiency of Man – to defend him against seeming to have any need of religion. They have observed that serious attitudes to the whole cosmos do tend to be religious, and because institutionalised religions have often been harmful, they have wanted to resist that trend. But in doing so they have set up a form of anthropolatry that is every bit as superstitious, as arbitrary and as over-confident as any of the religions they wanted to avoid. This unreal exaltation of Man has played a key part in bringing us to our present environmental crisis. We need to do all we can to clear it out of the conceptual schemes we must use in our attempts at salvage.

CONFUSED REDUCTIVISM

This kind of English-speaking moral philosophy, characteristic of the later Enlightenment, has had another, more general fault which is still giving us trouble. It is the tendency to insist on conceptual monoculture – on bringing all moral questions together under simple headings, reducible ultimately to a few key terms. It is felt to be scientific, but it isn't. Utilitarianism began this over-tidy enterprise, and, a few decades back, linguistic philosophers managed to narrow down the 'moral words' for a time to two – 'right' and 'good'. No doubt clarity is always a gain, but you can't till fields with a nailfile. Philosophers fairly soon noticed that this kind of thing was unhelpful. They now use a much larger and more flexible toolkit. But they do still tend to get obsessed by particular words. They have, for instance, repeatedly piled far more problems onto the concepts of 'rights' and 'justice' as well as 'value' than those words can stand, instead of looking round to see what other notions might be helpful. (What about 'importance'?) And they also have a tendency, dating from their most rule-bound epoch, to treat things as alternatives which are demonstrably not alternative but complementary – to dispute about whether we should use knives or forks instead of asking how we should combine them.

This divisiveness has already made trouble on environmental issues. Fierce debate broke out for a time between philosophers campaigning on behalf of animals and others supporting wildernesses – as if these concerns were simply rivals, rather than interdependent elements in a larger problem, elements which must be intelligently brought together. And there is now an equally irrelevant competition going on between various simple answers to the general question why we should bother about any of these things. The tendency is to say, 'We know that we ought to be concerned about the environment, but *we don't know why* until we find some single, simple explanation', and then to pursue the matter by backing some sweeping 'moral theory' intended to validate all duties wholesale.

This narrow disputatiousness is obviously likely to obstruct attempts to answer questions about the general principles to which we should appeal. The notion that there is just one right set is a mere distraction. We need to remember how big the questions are. We are bound to need many partial answers to them; no single password can possibly clear up the matter. This is particularly obvious when we have to turn hastily to these issues after having neglected them. But even in the long run, the place they should occupy in human life is never going to be simple. It must demand more, not less, conceptual schemes to describe it than we now use.

This would, after all, be true even on moral topics with which we are much more familiar. If somebody asks 'but why should we bother about our children?' or 'why have art?' or, 'why, really, shouldn't I kill you?' many people will be somewhat stuck for an answer. This is not (as cocky graduate students tend to think) because these people don't know the answer, but because they know too many answers. Such general queries make no sense unless we know just why they are being asked. Where does the particular questioner stand? What is being presupposed? What unusual conditions are raising the question and making it real? What good reasons for *not* bothering are being brought forward? What other background concerns are still being taken for granted? What specific conflicts, in fact, are we dealing with? Without this background, such questions are vacuous. General 'moral theories' – such as utilitarianism or Rawls's theory of justice – become vacuous too when they are wheeled out to answer them.

These theories have their place in explanation, but it is (again) a more limited one, in helping to arbitrate particular conflicts between other possible principles, not in ruling over all of them. No theory has the absolute dominion which utilitarianism so mistakenly claimed. None can make the whole moral scene intelligible. And of course when we turn to questions about the environment, these theories have still less prospect of being helpful, because all of them – including even Rawls's – were devised before the issue really came onto people's moral horizon. Enlightenment thinking has never said much about it. And the scale on which it confronts us now – the genuine planetary danger – is something unparalleled in the history of our species. There is no use in scouring our recent predecessors for ready-made solutions to it.

HOW THEN SHOULD WE TALK?

This does not mean, of course, that earlier ideas cannot be helpful. Since ethics grow naturally, rather than being bought like hats, there is already much material which we can gather, use and foster, rather than inventing some astonishing novelty. When we ask whether principles such as respect for life, stewardship and species' rights can be used, the answer is surely 'Yes', and plenty more. All have their own advantages and drawbacks. All will need further development, and all will surely get it as we think harder about these matters. All overlap on an enormous area of the action that is necessary. All, however, suit some contexts better than others.

For instance, the language of rights has a particular resonance for Americans, who may well accept it without question. In Europe, and perhaps elsewhere, its shortcomings in certain kinds of context are more obvious. Some brief explanation may therefore be needed to show how using it outside its familiar political and legal context is, in fact, unobjectionable. Again, talk of 'stewardship' readily suggests a God in the background; can atheists accept it? They surely can if it is pointed out that we are stewards for our posterity. And so forth.

Similarly over differences of cultures, these clashes, on the whole, seem to affect relatively minor matters. Simply because things are so bad, the main campaign ought not really to be divisive. Differences between the Western outlook and others should surely not be too troublesome this time, because we see that it is we ourselves who have, so far, been most out of step. Cultural imperialism at this point would be ludicrous. The distinctively Western anthropolatry of recent tradition is exactly what we need to abandon. We have indeed diffused this attitude widely, which makes trouble for us now. But many other cultures have not altogether lost the more viable views which they had before they listened to us. Among the larger, more dominant cultures, this was clearly true of Japan and India, and to some extent also of Islam. China may be more of a problem, but then it is so on other moral issues too, such as human rights. For such cases the prudential, anthropocentric notion of 'sustainability' is always there to fall back on. Anyway, we must all be prepared to learn from one another, rather than shutting ourselves into supposedly separate cultural boxes.

If we ask 'does any of the proposed principles have a claim to be universal?' my answer would be, 'certainly not in the sense of winning a competition, set up by moral philosophers, for a perfect, final, all-purpose formula'. But then that quest was always a mistaken and trivial one. The kind of universality that can reasonably be sought seems to have a wide appeal for thoughtful people, coherent with the other ideals that they accept – an appeal strong enough to lead to action, and rational enough to fit in with important elements in existing morality. On all major moral questions such appeals have many elements. They are made in different terms according to the kind of issue involved and the particular public addressed. Of course the relation between these different conceptual schemes must be watched and thought out carefully. But moral pluralism of this kind is neither confused nor dishonest. It is simply a recognition of the complexity of life. The idea that reductive simplicity here is particularly rational or 'scientific' is mere confusion.[10]

NOTES

1. A point admirably made by John Passmore in *Man's Responsibility for Nature* (London: Duckworth, 1974)
2. I have discussed their incoherence and unhelpfulness in *Can't We Make Moral Judgments?* (New York St Martin's Press 1991) and in *Wickedness: A Philosophical Essay* (London: Routledge, 1984)
3. David W. Pearce and R. Kerry Turner, *Economics of Natural Resources and the Environment* (Baltimore, MD: Johns Hopkins University Press, 1990), p. 238.

4. Jared Diamond, *The Rise and Fall of the Third Chimpanzee* (London: Vintage, 1992), pp. 324–5
5. Arne Naess, 'Intrinsic value: will the defenders of value please rise?', in Michael E. Soule (ed.), *Conservation Biology: The Science of Scarcity and Diversity* (Sunderland, MA: Sinauer Associates, pp. 504–15 at p. 508.
6. Ibid.
7. Paul P. Craig, Harold Glasser and Willett Kempton, 'Ethics and values in environmental policy: the said and the UNCED', *Environmental Values* 2(2), 1993: 137–59.
8. Ibid., p. 151.
9. See G. E. Moore, *Principia Ethica* (Cambridge: Cambridge University Press, 1903), especially Chapter 6.
10. A different version of this essay appeared in Mary Midgley, *Utopias Dolphins and Computers* (Routledge, 1996).

6

HOW TO BASE ETHICS ON BIOLOGY

Timothy Chappell

INTRODUCTION

The argument in this chapter[1] proceeds as follows:

1. Personhood is not what matters. We would get on better in ethics if we did not take the notion of a *person* to be of decisive and unique ethical significance. As Hume remarks (EPM I), we should reject 'every system of ethics, however subtle or ingenious, which is not founded on fact and observation'. But the notion of personhood is not so based.
2. Our need, at the foundations of normative ethics, for other and sounder concepts than that of personhood is especially clear in bio-ethics and environmental ethics. Specifically, what we need to replace the notion of a *person* in ethics is the biological notion of an *individual animal* (of whatever species).
3. How might an environmental ethics, or an ethics of animal rights, look if it did take the biological notion of the individual animal to be foundational, rather than the baseless notion of a 'person'? And how might the biological notion deal with such accusations as that of 'speciesism'? I make some suggestions about this on the basis of a point, which I shall call the *perspectival point*, about practical reasoning.

AGAINST THE CONCEPT OF PERSONHOOD

'Imagine a space traveller who lands on an unknown planet and encounters a race of beings utterly unlike any he has ever seen or heard of. If he wants to be sure of behaving morally towards these beings, he has to somehow decide whether they are people, and hence have full moral rights, or whether they are the sort of thing which he need not feel guilty about treating as, for example, a source of food. How should he go about making this decision?'[2]

Well, how would we give a clear and determinate answer to Warren's question[3]? What does the space traveller have to learn about these aliens to find that they are 'people' (a word which Warren uses as if it were the plural of 'person'[4])? Warren's own suggestion is that he has to learn that the aliens display, for example, 'consciousness, reasoning, self-motivated activity, the capacity to communicate, and self-awareness'. If (1) he discovers that they display all or enough of these personal qualities, then (2) he reaches the verdict that the aliens are 'people' and so (3) that they are the sort of creatures who have moral rights.

Warren's picture – and there are many writers on applied ethics whose picture is substantially the same as hers,[5] which is why I shall spend so much of this essay unpicking it – is of a three-stage procedure through which the space traveller goes. (I mark the stages in the last sentence but one.) About this picture I offer three observations. First, there is nothing in which stage 2 consists, except perhaps a conjuring trick. Thus, second, what happens at stage 3 cannot legitimately be justified by appeal to what happens at stage 2. If anything justifies stage 3, it must happen at stage (1). But, third, the question about stage 1 is 'Why should we fix on just these qualities as being the ones that matter morally in the special way required for the possession of "full moral rights"?' This question can be used to undermine, and replace, Warren's whole proposal.

To begin, then: there is nothing in which stage 2 consists because what is (supposedly) discovered at stage 2 is, logically, not independent of anything that is discovered at stage 1. The 'conjuring trick' of which I accuse Warren consists in making it seem otherwise.

To understand this point, we first need to contrast two ways in which claims like stage-1 and stage-2 claims might be connected. The first way is the *definitional* way. Connecting claims like stage-1 and stage-2 claims in this way, we say that if something has some feature F then by definition, and so *analytically*, it is an X. So, for example, to say of some figure that 'If it has four sides *then that is because* it is a quadrilateral', or vice versa, is simply to register a definitional connection. If some shape has four sides then by definition it is a quadrilateral: that is simply what 'quadrilateral' means. The second way of connecting such claims is the *explanatory* way. Connecting them in this way, we say that if something has some feature F then *that is because* it is an X. So, for example, if some chemical burns, that may well be because it is an acid.

There are some vitally important contrasts between these two ways of connecting claims like stage-1 and stage-2 claims. Notice, in particular, that no new information or explanatory power about four-sided figures is added by the making of a definitional connection. What the connection gives us is no more (and, of course, no less) than a piece of information about how we use the word 'quadrilateral' in English. Consequently, the notion of a quadrilateral does not (as I shall say) outstrip this piece of information about that notion. You've got that notion, and everything there is to it, once you've understood the definition of 'quadrilateral' as 'four-sided figure'. Anyone who thought that there was or even could be more to that notion – who thought, for instance, that quadrilaterals, just as such, tend to be blue in colour, or that we might be able to find out more about quadrilaterals, just as such, by examining a bigger or less statistically loaded sample of quadrilaterals – such a person would be making some bizarre sort of mistake.

Contrast the notion of an acid, and the kind of connection which is being made when I say that chemical K burns *because* it is an acid. This is a quite different connection. The notion of an acid *does* 'outstrip' the notion of a chemical that burns: for at least two reasons. First, because plenty of other chemicals besides acids burn, whereas by contrast it is only four-sided figures that are (all of them) quadrilaterals. (This suggests a quick test to distinguish definitional from explanatory connections. I wrote above that 'If some chemical burns, that may well be because it is an acid'. This is not absurd. But 'If something has four sides, that may well be because it is a quadrilateral' *would* be absurd.) Second: the notion of an acid outstrips the notion of a chemical that burns, not only because an acid is not defined as something that burns (it cannot be, since many non-acids also burn), but also because there is much more to what an acid is than simply the capacity to burn. (What is more, however much you discovered about what an acid is, it would always remain open that there was still more to learn.[6]) By contrast, there is *nothing* more to what a quadrilateral is than having four sides.

So when I say that the notion of an acid *outstrips* the notion of a chemical that burns, what I mean is that it is in no sense a merely definitional move to say that chemical K burns 'because it is an acid'. On the contrary, the making of such a connection registers a genuine causal explanation. For chemical K might have burned because it was strongly basic or alkaline; or because of a marked difference in temperature, either way, between K and whatever K burnt; or K might simply have been the catalyst which set off some other chemical with a capacity to burn; or K might have burned for all of these reasons; or K might have burned for none of these reasons, but because of some other chemical process(es) besides these which we don't understand; or K might have burned spontaneously or freakishly, i.e. for no good reason that anyone can give at all. Saying that K burnt because K is an acid is non-vacuous, and genuinely explanatory, because it rules out all these other possible explanations of K's burning.[7] (It also suggests a different view of the cases where K *fails* to burn: if K burns because it is an acid, then that capacity to burn will be defeasible in different ways from capacities to burn which are supported by other features than acidity.)

Now let us come back to the case of 'persons' as defined by Warren, and the connection she makes in her moves from a stage-1 claim such as 'This creature C has the personal qualities XYZ' to a stage-2 claim such as 'C is a person'. What kind of connection is Warren's: definitional or explanatory?

The answer to that seems at first to be that it is a definitional connection. Certainly, for Warren, it seems to be a matter of definition that anything which has any of the personal qualities she lists is a person. If so, it follows from this that there is nothing *more* to discovering that her aliens are persons beyond discovering that they display some one or more of the personal qualities which Warren lists. For some creature to possess those qualities, or at least some of them, *is* for it to be a person, just as, in the example we have already considered, for a shape to have four sides *is* for it to be a quadrilateral.

At other times, however, there is reason to doubt that Warren's connection between 'creature, of whatever sort, with the personal qualities XYZ' and 'person' *is*, after all, a merely definitional connection. In fact, I suggest, it is clear that she thinks that 'person' outstrips 'creature [. . .] with the personal qualities' in at least the following two ways. First, it is persons, not creatures with the personal qualities, to which she explicitly attaches moral status. In other words, she thinks that at least one further claim is (directly) deducible from 'X is a person' which is not (directly) deducible from 'X has the personal qualities'. Second, and more fundamentally, she seems to treat the presence of the personal qualities in her aliens as *evidence* for ascriptions of personhood, in the way that burning is evidence for ascriptions of acidity. The picture is a strikingly Cartesian one, in fact. For Warren ascriptions of personhood form the content of a scientific hypothesis, which is not simply entailed by the evidence for that hypothesis, but which on the basis of the evidence the (individual) investigator is typically able to formulate, as an induction, about at least some of the moving objects around him (and in practice, it is normally 'him'). But now it is patent that the forming of any such hypothesis will necessarily embody more than a mere definitional connection between personhood and the personal qualities. Rather, it now seems, Warren's claim must be that personhood is something over and above those qualities, in the way that acidity is something over and above the capacity to burn. On this view, in fact, the status of personhood is supposed to be *explanatory* of the possession of the personal qualities, just as the status of acidity is explanatory of the capacity to burn.

However, it cannot possibly be correct to see the connection as an explanatory one. Recall the 'quick test' which I suggested above as a way of seeing whether any connection is definitional or explanatory. We saw that 'If some figure has four sides, that may well be because it is a quadrilateral' is an absurd remark, since by definition there is no possibility of a four-sided figure's being anything but a quadrilateral. Surely the same point applies to the remark that 'If something possesses the personal qualities, that may well be because it is a person', and for the same reason. Since a person is by definition a possessor of the personal qualities, there is no possibility of a possessor of the personal qualities being anything but a person. Nothing, for instance, could be a *simulation* of a person, by having the personal qualities without being a person. Unless it is a real and not simulated person that we speak of, neither will we be speaking of real personal qualities, but only of simulated ones.

I conclude that the connection Warren is looking for can only legitimately be understood as definitional: to speak of persons just *is* to speak of possessors of the personal qualities. But how, it might now be asked, does this conclusion affect Warren's argument? I think the answer begins to be clear when we try rewriting her argument without the word 'person' in it. Suppose that what her space traveller has to do is decide whether the aliens he meets (not: are persons, but) *have any of the personal qualities*, 'and hence have full moral rights'. This supposition, I suggest, is not very close to making real sense; and the two main reasons why it does not add up are closely connected to the removal from the story of any genuinely separate notion of a person.

Consider first the role of the little word 'full' in the story as it now stands. If you take it that the connection between personhood and the presence of the personal qualities is an explanatory one, then it is easy enough to justify moving from any amount of display of the personal qualities, however small, to the ascription to a creature of full moral rights. For if you think that the connection between personhood and the personal qualities is explanatory, then you will also think that personhood is (so to speak) all or nothing. Anything that is a person at all is just as much a person as anything else that is a person: so it doesn't really matter how little their personhood is displayed or evidenced by way of personal qualities, provided there is at least *some* evidence.

Take the notion of personhood out of this explanatory connection with the personal qualities, and the feeling that personhood is or even could be all or nothing will become extremely hard to maintain. Indeed if personhood is connected with the possession of the personal qualities *as a matter of definition*, and if we still insist that persons are what we value, it is not clear why we should not begin to value creatures more or less according as they are more or less persons, i.e. in proportion to the degree to which they possess (as many as possible of) the personal qualities. If personhood is *only* the possession of the personal qualities, or only matters because it entails their possession,[8] then our attention switches to the issue of why and how those qualities are to be valued. And the question becomes: why *shouldn't* they be valued in a quantitative fashion?

But if they are, then the notion of *full* moral rights seems to go out of the window as well. Anything's rights will now depend, not on *whether* it is a person, but on *the degree to which* it is a person, and full rights will just mean the highest moral status, which will probably be possessed by only a few superlative creatures who possess the personal qualities in some excelling degree. This picture is clearly nowhere near the picture of human rights which, pre-theoretically, we wanted to have.

Second, take the word 'hence'. An argument which proceeds by deciding whether some aliens are persons 'and *hence* have full moral rights' is at least the ghost of a good argument. (More of the good argument of which it is the ghost in a minute.) By contrast, an argument which proceeds by deciding whether some aliens have the personal qualities, 'and hence have full moral rights' just seems like a *non sequitur* – no real argument at all. In what *sense* 'hence'? What underlies the notion that the possession of just these qualities is a sufficient condition for the possession of full moral rights? What was meant to underlie it was a substantive conception of the person, connected with the possession of the personal qualities in what I have been calling the explanatory way. But if we take away this explanatory connection, and replace it with a merely definitional connection, then we no longer have any idea what is supposed to *explain* the privileging of the personal qualities. The questions of why these qualities should be the only ones that matter, or the ones that matter above all others, or ones that matter equally wherever they occur – these questions becomes very difficult to answer if we are not allowed to say that the point about such qualities is that they reveal the presence of a *person* who stands to those qualities as cause and explanation. But there is sufficient reason by now to believe that we do not have the right to make that explanatory connection.

As already pointed out, this leaves the presence of the personal qualities (or equivalently, personhood as now reinterpreted) out on its own, logically isolated, as a moral criterion. Of course, even so, the presence of such qualities might still be taken to be what counts morally and what makes anything which has such qualities a candidate for equal moral rights. But this would be a bare stipulation, explained by nothing else. In particular – as already noted – the notion of the *equality* of the possessors of such qualities would be very hard to justify without appealing, implicitly at least, to the idea that such possessors ought to be equal because they are all equally persons, or all equally possessors of the personal qualities. But as we have seen, in the relevant sense that is no longer true once the logically independent notion of personhood has been dropped (as it must be, for reasons we have also seen). For different persons were all conceived, in the Cartesian way or something rather like it, as being equally persons, no matter how much or how little they displayed or possessed the personal qualities. By contrast, different possessors of the personal qualities are *not* all equally possessors of the personal qualities. Some possess more such qualities; some display the qualities they possess to a greater extent. So if there is reason to accept the equality of the possessors of personal qualities, it cannot be found by any sort of appeal to personhood.

This conclusion suggests the ethical question of where a reason for valuing the personal qualities *might* be found, if not in their revealing a person. It also suggests a parallel causal question, namely the question of what causally explains the possession of the personal qualities, if personhood does not. The answer to the causal question gives the answer to the ethical question; but the answer I shall give shows why it is not just the personal qualities that we have reason to value. And this brings us to the collapse of Warren's proposal.

What causally explains the presence of the possession of the personal qualities? That is to say: what is there that is such that it stands in that explanatory connection with the personal qualities which, we have seen, personhood does *not* stand in? The answer which I want to propose is: being *human*. The reason why creatures display personal qualities is, typically, because those creatures are human, and displaying the personal qualities is a crucial part of what it is to be (a mature and healthy) human. 'If something possesses the personal qualities, that may well be because it is a person' did not pass our quick test for an explanatory connection because it was absurd to try and say this sort of thing about what is clearly a definitional connection. But 'If something possesses the personal qualities, that may well be because it is a *human*' *does* pass this test. This connection clearly is a real explanatory connection, in a sense in which the other connection, which appealed to the notion of personhood, is not. (As a matter of fact, it seems very doubtful whether personhood – in any sense which goes beyond the possession of at least some of the personal qualities – admits of explanatory connections with *any* other concepts at all: this indeed is a key part of what is wrong with the way the concept of personhood is used by writers like Warren.)

What then is our reason for taking the possession of the personal qualities to be important? Can we give one, or are we stuck with a bare stipulation that their possession, in itself, just *is* morally valuable? Once again, my suggestion refers us back to the notion of being human: the possession of the personal qualities is morally important because it is characteristic of human beings. This too is a real explanatory move, in a sense in which it would *not* be a real explanatory move to say that the possession of the personal qualities is morally important because it is characteristic of *persons*. Since there is no going notion of personhood which is not definitionally but explanatorily connected with the notion of the possession of the personal qualities, someone who said this would really be saying no more than that the possession of the personal qualities is morally important because it is characteristic of those who possess the personal qualities. That idea may be what Warren is committed to. But it is not much help theoretically speaking, since it moves in a small and uninteresting circle. If we can do better than this in our moral epistemology, we should. I am in the business of suggesting that we *can* do better, by linking the moral importance of the possession of the personal qualities with the moral value of the humanity which their possession characteristically reveals.

This is the good argument whose ghost appeared above. The ghost-argument is the form of argument which proceeds by deciding (on the criterion of the possession of the personal qualities) whether some creatures are persons, 'and *hence* have full moral rights'. The argument-form of which this is the ghost can now be displayed. It proceeds by deciding whether some creatures are *humans*, 'and *hence* have full moral rights'.

However, two obvious points about this argument-form need to be noticed at once. First, if what we have to decide is just whether a creature is a *human*, there are plenty of other ways of doing this besides looking for evidence of the personal qualities. The personal qualities matter, I have suggested, because they help us to identify humans, and humans matter morally. But if it is humans we are looking for, then the personal qualities may turn out to be neither necessary or sufficient as evidence: not necessary, because there may be creatures which are humans but do not display the personal qualities, e.g. very young babies; and not sufficient, because there may be creatures which do display the personal qualities and yet are not humans, e.g. (perhaps) Warren's aliens.

The fact that the personal qualities are not necessary for humanity gives us further reason for doubting that possession of the personal qualities is *all* that counts when we are trying to assess whether any creature 'has full moral rights'. If I was right to claim, above, that the ethical importance of the possession of the personal qualities depended on the fact that such possession characteristically reveals humanity, then it will indeed follow that anything else which proves equally effectively diagnostic of humanity will be equally important as a criterion (or rather as a diagnostic symptom) of moral significance. In this way our criterion of what makes something morally significant will begin to get wider. It will not just include possession of what Warren counts as the personal qualities. It will be a conjunction also including all sorts of other features of humanity: for instance, capacity for pain[9] (and human capacities generally), human physical form and the possession of human DNA. To put it another way, we will begin to value not merely the (usually) human *person*, as Warren seems to, but (more broadly) the human *animal*. For – as we can now see – what humans are is not persons who happen to be animals, but rather animals who happen to display the personal qualities.

This in turn suggests the second point: which is that there is no reason to think that what we value about human beings is exclusively captured by making the observation that they are persons. (This is so even though, usually, the observation is true enough, if it is understood aright as meaning that those humans are possessors of the personal qualities.) It is perfectly legitimate – and it is in fact part of our ordinary moral thinking, until we are 'educated' out of it by philosophy or by religion – also to see moral value in the *animality* and *physicality* which are essential characteristics of human beings. (Here consider again human pain and pleasure, and also what is necessarily involved in, for example, human perception, or sexual intercourse, or childbirth.) There is mileage in the thought that human life and experience is essentially animal, and essentially physical, life and experience. If there was a natural kind *person*, the life and experience of members of that kind would not be *essentially* animal or physical, even if it was *as a matter of fact* both animal and physical. If this is right, then it is another reason for thinking that humans are not persons – besides of course the point which I have already been arguing, that there is any case no such natural kind as *person*.

VALUING ALL SORTS OF ANIMALS

Being human will, then, be sufficient for moral significance.[10] It does not, of course, follow that it will also be necessary. This brings us to what Warren has to say about aliens.

I have suggested already that what we value when we are valuing humans is not just the *person* but the *human animal*, and that to value human animals is to value humans for a wider range of reasons, and on the basis of a wider range of considerations, than are available to the theorist who insists on the (anyway rickety) notion of personhood as criterial of moral significance. Expressions of human value will tell stories about what it is like, both from the inside and from the outside, to be a human animal. They will appeal to the vividness of lived experience, to the technicolor of phenomenological feels, to the sensations and the emotions which all humans know in their own lives, or can come to know. Such expressions will *display* before us the facts of the natural history of humans, and invite us to see the significance of those facts. As already pointed out, much of what these expressions will tell or depict will be *essentially physical* in its content, articulation or preconditions. (Consider also a further point: that while there is such a thing as the natural history of humans as such, there is no such thing as the natural history of *persons* as such.)

These are the sorts of considerations which will underwrite our reasons for thinking that humans are valuable *as animals*. Now the important point here is, of course, that there is no reason in principle why such an account could not also be applicable to *other sorts of animals*, such as Warren's aliens. And if it was – if facts about and reflections on the natural history of those aliens gave us reason to think of them as morally significant in the same way as we are – then *that*, and not anything to do with personhood as such, would give us reason to ascribe to them the 'full moral rights' which we recognise as our own also.

Ascriptions of different sorts of moral status to different sorts of creature depend, then, not on Warren's over-simple question whether the creature under discussion is or is not a person. Rather, they depend on the deliverances of a much deeper and broader consideration of the whole natural history of that creature – not just its psychology (if any), but its physical constitution and all: what its life is like when it goes well (and when it goes badly); what its habitats and its habits are; 'what it is like', in Nagel's phenomenological sense, to be such a creature; and so on. Such reflections will give us a view of what good living is for such creatures, of what it would be like to promote good living for such creatures, and of how the good living of such creatures is related to that of other sorts of creature, ourselves included.

But of course, one thing that happens when we go down this line of thought is that, as the allegedly clear and simple division between persons and non-persons disappears, so does the allegedly clear and simple division between those creatures which have 'full moral rights' and those which do not. Since there are (potentially at least) all sorts of creatures around exemplifying all sorts of ways of good living, it follows that there are all sorts of moral status around: not just *two*, person and non-person. Since the ethical importance of personhood is (it has turned out) just the shadow cast by the ethical importance of humanity, we can be clear enough that *any* human will actually be ethically important in the sort of way in which Warren supposes that only humans who are persons are ethically important. What we cannot be so sure about, in advance, is whether or not creatures which are not humans, such as Warren's aliens, will be ethically important in exactly the same way as humans are. Here, indeed, Warren is at least right to the extent that it will be an important fact if those aliens do turn out to display what we call the personal qualities. But that fact will not be important because it reveals the aliens as being *persons*. It will be important because it reveals the aliens as being – to the extent that they display the personal qualities – *significantly like humans*. If they are *very* significantly like humans, in possessing the personal qualities and/or in other important ways, then it is probable that they will be morally important in a very similar way to humans.

However, first, since their possession of the personal qualities is not the only thing that matters morally about humans, it follows that there are other ways in which the aliens might turn out to be important besides by possessing those qualities. Moreover, second, the fact that some kind of creatures turn out to be very different from humans may show that they are not morally significant *in the same way as humans*: but it does not show that they are not morally significant *to the same degree as humans*. They may have some other, quite different, sort of moral significance which is simply not in competition with the moral significance of humans. Nothing seems likelier than this in the case of alien species which (so to speak) nature never intended to meet up with humans. And, what is more, nothing seems likelier than this in the case of many other species which are actually present on the Earth, but which (so to speak) nature never intended to meet up with humans either, placing them in environs which in many ways are as foreign to humans as other planets would be: for example, sperm whales.

I hope that, at this point, it will become obvious – perhaps rather suddenly – how my discussion of personhood is relevant to some of the central questions of environmental philosophy. (Evidently it is also relevant to Warren's issue, the issue of abortion, but I shall not here discuss that issue any further.) The key suggestion which is emerging from the argument is this: that concentration on the question whether or not, for example, aliens, or sperm whales, are *persons* 'and hence have full moral rights' is a very natural emphasis for us in our post-Cartesian philosophical milieu; but it is also, for a number of reasons, an entirely misleading emphasis. It is misleading – I have argued – because the question whether or not anything is a person is a question which, since *persons* are not a natural kind, fails to go to the heart of the matter. Anything is a person if and only if it possesses the personal qualities. But those qualities are important to the argument just because they are, in virtually all the cases we actually know of, diagnostic of (and explained by) humanity; they are not even the only indicators of humanity; and anyway, there is no reason to think that *being human* is the *only* way of being of pre-eminent moral significance, even though it is certainly *one* way.

It follows, as I have said, that talk of a simple, all-out, on/off distinction between persons and non-persons, and full moral rights and no moral rights, is not soundly based. Such talk always looked altogether unpromising for the ethics of nature. (Witness Warren's rather alarming suggestion that her space traveller can *eat* the aliens, provided they turn out not to be 'persons'.) We can now see not only why such talk is unpromising: namely, because of its necessarily discriminatory anthropocentrism, that is to say, its speciesism. We can also see how to replace it: namely, by an ethics which allows, much more liberally, that there may be all sorts of reasons why something has a pre-eminent (or a lesser, but still considerable) moral significance, and that these reasons do not necessarily have to do with personhood at all, provided they are intelligibly based in other features of the natural history of the living species in question.

One further advantage of such a basis for ethics is the following: it allows us to base ethics on biology, and in a way, moreover, which makes sense of an important corollary of the notion of ethical *supervenience*, and hence allows us to build a bridge (or at least, a Bailey bridge) over the is/ought gap. The thesis of supervenience says that every difference in ethical status must be underwritten by a difference in natural status: that is, it is arbitrary to hold different moral views about two situations or things which, described in non-ethical terms, come out as similar in all relevant respects. The corollary of supervenience which I have in mind – call it the corollary of proportionality – says that the relative weights of judgements of ethical importance or salience depend upon, and are in fact proportionate to, the relative weights of judgements of natural importance or salience. That is, how much a thing, fundamentally, *matters* depends upon what that thing, fundamentally, *is*, and the interrelations of the different sorts of *mattering* of which any particular thing is capable mirror the interrelations of the different sorts of *being* which can be ascribed to it. We may be able to describe the thing in question in various ways which highlight various sorts of ethical value which we might find in it. But the judgement about its value which goes deepest is the one which runs in parallel with the judgement about its *nature* which goes deepest.

This also, incidentally, suggests a way of dealing with the is/ought gap, because it allows us to sidestep[11] the question of how there could ever be *inferences* which crossed that gap. Given that we do get across it *somehow* – and given that we do accept supervenience – we may also go on to accept the corollary of proportionality. But then there is nothing to stop us from ceasing to worry about the is/ought gap for the moment, and getting on with some first-order ethics. We no longer need to know *how* our attitudes to different sorts of things are to be justified: we can just get on with the project of sorting those attitudes according to their relative importance, which, by proportionality, depends on the corresponding relative importances of the natural kinds of objects to which those attitudes are responses. The problem is now simply to ensure that the judgements we make which go deepest about the value of things *do* run in parallel with the judgements we make which go deepest about their *nature*. As ethical problems go, this is a relatively small and manageable problem!

How does all this apply to humans? As already pointed out, it is actually rather well-known, by this stage in human history, that what we really are is human beings, and that what humans really are is a zoological species called *homo sapiens*. Since there can only be one basic truth about what we really are, isn't this answer flatly inconsistent with the alternative answer, favoured by Descartes, Warren and others, that what we really are is *persons*? Yes. Of course it is. And so much the worse for that alternative.

Hence in the case of any human being, the judgement about its nature which goes deepest is the one which answers the question 'What is it?' asked concerning that human being with the words 'It is a human being'. It is also possible, normally, to say that the human being in question is a person (and, perhaps, a father, a philosophy lecturer, a husband, a member of a rugby team, and so on). All of these different judgements may well have some sort of ethical importance of their own. If so, each of these judgements needs to be related to the others in the sort of way suggested by the corollary of proportionality. But – to say it again – the fundamental judgement about the being in question is that it is a human – and not a person. The basic natural kinds which we encounter in doing ethics are *natural* kinds, zoological kinds, and 'person' is not the name of any of these.[12] This is why the fundamental rights of humans – considered just as such, and not considered as rugby players or philosophy lecturers and so forth[13] – are correctly called *human* (not personal) rights. It is also why, in the last analysis, 'person' is a kind-term which it may well be better simply to drop from our most basic ethical thinking: especially, as I say, when it is the ethics of human relations with other animals that concerns us. If we understand the *metaphysical* superficiality of the question whether any animal is or is not a person, we will be well placed also to understand the *ethical* superficiality of that question. What matters about sperm whales or chimpanzees or lions is not whether or not they are in any sense *persons*: it is what they are *like* in their own right, and apart from the anthropocentric (and indeed non-handicapped-thirtysomething-adult-centred) notion of a person.[14]

PRACTICAL REASON AND OTHER SPECIES: THE HUMAN PERSPECTIVE

Here it will fairly be objected that these various suggestions do not give us very much to go on in practice – not even the most specific of them, such as the corollary of proportionality. What actual ethical conclusions will result from such biologically-based reflections? And what will we say when, for instance, the moral realms of two very different sorts of creatures such as sperm whales and humans *do*, however 'unnaturally', come to clash? How are such clashes to be dealt with, according to my suggestion that the basis of the ethics of nature is in the natural histories of the species in question? This is an issue which I shall not try to settle here in any detail. (But I will offer one quick observation *en passant*. If the present proposal makes it harder than it was under the person-based approach to set up determinate rankings of relative moral importance between different species, as no doubt it does, that will not automatically be a count *against* it. Perhaps it just shows that the present proposal more accurately reflects the richness and confusing profusion of moral reality than the simplistic division of everything into persons and non-persons did.)

However, I want to finish this essay by making a point about human practical reason (and possibly non-human practical reason, too) – the perspectival point. This may go some way to suggesting the kind of approach to practical problems of prioritising that can be developed on the present basis; and which will also show the extent to which at least one sort of 'speciesism' is not merely discriminatory anthropocentrism, as Warren's sort certainly is, but rather is methodologically inevitable.

The perspectival point about human practical reason is, in a slogan, simply this: all human reasons are *human* reasons. Our approach, as humans, to the question of how to treat other species is necessarily *our* approach. We cannot come at the question from some God's-eye point of view. Nor, beyond a certain degree of imaginative and sympathetic identification, can we adopt the point of view of any other species. (Presumably the same would apply to any other species which like us was in the position to put the question of how other species should be treated.)

To see this, consider the following model of practical reasoning. I take it that we can get from thought to action in something like this way (my description is, of course, over-simplified): start with information about the natural history of humans; from that, get some ideas about what it is like for human life to go well; from this in turn, deduce some reasons which humans have, just *qua* humans; and then finally add – *not* a desire, but simply *the first-person perspective*: the fact that *we* are humans, or that *I* am a human.

In this story the crucial move is the addition not of a desire or other 'pro-attitude' (as in any Humean story), but of a viewpoint. On this view the crucially motivating aspect of human reasons or the attitudes which they ground, for me, is not necessarily that I *want* to act on them; it can also be simply that they are *human* reasons or attitudes, and I'm a human: therefore (as it is at least possible for me to see) they are *my* reasons or attitudes.

Such a story is, I think, a plausible one. And it is an interesting one too, for a number of diverse reasons. First, because its possibility would refute Hume's thesis that all motivation necessarily depends on antecedent desires. Unless we have already accepted Humeanism about motivation, there will be no good reason why just these ingredients – the human reason, and the first-person perspective which allows me to see that it is *my* reason – can't be enough to motivate action on their own. Second, because its possibility would also refute Williams's thesis[15] that there are no external reasons. Reasons that derive from human well-being in the way I have sketched are apparently 'external reasons' in Williams's sense. For although nothing is more natural and normal than that such reasons should appear in an agent's S (his 'subjective motivational set'[16], it is not their appearance there which makes them reasons for the agent. They are still reasons for him irrespective of whether or not they appear in his S. If this is right, then reasons of this sort are a counter-example to Williams's claim.

Thirdly, and most importantly for our present purposes, if this sketch of (at least some of) the workings of practical reason is correct, then it shows a clear sense in which our dealings with other species are necessarily conditioned by our own status as humans – and hence, as one might want to say, a sense in which speciesism is correct. For from the view of practical reason just outlined, it follows that one of the most important and general sorts of human reasons are species-specific reasons: reasons which arise from our own nature as members of the human species. And that this is some sort of limitation on how we can possibly rationally interact with (members of) other species is, I think, quite clear.

However, how *much* of a limitation it is, is less clear. One way in which it is certainly not a limitation is that it does not limit us to what might be called *species-egoism*, i.e. a ruthless preference for human interests in every case where humans' and other species' interests clash. In advance of any particular account of what reasons humans have – and to give such an account in anything like its proper fullness could take hundreds of pages – it is no clearer why human reasons in general should be species-egoist than it is why any individual's reasons should be individually egoist. If the human individual can have concern for others as one of his own basic and underived reasons, then *pari passu* the human species can have concern for other species as one of their own basic and underived reasons. In fact, I think, we do have just such a basic and underived reason: this fact is what excludes speciesism – in one sense – from the picture. But, to repeat, this reason too is always a *human* reason. And this last addition, no doubt, brings speciesism – in another sense – back into the picture.

NOTES

1. I am grateful to John Harris for his criticisms of an earlier version of this paper, and to Keekok Lee, Cynthia Macdonald, Eric Olson and a Moral Science Club audience in Cambridge, for their comments on some of the ideas presented here. Naturally, none of these entities are in any measure accountable for my continued adherence to those ideas.
2. Mary Anne Warren, 'On the moral and legal status of abortion', in Hugh Lafollette (ed.), *Ethick in Practice* (Oxford: Blackwell, 1977), pp. 79–90.
3. I shall set aside as a distraction the point (important though it may well be) that these beings can't, *pace* Warren, be *utterly* unlike any our space traveller has seen or heard of, since

if they were, he would fail to identify them as 'beings' – presumably Warren means *living* beings – at all.

4. Another distraction is the use of 'person' as a synonym of 'human'. This is very common in US English. (One example, from an American children's science book belonging to my daughter: 'The dinosaur Deinonychus was about three times as tall as a *person*'). This use of person is just fine – provided we remember that it is irrelevant to the present argument, since the 'person' (i.e. human) who is three times smaller than Deinonychus need not be a person in Warren's sense. We must not allow our intuitions about person = human to influence our intuitions about person = possessor of Warren's personal qualities. No doubt arguments like Warren's do commonly gain part of their apparent attraction from implicitly and illicitly trading on the other meaning of the term 'person'. But to see the real value of those arguments, we have to keep the two different meanings clearly apart.

5. See, for example, John Harris, *The Value of Life* (London Routledge, 1985), Chapter 1; Peter Singer, *Practical Ethics*, 2nd edn (Cambridge. Cambridge University Press, 1993), Ch 4; Michael Tooley, 'Abortion and Infanticide', in P. Singer (ed.), *Applied Ethics* (Oxford. Oxford University Press, 1926); Jonathan Glover, *Causing Deaths and Savings Lives* (London. Penguin, 1977), Chapters 3 and 9.

6. Compare the Putnam/Kripke view of the reference of natural-kind terms: see H. Putnam, 'The meaning of meaning', in K. Gunderson (ed.), *Language, Mind and Knowledge* (Minneapolis. Minnesota University Press, 1979), and S. Kripke, *Naming and* Necessity (Oxford: Blackwell, 1930), pp. 134–9. As Terence Wilkerson describes Putnam's view (in his *Natural Kinds*, Aldershot: Avesbury, 1995, p.90): '. . . We naturally find ourselves focusing on a group of objects that are superficially similar in colour, shape, habit, geographical position, etc., and we begin to think of certain objects as typical of the whole group. The general name is introduced originally as an indexical, as an expression which allows us to *point*, literally or metaphorically, to objects in the group . . . But (and this is a crucial point) according to Putnam, those properties do not determine membership of the kind, and the list is not a list of defining properties of tigers, in any relevantly formal sense of "definition". They merely help us, in Kripke's words, to "fix the reference" of the word "tiger".' In these terms, the present point is that *person* should not (unlike *human*) be seen as picking out any natural kind, *precisely because* a full list of the properties which constitute personhood *does* determine membership of that alleged kind.

7. Just likewise, incidentally, saying that opium puts people to sleep because it has a *virtus dormitiva* is not vacuous either, whatever Molière may have thought. For opium might have put people to sleep for other reasons. For example it might have had a *virtus* which gave people sleeping sickness; or else maybe all the people it has ever been administered to might by some massive fluke all have had a *tendentia dormitiva* of their own. In both these cases it is strictly false that opium is putting people to sleep because of its *virtus dormitiva*. But then we can describe what it is like for it to be false that opium has a *virtus dormitiva*. And if that is so, then it clearly follows that the claim that opium has such a *virtus* is not just vacuously true – and not just a high-faluting equivalent of 'Opium usually puts people to sleep' either.

8. These are both moves which, in conversation with me, John Harris has displayed a preparedness to entertain.

9. *Pain*, incidentally, is a most curious conceptual absentee from Warren's account!

10. 'Sufficient for' in the strict sense of 'being a sufficient condition for'. Here I cannot resist two comments on Warren's criticisms of John Noonan's discussion of abortion in his *The Morality of Abortion: legal and historical perspectives* (Cambridge, MA: Harvard University Press, 1970) Warren writes that 'Noonan argues for the classification of foetuses with human beings by pointing to the presence of the full genetic code, and the potential capacity for rational thought . . . [but] what he needs to show, for his . . . argument to be valid, is that foetuses are humans in the moral sense, the sense in which it is analytically true that all humans have full moral rights. But in the absence of any argument showing that whatever is genetically human is also morally human, and he gives none, nothing more than genetic humanity can be demonstrated by the presence of the human genetic code.' *First comment*: If Noonan is in this predicament then so is Warren. In the absence of any argument to show that whatever is factually a person is also morally a person – and Warren gives none – nothing more than factual personhood can be demonstrated by the presence of the personal qualities which

Warren identifies. *Second comment*: Warren's account of Noonan's argument is inaccurate anyway. What Noonan says is only that 'a being with a *human* genetic code is man'. He does not make possession of the *full human* genetic code the necessary and sufficient condition for humanity, for the good reason that if he did, then genetically abnormal human infants (e.g. those with Down's syndrome) wouldn't count as humans, which would be absurd. However, Noonan's criterion of humanity may still not be quite right, since even thus understood, it seems to entail that if there could be transgenic pigs (i.e. creatures which were phenotypically purely porcine and genotypically purely human) then they would count as humans, which would also be absurd. The moral of this story is an interesting one: it is that there is more to being human, or a member of any other species come to that, than DNA.

11. I stress, however, that the manoeuvre *is* a sidestep. The problem of how to make inferences from is to ought is not solved by it – and that problem does need solving, even if we can often get on, pro tem, without having a solution to it in our hands. For an attempt to solve it, see my 'The incompleat projectivist', *Philosophical Quarterly*, 48, January 1998, 1 ff.

12. This point is related to the point made above about *person*'s relative lack of explanatory power compared with *human*.

13. In virtue of these roles, humans can of course have further particular rights or duties, the interrelations between which will, by the corollary of proportionality, be determined by the 'fundamentalness' of those roles. If it is a more *metaphysically* fundamental fact about me that I am a father than that I am a philosophy lecturer, then we may expect a corresponding *ethical* ranking: i.e. we can expect my duties *qua* father to override my duties *qua* philosophy lecturer. As indeed they do.

14. I write, by the way, as a non-handicapped thirtysomething adult!

15. See B. Williams, *Moral Luck* (Cambridge: Cambridge University Press, 1981), pp. 101–13.

16. Ibid., p. 101.

7

RESPECT FOR THE NON-HUMAN

Timothy L. S. Sprigge

THE MORAL STATUS OF THE NON-HUMAN

Among the most divisive questions in ethics today is the moral status of the non-human. Some think that animals (henceforth = non-human animals) have rights which are far from adequately respected in current practice in any country. Others deny this with various degrees of vigour. Some think that nature, or perhaps rather the biosphere, should command our respect and concern, and not merely as a domicile in which we need consider nothing other than our own human interests. And, again, various natural things which are not individual organisms, such as species, individual ecosystems, lakes, mountains, wildernesses, forests, stretches of scenery, are deemed by some to be loci of intrinsic value insufficiently recognised as such; likewise certain beautiful artifacts.

Two questions about various such non-human things recur. Can they possess (positive) intrinsic value, meaning by this a value which is not a matter of their use, whether for 'practical purposes' or as a source of aesthetic or recreational enjoyment, but is simply the fact that it is a good thing that they exist in virtue of what they inherently are? (It is less often asked whether they can have negative intrinsic value, a rather significant fact. When not qualified as negative 'intrinsic value' is to be understood as qualified by 'positive'.) And can they, and do they, have moral rights (which should in some cases be made legal rights)? The first question arises typically about (non-human) animals, the second about various non-human components or aspects of nature (however precisely that last expression is to be understood).

So although it is perfectly possible to ask also whether animals have intrinsic value, and whether various non-animals (= neither human nor animal) have rights (considered briefly at the end of the essay) I shall initially go for the more usual issues of animal rights and intrinsic values in nature.

DO ANIMALS HAVE RIGHTS?

What are rights?

Let us consider some examples of what would quite widely be granted as basic human rights.

First, there is the very generic right not to be treated merely as a means, but also always as an end in oneself. There is no need for us to offer a further analysis here of this essentially Kantian idea.

A more specific example of what many would regard as a basic human right is the right not to be tortured, not even for the extraction of information. I, at any rate, would not approve a moral outlook which would see torture as a ready instrument for getting hold of certain facts, however important. (Compare the use of research animals.)

In considering this some philosophers will set about finding examples of cases where torture would seem justifiable, as, for instance, if some captured terrorist was known to know where some terrible outrage was to be committed, which could only be prevented by obtaining this information from him by torture.

I shall not go into such cases, because I believe that a right need not be conceived as something which it is never morally acceptable to override. Rather is it something the denial of which to the rights-holder is a very grave matter, such that we should not organise our life around any plan bound to require its being overridden. There may be rights which are so absolute that they should never be overridden,[1] but we lose an important concept if we reject the notion of rights which are not absolutely absolute, so to speak. Rather a right is a moral barrier which should not be crossed in any situation of a type whose recurrence we accept as a normal part of life.

But what does this talk of rights, whether absolutely absolute or not, really amount to? Suppose someone says that every child capable of benefiting from it has a right to education up to a certain level, what exactly is meant? One view is that it is simply a way of making certain statements about the duties towards each child of certain other persons, or of society and its official representatives and agents. Most probably, it is a way of saying that the national or local government has a duty to make provision for the education of every child within its region, or to compel other persons, such as the parents, to do so; it may even be taken as implying that it has an obligation to compel the child to attend school, or some other place of education. (Thus rights are not necessarily things one has a right to waive.)

There is much to be said for such a reduction of statements about one individual's rights to a statement about another's obligations. Certainly it is unclear what a right amounts to unless the obligations it imposes upon others can be specified Yet such a reduction fails to do justice to our feeling that, when someone has a right, this is a fact in the first place about them and not about others.

Perhaps we can remedy this by saying that an individual has a right to some benefit if there is *something about them* which imposes certain moral obligations on moral agents (either in general or just those in some specifiable relation to the rights-holder) of concern for their welfare. (These may be merely negative rights not to harm them or positive rights to assist them, according to a vast range of circumstances.) What this something about them is is a substantive moral question rather than a matter of mere definition, though it must be something which makes talk of their welfare intelligible. My own answer to that substantive moral question is that the main something in question is that of being a centre of consciousness, susceptible to pleasure and pain, and capable of happiness (a life experienced in a synthesised unity over a longish period as worth while) and unhappiness (a life similarly experienced as an uncompensated burden).

So do animals have rights?

Do animals have rights in this sense? In approaching this question we must have at least a rough idea of what is to count as an animal in this context. Everyone who speaks in favour of animal rights clearly counts all (non-human) mammals as animals but it is not clear whether they mean to count insects as such, while they are unlikely to count bacteria. My rough and ready suggestion is that we count all mammals, birds, reptiles and fish as animals and count other animals, in a strictly scientific sense, as animals in the sense relevant to discussion of animal rights only if their capacity genuinely to feel pleasure and pain, and perhaps happiness and unhappiness, is not less than that of whichever of these has the least such capacity. (Whether some lower levels of sentience than this still matter ethically is a question I shall bypass.)

Our definition does not logically imply that all animals are sentient, or even that some are. If fish are non-sentient, then bacteria, even if they are non-sentient too, are as sentient as fish and thus animals in our sense. And if none of mammals, birds, reptiles and fish are sentient then all animals in a scientific sense are animals in our sense. However, I shall take it for granted that all animals, in our sense, are sentient, since I think that the denial of a capacity to feel pleasure or pain of any of these creatures is absurd. To argue this, however, is impracticable here.

If animals are, indeed, thus sentient and my definition and substantive moral claim are agreed to, does it follow that animals have rights of some kind?

One way of resisting this conclusion from those premises is to say that though animals feel pleasure and pain, they do not enjoy happiness and unhappiness in the sense adumbrated. While a human being lives with a sense of how well or badly their life is going over time, animals, it is sometimes said, live entirely in the present.

I do not accept that this is so of animals in general, though it may be so of some. A cat's mood at each particular moment (each specious present) certainly seems to register how things have gone for it over some longer time. Animals trapped surely get more and more desperate at the length of their torture; they do not merely experience a series of atomic moments of pain. Moreover, animals can certainly be bored.[2] The whole business of any sentient being's experience of time is highly problematic. Some will think that nothing like our human sense of it could exist in the absence of language. But I doubt this. It seems to me that our experience moment by moment is intrinsically connected with what our experience has been for some time past, so that a period of time longer than a specious present can be said to be experienced within such a present. There is something wrong in the suggestion of Marcus Aurelius that all suffering is momentary, because every experience is so. I cannot delve into this difficult problem further but must simply give it as my opinion that both humans and at least some animals do in a manner experience a longer duration within each momentary specious present.

But perhaps the experience of some lower animals is merely momentary so that, though they feel pleasure and pain, they cannot experience happiness or unhappiness. Even so I would claim that they have some rights, for the mere capacity to feel pain and pleasure is a fact about a creature which imposes certain obligations on us. However, I would agree that a creature with no intensification of its momentary experiences by what preceded would have much less by way of rights than animals with a fuller experience of time.

The conception of animal rights connects up with our later theme of intrinsic value inasmuch as I would say that enjoyed experiences on the part of conscious creatures are the paradigm cases of intrinsic value, while seriously unpleasant such experiences are the paradigm cases of negative intrinsic value. They are, indeed, precisely what ethical theory needs for its foundation, factual characteristics of the world which are intrinsically prescriptive (of behaviour to promote, extend, prevent or curtail them) something which, if adequately recognised as equally true of the experiences of others, including animals, as of ourselves, must bring recognition of their equal right to happiness with us. I shall gesture towards this point again in the section on deep environmentalism and the value of the non-sentient below, but cannot defend it in this article against inevitable objections.[3]

To show along these lines that animals have rights, I do not need to establish the whole creed of a typical animal rightist, only to persuade the reader that there are at least some examples of animal rights.

To do this, let us ask ourselves whether cats, for example, have a right not to be hurt for the amusement of humans, as, sad to say, they often were in the past, when it was a favourite entertainment to lower a net full of cats into a bonfire, and to laugh at their howling.[4]

It seems to me evident that those who did this could not really appreciate the fact that pain, of a kind not fundamentally different from that experienced by a human in being burnt, was caused thereby (just as indifference or enthusiasm for another human's suffering turns on a distorted conception of that – either as shadowy, compared with our own, or as vibrant in some misconceived manner).

It is time to defend this very modest claim about the rights of animals against some common objections. Some of these are more to my use of 'rights' than to the claim that animals have them in the sense I have specified. For, so it may be said, using the expression so as to give it this extension suggests that the moral status of animals and that of humans is much closer than in moral truth it is. This is a legitimate challenge, since the word 'rights' has a highly flexible sense, while possessing an emotive power, which is up for grabs between different moral outlooks. So it is not enough for me to entrench myself in my own definition of 'rights', I must also defend the moral position which has inclined me to this usage. So let us now turn to objections to the notion of, or the expression, 'animal rights', even in such a case as that of the tortured cat, where, it is to be hoped, it will not be denied that such torture is wicked.

Objections to animal rights

A likely objection to what I have been saying is that even if it is wrong to do certain things to animals, such as torturing a cat for fun, it is inappropriate to express this fact by saying that the cat has a right not to be hurt. If this follows from my usage of 'rights', so it may be said, that only shows that this is a bad usage.

1. Let me deal first with those people, whom I have encountered, who on further probing dislike talk of animal rights because they dislike the whole language of rights as a way of expressing ethical opinions, whether about human to human, or human to animal, behaviour.

To this my main reply is that I would not mind too much if the whole language of rights were dropped and we just spoke of what it is morally acceptable or unacceptable to do to fellow conscious creatures. The trouble is that the language of rights is strongly entrenched and if we allow talk of human rights and not of animal rights we suggest that the reason why it is wrong, say, to torture a cat for fun is essentially different from why it is wrong to torture a fellow human for fun. So as long as talk of rights persists we should talk of animal rights.

There is, however, something more positive to be said about the language of rights which is that it centres attention on the individual said to have the rights and bids us think about the moral implications of its being the kind of individual it is, and not just on the nature of the relevant moral agents.

I turn now to the objections of those who speak of human rights but reject talk of animal rights.

2. One reason for this may be the quasi-Kantian one that the something about fellow humans which, properly conceived, requires us to respect their welfare is not their capacity for pleasure or pain, or for happiness and unhappiness, but their status as rational beings. Thus talk of animal rights assimilates what should not be assimilated. It suggests, for example, that the reason it is wrong to torture a fellow human for one's own amusement is radically different from the reason why it is wrong to do so to a cat (even granting that the latter is wrong). For the reason why it is wrong to torture a human being is that it fails to respect their status as a rational being, while the reason it is wrong to torture an animal is merely to do with pleasure and pain. (Kant, himself, of course, thought that it was because it encouraged cruelty to humans, but I am coping with a supposed worthier – in this respect – opponent.)

This is an old argument but I am among those who think this position radically misconceived. Thus I turn the argument on its head. The prime reason it is wrong to torture a cat for fun is essentially the same as the prime reason why it is wrong to torture a human being for fun, namely that the pain or suffering of a conscious creature is the paradigm case of what is intrinsically bad, and that it is therefore shameful deliberately to produce it for no better reason than one's own amusement. It is therefore best to use the expression 'rights' either in both cases or neither, since otherwise one suggests that there is a moral difference where there is not. Of course, this is a matter of substantive moral disagreement but I have indicated why I consider the animal rightist more in touch with the most relevant facts.

3. Some people say that the notion of rights only makes sense in the context of duties. An individual only has rights if they have duties. This is sometimes said as a reproach to people who go on too much about their own rights.

Now there is liable to be a confusion here. The concept of rights, on the one hand, and of duties and responsibilities on the other, are certainly interconnected in the sense that one individual's rights are another individual's duties.

But that does not imply that an individual without duties themselves may not have rights. Human babies are an example. If you object to the notion of animal rights on the ground that animals have no duties, you must say that human babies have no rights – no right not to be burnt for fun, for example. And I don't think most people who talk about rights at all would be happy with this.

4. A somewhat similar objection is that it is linguistically improper, and a blurring of an important moral distinction, to speak of individuals as possessing rights except where they are capable of appreciating that they possess these rights and of claiming respect for them.[5]

An initial response is that, even if this view about the proper use of the word 'rights' were accepted, it is not obvious that this precludes cats having rights. A cat who is being hurt will struggle and scratch. Why is not this a claiming of its rights? Is it even clear that the cat does not really feel a kind of righteous indignation? But let us accept, for the sake of argument, that the cat has no sense of the moral significance of the situation.

I can see that the word 'right' can be given this restricted sense. The word's meaning in standard English is, as we have already noted, too flexible to settle such matters by a mere appeal to usage, though it is none too easy to find a plausible definition which allows rights to babies and imbeciles, but not animals. The main point I would make against any such usage is the ethical one that it encourages us to draw a sharp distinction between different sorts of moral obligation towards other conscious beings, as resting or not resting on rights, where there is minimal distinction in what really makes the actions which go against it wrong.

Of course, if one thinks that the only reason it is wrong to hurt a cat is that it foments a cruel disposition which could later vent itself upon humans, one holds a view which it is quite proper to express by saying that it is wrong to hurt the cat, but that it does not have rights.[6] Such a view, however, though suitably expressed in these words, is an appalling and irrational one resting upon failure to recognize the essential identity of the consciousness in all sentient beings.[7] It is just the importance of distinguishing the real ground there is for saying that it is wrong to hurt the cat, from anything of this kind, that makes it so important to say that the cat has rights, so long, at least, as one uses the expression 'rights' in it connection with one's views about what it is wrong to do to humans.

Doubtless one may only talk of individuals as having obligations where there are certain possibilities of reflection, of action going against the grain, and appreciation of values not immediately present. Whether this means that no non-human animals have obligations is hard to say. But this is no reason for hesitation in the ascription of rights. That an animal lacks the ability to appreciate properly the reality of the consciousness of other beings in a manner which would prompt moral restraint in dealing with them does not affect the fact that it is conscious in a manner which *we* can appreciate as giving grounds for restraint in our dealings with it, and that this is the same kind of fact about the animal as we recognise in humans when we talk of their rights.

5. And doubtless this is really the heart of most denials of animal rights, namely that people just do not believe that the pleasure and pain, or happiness and unhappiness, of animals is really at all the same thing as is that of humans.

There are indeed problems in really bringing home to oneself the likely character of animal experience. To imagine an experience which has no linguistic element is difficult. But I cannot pursue this matter further here, beyond remarking that I believe it a false phenomenology which makes us reject the idea that there is a basic positive or negative hedonic character to experience which does not depend upon language, and the presence of which is amply evidenced in animal behaviour. After all, it is all too easy, and the basic source of human to human immorality, to think that the pleasure and pain, or happiness or unhappiness, of fellow members of one's own species is not the same kind of vivid reality which they are in one's own case.

Those who insist on the utter difference of human and animal consciousness (so far as they admit the latter at all) often have in mind the presumed fact that animals are not self-conscious, even if they genuinely have experiences. Well, self-consciousness has several different meanings, and animals of different species may be presumed to have different levels of it in most of these senses. It is often thought significant that only certain apes seem capable of recognising their reflections as themselves. But though most animals may have little sense of themselves as objects for other subjects (one crucial form of self-consciousness which, indeed, might seem to be possessed by every animal which hopes to pounce on its prey from an unobserved position) they must all in some manner contrast the world within which they move and themselves as moving within it. No more, indeed much less, than this seems requisite for having a good and a bad time.[8]

The three basic animal rights

If I am now asked what the basic animal rights are I suggest that they could be summed up under the following three heads:

1. Each animal has a right not to be subjected to serious suffering, except for its own sake (e.g. medical treatment) by moral agents (i.e. human beings).

2. Each animal, in so far as its life is under the control of human agents, has a

right to a life worth living, and in particular to an environment in which it can indulge in a fair amount of its inherited behaviour patterns.

3. Each animal has a right to some respect by human beings as a fellow conscious subject.

I do not say that these are the only basic animal rights, but they are the main ones. They may be thought vague but they are not vacuous.

If you challenge me as to my grounds for ascribing these particular rights to animals, my quick answer is this. We do grant that humans have comparable rights to these, and the basic reason is that each human being is an individual capable of enjoying its life or being miserable. But this is equally true of animals, so they must have kindred rights.

You may notice that I did not specifically list a right not to be killed as among the animal rights. Yet a right not to be killed by another human being, with the debatable exception of war or capital punishment, is regarded as a very basic human right.

I shall by-pass this subject for now beyond allowing on the one hand:

1. that in principle, if not often in fact, killing animals can be done without causing suffering, while this is in general impossible with human beings in virtue of their greater capacity to grasp what is going on;

2. that in some cases, but by no means all, violent animal death does not cause the same sense of bereavement and/or anxiety which a violent human death does;

and on the other hand;

3. that a readiness to kill other creatures too lightly, and as a matter of routine, does not exhibit much respect for them as fellow conscious subject.

ARE THERE INTRINSIC VALUES IN NATURE?

Deep environmentalism and the value of the non-sentient

I turn now to the second main question I raised about the moral status of the non-human. Can non-sentient things, in particular things or aspects of 'Nature', possess intrinsic value? And granted that they can, does it not follow that we have certain direct obligations towards them, such as we have to sentient creatures, in virtue of what we call their rights, whether we choose to use the term 'rights' in this context too or not? If so, let us say that they, like individuals with rights such as humans, or, as we have argued, animals, are likewise 'morally considerable'.[9]

Some environmental ethicists, as, for example, Paul Taylor and Holmes Rolston III,[10] suggest that those who limit their moral concern to humans and animals and do not recognise the intrinsic value and consequent moral considerability of such apparently non-sentient things as trees and plants, forests and ecosystems, and species as historically evolved individuals are guilty of a prejudice in favour of sentience which is as morally obtuse as the prejudice in favour of rationality which has made some thinkers deny the moral considerability of animals.

What's so special about sentience? they ask. Why should this one attribute of one particular class of individuals, namely animals, be the sole thing which can confer moral considerability? Surely, some of them say, the cut-off point must be life rather than sentience, for everything that is living can flourish or flounder, and has a telos which we should recognise in our own striking of the moral bank balance.[11] There are others who go further still and reject a prejudice in favour of life too, being prepared to find value in what is neither living nor sentient, and not merely derivative from the values realised in such life as it may contain (e.g. a cataract).

I shall refer to this outlook as 'deep environmentalism' rather than by the more usual expression 'deep ecology' because the latter term seems now to be used for one particular position within the broad swathe of views which urge the moral 'considerability' of things in, or aspects of, nature or even Nature itself (however exactly this is understood; – it tends to mean 'the biosphere') in virtue of facts other than the quality of the conscious lives of sentient individuals bound up with them.

Personally I find this talk of a prejudice in favour of sentience somewhat amazing.[12] But if one *is* going to say that life possesses value even when devoid of consciousness, I sympathise with those who deny that life is the final cut-off point for moral considerability. It will be said that only the living can flourish or flounder, or be in any sense teleological. Whether this is true or not, it seems to me that a flourishing, floundering or teleology on the part of living things which is no more than a habit of moving in conformity with certain lawful patterns (whether the laws have a teleological character or not) is no better than moving about in the way plenty of inanimate things do. It is simply matter in movement. Why should value be confined to that particular type of pattern of movement and not attributed also to some of the many other such patterns found in the universe? Certainly looked at from the outside there are all sorts of patterns and processes in nature which have as much fascination as do processes involving life. Why should there not be intrinsic value and moral considerability there too?[13] Once one has abandoned the notion that value requires sentience I do not see why one should not go further and say that it does not even require life. For without consciousness life is just a complex physical process, no more and no less capable of value than various other such processes.

Deep environmentalists who put this special stress on life answer that value is determined by the pursuit of goals, and also requires a contrast between a flourishing state of something and a non-flourishing state. But they value a living organism itself, not just what it is after, and it is doubtful whether the organism itself can be described as the object of any being's goal, as being good for something. Holmes Rolston, perhaps,[14] wants to hold that the process of evolution has a goal, and that each species is a stage in its realisation. But it is doubtful how far this point can be sustained. At any rate, upon the whole it is difficult to see why, having decided that there can be value without sentience, one does not conclude further that there can be value without life.

Even if we are bound to be more fascinated by the living than the inanimate,[15] even when sentience is supposed absent in both cases, it does not follow – if value judgements neither express nor necessarily concern any sort of feeling – that it is only or pre-eminently the former which possesses intrinsic value.

But how reasonable is the claim that there can be value without sentience? Its proponents see our putting such a high value on sentience as merely a preference for our own kind, understood more extensively, as animal rightists chide us for when we think that it is only those conscious beings whose consciousness is of the same rational linguistic kind as our own who really matter. But this will not satisfy most of those who think that there can be no value without sentience.

Sometimes the limitation of value to the realm of sentience is said to stem from a confusion between valuers and what is valued. The valuer must be sentient, it is said, but what he values need not be, and may even include situations from which all consciousness is supposed absent, or hypothetically, even a world in which sentience never arose at all. For this view, in effect, all value is in the eye of a sentient beholder, but the beheld and valued need not itself be sentient.[16] However, philosophers like Rolston and Taylor will have no truck with this rather weak defence of the independent value which can be present in nature, even apart from sentience, and take a much more robust view of the reality of value as a factually existing feature of the world which can exist independently of any act of evaluation at all.

My own reason (already hinted at) for claiming a special relation between value, both positive and negative, and sentience is this. To think it a good or a bad thing that something is happening is, indeed, to have certain feelings. But having these feelings is envisaging the situation as having certain value qualities. What seems a good thing to me is presented to my imagination or perception with a certain positive sparkling quality, in, so to speak, glowing rosy colours. Similarly, what seems a bad thing to me presents itself to me in a certain grim or gloomy colour.

It is a mistake to conclude from this that value, positive or negative, is only ever there in the eye of a beholder. For this is to ignore the fact that experiences of joy or misery really do have the relevant sparkling or gloomy colour. When I see or imagine someone else doing something, the real heart of the external situation is what it feels like from the inside to that person themselves. Now as it feels from the inside, the situation will possess a real, not merely an imputed or imagined, positive or negative such value quality, consisting in the person's joy or misery as they act. Thus I grasp or fail to grasp the situation as it really is according as to whether the light in which it presents itself to me corresponds to what it feels like, and therefore really is like, at its source. To hold that value only exists in the eye of the beholder (or, alternatively, that judgements of value are not really judgements of fact at all) is to ignore the simple fact that they ascribe qualities which can really be there when their topic is the experience of a subject. For this may really possess in itself, and not merely for a beholder, those qualities which I imagine to be there when I think something a good or a bad thing. To put it in traditional empiricist terms, it is certain qualities of joyful or miserable experiences which are the impressions from which we get the very idea of value, and they can only exist as features of sentience, however much we may cast them in imagination upon situations supposedly devoid of it. I conclude from this (perhaps contentious) line of thought that it is not mere kingdomism (cf. speciesism) which leads us to think the idea of value without sentience absurd.[17]

Does that mean that we must totally reject the claims of such deep environmental ethics? I think not. For it stresses the importance of three types of value whose existence is compatible with the inseparability of value from sentience. These are aesthetic value, understood in a broad sense, and what might be called inner value and mystical value.

First, aesthetic value. When I look at a beautiful painting, the object which I am admiring possesses its beauty as an intrinsic feature of that which I am contemplating. It is not merely producing pleasant sensations in me, which can be separated off from the painting itself. All the same, the painting, as an aesthetic object, is not something which can exist outside anyone's consciousness. It is only when someone looks at it that it comes into existence as an aesthetic object possessed of beauty. And that beauty is, in fact, a special sort of pleasure. However, it is not pleasure as a quality of a spectator's merely subjective feelings or sensations but as a feature of the not-self side of our consciousness. For one's consciousness as a whole normally contains a self side which is the home of subjective sensations, and is largely private to oneself, and a not-self side which is the world in which one lives as one experiences it. This is, to a great extent, shared with other people. Beauty and the objects which possess it belong, I suggest, to this not-self side of consciousness.

Now a great deal of the value we find in nature is of this aesthetic kind. Suppose two people are glorying in the beauty of a mountain scene. There are two mistakes to avoid in analysing this situation. On the one hand, it is wrong to think that each is just enjoying their own private sensations. For each is sharing their wonder with the other and rightly believing that they are both entranced by the same reality, one which takes them beyond their private personalities. But, on the other hand, the reality they find so beautiful can only have real existence as an object of human consciousness, as an element in a more or less common not-self. If there were no creatures with suitable sense organs, the panorama they find beautiful would simply not exist. It is not, as is sometimes suggested, that the panorama would still be there, but that its beauty would not. The very panorama itself would not be there. There would simply be certain causes which might have produced it in someone's consciousness had there been someone suitably situated. The scientist will describe these causes ultimately in terms of atoms and so forth, while the metaphysician may postulate something more fundamental still of which these are only our conceptual transcript.

I suggest that a great deal of what people hold to be intrinsically valuable in nature consists in panoramas possessing certain aesthetic qualities. It may be, indeed, that these panoramas owe their intrinsic value to something more than sensuous beauty. When someone with the appropriate grasp of an ecosystem is filled with wonder and holds it to have intrinsic value, then the synthesised picture of it all in their imagination has a more severe intellectual beauty than that of, say, a sunset. All the same, it only exists for a consciousness. For, although there is certainly some reality there apart from human consciousness to which they are responding, it cannot be precisely equated with the system as they imagine it. Certainly, if our view of what the underlying reality is in itself is to be based on science, it is more plausible to conceive it in terms of the units of physics that of those the ecologist deals in.[18] For species, ecosystems and tracts of land seem to be unities on a scale which only exist for a contemplating consciousness and which thus belong to 'the manifest image', rather than to the underlying reality. One can argue over the details of the point, but, upon the whole, it seems clear that what is there independently of our thought and imagination cannot be equated with the ecophilosopher's picture of that to which they ascribe intrinsic value. Even the variety of species of bird, and their inter-relations, in the British Isles consists, so it seems, in a multitude of separate facts, and exists only virtually as a unity until it is apprehended as such by the student of nature, unless, indeed, it is contemplated as a unity by God, something to which not all deep ecophilosophers would be willing to appeal.

My conclusion is that one kind of intrinsic value which may be truly ascribed to nature is aesthetic value, and that this attaches to nature as a multi-sensory panorama which transcends any one human being's consciousness, but does not exist except as a (more than merely visual) spectacle for human beings. The deep ecologist who puts their case for the moral considerability of nature on this basic would then, I suggest, be making basically the same kind of case for the conservation of wild nature as someone who campaigns for the conservation of beautiful cities. A beautiful city is something which, as a beautiful panorama, is a value transcendent of any one individual's awareness, but it does not transcend human consciousness, for the city, as a part of the human 'life-world', as opposed to as a mere complex of invisible atoms, only exists for human consciousness. I am more than happy to agree that such things have a kind of moral 'considerability'. They do make certain demands upon us. We should not destroy beautiful things, even if they cannot be actual as genuine beautiful things except in a human consciousness. And this is true of much of wild nature.

But if there are positive aesthetic values in nature, are there not also negative ones, requiring a Capability Brown? Or is perhaps everything in nature properly regarded beautiful, so that negative value pertains only to pain and suffering? This is an issue I cannot explore here.

Value pertaining to the felt inner life of nature

An identification of the intrinsic value they claim for parts, features or aspects of nature with beauty will not satisfy most deep environmentalists. They want us to afford wild nature the kind of respect which we are supposed to feel for other people, and, as animal rightists claim, for other animals, not that which we feel for a painting, piece of music or even for a beautiful building. For when I respect another person and regard them as having rights, I do so for what they are in themselves, not for the spectacle which they present to an observer. And they want us to respect all forms of life in essentially the same way as this.

Richard Taylor, for example, wants us to feel about the striving of every living individual, sentient or not, for its its good as we do for a child trying to find its way in life as it grows up.[19] Well, in so far as what is in question is the good of wild animals there is, in principle, no problem here. One may well feel that the different ways of experiencing the world which pertain to every kind of animal add to the totality and variety of value in the world. But here the value is actually felt – and, though life in the wild has its horrors, one may feel that the overall experience of a wild animal has normally sufficient that is positive in it to be worthwhile. For Taylor the flourishing of every shrub, plant and tree is intrinsically good, while others, such as Holmes Rolston, wish us to feel in the way about nature, or the totality of life on the planet, as a speciating process.[20]

Is such an ethic absurd? Well, it seems a dubious one, so far as those things in wild nature go which are not normally thought of as conscious or sentient. Value, I have suggested, is only coherently conceivable as something felt, that is, as some kind of pleasure or pain, joy or misery. (Perhaps I should emphasise that I do not think of pleasure and pain as sensations detachable from the wholeness of their many different species.)[21] Such value can exist as the felt state of some conscious being, or it can exist as a kind of objectified pleasure or pain in some shareable spectacle which can figure in the consciousness of such beings. But if such things as trees have a value other than as a spectacle which can be present in minds like ours, it must be because they, or their components, do possess some kind of consciousness or sentience.[22] Thus I can only think of value as pertaining to things in, or aspects of, nature not normally thought of as sentient, if, in fact, sentient experience is present there, either in their parts or in themselves as wholes. In short, to ascribe moral considerability to parts or aspects of nature normally thought of as non-sentient requires a panpsychist view, according to which the universe is much more pervasively filled with feeling than modern scientific man tends to believe it is. Some return to something like animism is required if nature as it is in itself, and not as a spectacle for humans, is to be considered of intrinsic value.[23]

Personally, indeed I think that panpsychism, animism of a sort, if you like, is true.[24] I cannot argue the matter here, but I do think that the whole of reality is full of feeling or sentient experience, and that what presents itself as an external physical object must either itself have a feeling of its own being, or be composed of what does so or both. This, as I see it, gives us three types of thing. First, the ultimate units of matter, whatever they are. These have a feeling of their own individual being and do not contain anything simpler which does so. Then there are things which are composed of these simplest units but, not being real individuals in their own right, possess no sentience or consciousness as wholes. This is true of many things, for example of chairs and tables. Then, thirdly, there are things like humans and animals, which are not only composed of the ultimate units of matter, each with its own charge of feeling, but also have their own overall feeling of themselves and what they are up to and among. A crucial question for a deep environmentalist who took this view would be whether some of the units in nature, besides humans and animals, are similarly sentient as wholes rather than merely composed of minute parts which are so.

Now as a panpsychist I am not in principle averse to the idea that there is value in nature apart from the life of humans and animals. And though deep environmentalists are often eager to disclaim any tincture of panpsychism, they tend to write in ways which make doubtful sense without it. So maybe their conviction that there are values in natural processes arises from an intuitive sense, which they possess despite themselves, that there is some kind of real feeling there. In particular, when they think that all life has value and that a tree (for example) has a real good of its own, they may be implicitly supposing that the tree does feel its own processes from within. So I do not deny that there can be value in nature independently of commonly recognised sentience, only adding that it is hard to make sense of this claim without moving towards panpsychism (or at least broadening our conception of the distribution of sentience).

So we can allow the deep environmentalist the possibility of two types of value in nature, that which pertains to it as an aesthetic spectacle, and, if they are willing to move in the direction of panpsychism, that which pertains to its inner felt life, such as may be thought to have its own rights.

But I suspect that, even for the panpsychist, where it is not the welfare of individual organisms that is in question but the alleged value of units such as total ecosystems, species or terrains, appeal must be mainly to aesthetic value. For, even if there is a world of inner feeling in nature, we must remain so ignorant of its character, except when it rises to the animal or human level, that we can hardly take the values realised there into account in our moral reckonings.

Mystical values in nature

But the contrast between the value a sentient individual possesses as a spectacle for another and that which it possesses for itself need not be a sharp one. For a spectacle may be a better or worse clue to that of which it is the spectator's subjective version. The spectacle which you present to me, for instance, is in a very subtle relation to what you are in yourself. Certainly, the value of you as an object in my world is not to be prised apart from my sense of the value your life has for you. Similarly with animals. So perhaps the great spectacles of nature do owe some of their wonder to the fact that they induce a kind of empathy with hidden processes of feeling going on there.

However, it is a rather simplistic view even of works of art that they are merely beautiful forms which can occur as objects of delight within our consciousness. Art can stir up some deeper sense within us of the truth of things than we can otherwise obtain. Now what appeals to many environmental ethicists about wild nature is often the kind of mystical or quasi-mystical experiences which people tend to feel in being alone in places of great natural beauty, or wildlife free from human domination. But what is the real status of these experiences? Are they merely feelings which people find profoundly satisfying or do they also put us in touch with some deeper level of reality?

If nature, that is, the whole physical universe, really consists in numerous interacting streams of experience, of which our stream of consciousness is only one special instance, one may ask: what holds all these streams of experience into a unity so that they are not separate worlds in no real contact with each other and obeying no common laws? Perhaps the only real answer is that nature as a whole is all contained in one vast super-consciousness, which we can call God or the Absolute. Such at any rate is my view. Now for the needs of daily life, we have had to develop a strong sense of our separateness from the rest of things. But this is really an illusion. Our separateness from other human beings is one kind of illusion, which breaks down to some extent so far as we develop morally. But our sense of separateness from the remainder of the physical world is also an illusion. Perhaps in nature mysticism this illusion also partly breaks down, and fills us with peace because there is something painful in this sense of human separateness. And perhaps this is not just a feeling but a real collapsing of barriers so that certain non-human modes of experience flow in across the defences we normally keep up against them. If so, human beings may need areas of wild nature which they can visit to be refreshed by the experience of their oneness with a reality beyond the human. Consequent on this there is, of course, the problem of how to make this experience widely available without making it impossible through human crowding and and touristic modifications.[25]

Having introduced the notion of a divine mind should I not qualify my earlier suggestion that works of art and the wonders of nature as we perceive them may genuinely exist only when perceptually and sensibly present to human consciousness, though of course their noumenal backing remains? Should I not rather say, with Berkeley, that they do continue to exist in the mind of God? I am not dead against this Berkeleyan claim, but it is perhaps more likely that God's awareness of them in the character in which we perceive them is only via the human awareness of it, and that what they are for Him, Her or It otherwise are rather those streams of experience (of the specific character of which we can know little or nothing) which are their noumenal backing.

DO ANY NON-SENTIENT THINGS HAVE RIGHTS?

Suppose an area of outstanding natural beauty, or of ecological complexity of a value-conferring type, is threatened with destruction, in order, say, that a new road be built, and conservationists protest at the desecration. The deep environmentalist will probably contend that destruction of such a 'masterpiece of nature' is prima facie wrong, and often wrong all-things-considered on the final moral balance. I have given my opinion of this claim. On the one hand, the reality in question is a phenomenal object in the human 'life-world', and as such it has the same kind of value as that of a fine work of art. Like a work of art it only has genuine existence as a content of an appreciating consciousness, but like a work of art it may be rather the consciousness which owes its value to it rather than vice versa. (In comparing beauty in nature with that of a work of art I do not mean to deny important differences arising typically from the difference of our physical condition in enjoying each; the beauties of nature are enjoyed by many, especially for those not labouring there, in the context of healthful exercise while art may require a quite different type of physical self control.) So there is a direct duty to keep it there as a possible object of human awareness. Now certainly there is a noumenal reality, of which it is the appearance, and that may have an intrinsic value which does not depend on its being the object of any external individual's awareness. But though there may be such a value we do not have that access to it which would allow us to weigh it in the balance with other values, and seem therefore confined, so far as anything which could be called its intrinsic value goes, to a concern with the (in a broad sense) aesthetic value which it possesses as an object of human consciousness.

However, a further value may be claimed for certain scenes in nature, namely their power of generating a liberating sense in us of union with some greater whole than we can describe in the terms of everyday life. This should not be called a merely instrumental value, since that implies a distinction between the experience caused and its cause which may have briefly ceased to hold. Only a hint of such an experience is common for most of us, but even that hint may be among the most worthwhile things we know.

All this does amount, I think, to granting that certain parts or aspects of nature may have a certain sort of moral considerability, not reducible to the moral considerability of any sentient beings for whom they provide a home or a resource. But should we conclude that natural objects such as trees, lakes, mountains, wildernesses, forests, stretches of scenery, species, ecosystems, some of them, or all of them, may have rights?[26]

In favour of speaking of their rights, one may say that they make certain moral demands for respect and conservation in virtue of what they intrinsically are. Just as it would be wrong to destroy all copies of some great work of literature and thus (if memories are not powerful enough) destroy its existence as a possible object of consciousness, so it would be wrong to destroy a 'masterpiece of nature' as a possible object of human experience. One might even say that the book has a right to be read and the natural masterpiece a right to be seen.

But, on the other hand, the reason why such things make moral demands upon us, and are thus morally considerable, is so very different from the way a fellow human or an animal does so that it may be better to reserve the language of rights for the latter. For even if, as I believe, consciousness is there at the noumenal level in all nature's masterpieces it is too hidden from us in everything but individual humans or animals to be the basis of the respect we owe them. Just as the denial of animal rights too much contrasts their moral considerability with that of humans so would the affirmation of the rights of trees too much assimilate their moral considerability to both of these.

It is especially important to keep the special kind of respect which should be given only to conscious individuals at a time when the development of artificial intelligences and robots tempts many to confuse certain types of physical complexity with the presence of consciousness. (Nor, I take it, can they evoke that sense of oneness with the whole of things which we considered in the last section. The respect due to them is more like that due to a well designed car – but I cannot go into that.)

Thus the prejudice in favour of sentience which some deep environmentalists condemn is an enlightened prejudice, provided it does not make us ignore the kind of intrinsic value which things other than humans and animals may possess.

But what is the relation between intrinsic value and the rights of humans and animals? Our previous discussion suggests that it is the fact that their experiences may be intrinsically good or intrinsically bad which grounds their rights. But do not they themselves, and not merely their passing conscious states, have intrinsic value? Well, clearly as objects in the world they may have intrinsic value in the various senses distinguished as pertaining to various sorts of non-animals. They may, for example, be beautiful.

But something is missing here, is it not? Is an ugly person in pain merely a disvaluable object having disvaluable experiences? Well, perhaps they may have beauty of character, and thus be aesthetically valuable in this way. But what if their character is an ugly one? There is a strong inclination to say that even so, simply as persons, they have an intrinsic value, in virtue of which they should be helped and respected, which we have not yet properly addressed although it is, in fact, the basic reason why they have rights.

What we are seeking for here, I believe, is the notion that they should be objects of our love in the sense of affectionate concern, and this, if not exactly intrinsic value as we have been using that expression, is still something which follows necessarily from the truth of what they are and as such is intrinsic to them. One does not see them truly unless one feels respect for them and concern for their fate. And the same is true of animals, who are centres of consciousness living in fear and hope in essentially the same way as we do. (The consciousness which pertains to the noumenal reality behind inanimate things is, as we have seen, too hidden to be felt about in its individual instances in this way. Whether and how the Absolute, that is, the total unitary Consciousness of the Universe, should be loved is a more distinctly religious question which cannot be considered here.)

So important is love in this sense that if we loved all conscious individuals as they should be loved, the notion of rights might be allowed to go by the board, for rights are best spoken of where love is likely to fail. But should not aesthetic objects of great beauty be loved? Yes, they should, but it is a different sort of love from that respect and concern we should have for all conscious creatures or the more intense version of this emotion which the normal person can only feel for a few such individuals.

NOTES

1. This is doubtless true of the inspirational (rather than concretely specific) generic right just spoken of.
2. See Françoise Wemelsfelder, *Animal Boredom*.
3. See T. L. S. Sprigge, *The Rational Foundations of Ethics* (London: Routledge, 1983), Chapters V, VI and VIII; also for a slightly different perspective on the point see my 'Metaphysics, physicalism and animal rights', *Inquiry* 22, 1979. 111–15 (Appendix I).
4. Norman Davies, *Europe: A History* (Oxford, 1996), p. 543.
5. For objections of this type to animal rights, see D. G. Ritchie, *Natural Rights* (London: George Allen & Unwin, 1889) or the extracts from it in Tom Regan and Peter Singer (eds) *Animal Rights and Human Obligations* (Englewood Cliffs, NJ: Prentice 1976); H. J. McClosky, 'Rights', *Philosophical Quarterly* 15, 1965); John Passmore, *Man's Responsibility for Nature* (London: Duckworth, 1974), p. 116.
6. Cf. Alexander Broadie and Elizabeth Pybus, 'Kant's Treatment of Animals', *Philosophy* 49, 1974.
7. There is at least an identity in the (generic, but not vague) universal or essence actualised in each case. It is also arguable, though not here, that there is a Cosmic One who is the one ultimate subject of all experience. But I cannot argue for metaphysical monism of this kind here.
8. For more on this see my 'Non-human rights: an idealist perspective', *Inquiry* 27, 1984: 444–6.

The present paper includes extensive extracts from this article, as also from my 'Some recent positions in environmental philosophy examined', *Inquiry* 34, 1991.

9. This expression was introduced into discussions of the present kind by Kenneth Goodpaster in his 'On being morally considerable', in Donald Scherer and Thomas Attig (eds), *Ethics and the Environment* (Englewood Cliffs., NJ. Prentice-Hall, 1983), pp. 30–41. Something is morally considerable if a moral agent may have direct duties towards it, that is, duties not more fundamentally owed to some other individual such as its owner.

10. See Paul Taylor, *Respect for Nature: A Theory of Environmental Ethics* (Princeton, NJ: Princeton University Press, 1986) and Holmes Rolston, III, *Environmental Ethics: Duties to and Values in the Natural World* (Philadelphia: Temple University Press, 1988).

11. A tree is not sentient, says Holmes Rolston, but it does 'care in the only form of caring available to it, and why should I take no account of that form of caring because it is not my form of caring?' (Rolston, *Environmental Ethics*, p. 106.)

12. Among others, besides Taylor and Rolston who attack the idea that only the sentient can matter morally in any fundamental way, is Kenneth Goodpaster. See Scherer and Attig, *Ethics*, pp. 30–41.

13. See, for example, Tom Regan, *All that Therein Dwell* (Berkeley: University of California Press, 1982), p. 200.

14. Thus he talks of the 'creative toil' of speciating Nature. See Rolston, *Environmental Ethics*, p. 157; also p. 143 ff.

15. Edward O. Wilson, *Biophilia: The Human Bond with Other Species* (Cambridge, MA: Harvard University Press, 1984).

16. See J. Baird Callicot, 'Animal liberation: a triangular affair', *Environmental Ethics* 2, 1980, reprinted in Scherer and Attig, *Ethics*.

17. See Sprigge, *Foundations*, Chapters V and VI.

18. Compare William James in *A Pluralistic Universe* (New York: Longmans, Green & Co.) at p. 194.

19. See Taylor, *Respect*, pp. 155 ff.

20. See Rolston, *Environmental Ethics*, p. 137.

21. See Sprigge, *Foundations*, Chapter V.

22. As I use the terms they are synonymous, but because the term 'consciousness' in such a context makes some uneasy who may still really agree with my message, I allow them the less alarming term 'sentience' as an alternative.

23. Compare Lynn White Jn. in 'The historical roots of our ecological crisis', *Science* 155(37), 1967: 67, and for its contradiction Robin Attfield in 'Western traditions and environmental ethics', in Robert Elliot and Arran Gare (eds), *Environmental Philosophy*, (Milton Keynes: The Open University Press, 1983) and in his *The Ethics of Environmental Concern* (Oxford: Basil Blackwell, 1983), especially Chapter 1.

24. I have argued in favour of panpsychism in several places, most fully in T. L. S. Sprigge, *The Vindication of Absolute Idealism* (Edinburgh: Edinburgh University Press, 1983).

25. I might remark in this connection that a 'hands-off' ethic towards the wild, such as is urged by some environmental ethicists, risks drawing such an excessive contrast between wild nature and the humanly modified that they undercut their initial claim that humans are a part of nature. To believe that our sole role in nature is that of intruders who should stick to, and reduce, their own realm might seem in its way as much of an alienation from nature as are the purely exploitative attitudes which these thinkers deplore. The best answer may lie in that special sense of oneness with the wider system of things which humans can obtain when away from human restrictions, even though nature is just as much there in much of the apparently humanised world.

26. For a discussion highly relevant to this see Christopher D. Stone, *Should Trees have Standing? Toward Legal Rights for Natural Objects* (Tioga CA: Publishing Company, 1988).

8

CONSERVATION AND ANIMAL WELFARE

Kate Rawles

I recently spent three months' sabbatical leave at Green College, Oxford. While there, I talked to a great many people involved with environmental issues, but largely shunned the company of philosophers. As a result, I learned that hardly anyone, environmental scientists, politicians, campaigners alike, had come across environmental philosophy. No-one that I met had a clear idea of why it might be useful.

I have thought that philosophers should be talking outside their own discipline for a long time, and of course the idea is not a new one. But this experience served to underline the need, especially with an area like environmental philosophy, for communication beyond a particular academic discipline. In Britain, while philosophers do publish in journals such as *Environmental Values*,[1] *Ecos*[2] and *Biodiversity and Conservation*,[3] increased pressure to publish in peer-reviewed, central-to-the discipline journals means that, in general, we are inclined to write for publications little read by non-philosophers.

I believe that environmental philosophy has much to offer the environmental movement. This chapter is written in the spirit of trying to communicate philosophical ideas to a non-philosophical audience. Moreover, it summarises a much larger project. Hence a lot of issues in it are sketched in broad strokes with a great deal of detail still to be filled in.

INTRODUCTION

As human numbers increase, and the percentage of humans aspiring to a high-consumption lifestyle also grows, so does the impact of our species on the earth's other residents.

According to the report just published by the United Nations, clearing of forests and other habitats now threatens 11 per cent of all known mammals, 18 per cent of birds and 5 per cent of fish with extinction. (The percentage of insects and micro-organisms threatened is not really known: although estimates suggest that there are between 2.7 and 16 million species of algae, bacteria and fungi, only a tiny fraction of these, about 175,000 have been identified. This is of course interesting in itself, raising the possibility that we may extinguish a large proportion of micro-organisms before we have given them names.) Between 40 and 1,000 species of animals and plants become extinct each day, this being between 1,000 and 10,000 times faster than the so-called background rate of extinction. Other well-rehearsed figures include the 40 per cent of photosynthetic production on land appropriated by humans while, also daily, an additional 2,700 tons of chlorofluorocarbons and 15 million tons of carbon join the atmosphere, and the number of humans on earth increases by a quarter of a million.[4]

Of course, one needs to be a bit careful about what these figures are actually taken to mean. But my general point is that, against this sort of background, one might expect to find animal welfare campaigners featuring as the firm allies of conservationists, with both standing up for non-humans in the face of what looks very much like a shared human threat.

In fact there are many rifts and disparities between these two groups, both in practice and at a more theoretical level. In this paper, I want to look particularly at the way in which those who are concerned with the lives and well-being of non-human animals – animal welfarists – take issue, often fiercely, with the attitudes and actions of conservationists. (I am talking, throughout the paper, about conservationists who work primarily with living systems and species rather than with ancient buildings and monuments.) My aim is twofold. First, I want to sketch the nature of the theoretical commitments which underpin these two groups, and to reveal how very different these commitments are. These theoretical differences, I suggest, explain why welfarists and conservationists disagree at the level of practice and policy, and it is here that work will need to be done if practical resolution is to be effected.

Conservationists may be inclined to dismiss the animal welfare perspective altogether. My second aim is to argue that outright dismissal is hard to justify. While there are considerable problems with the arguments traditionally employed by animal welfarists, particularly those which use the language of rights, or which assert equal consideration for all animals, the basic claim that we have ethical obligations to individual sentient animals is sound. It should continue to be incorporated into conservation policy.

DEER-CULLING

The Scottish Highlands include some of the most beautiful and, I would argue, wild, tracts of land left in Britain. Ensuring that this land and its non-human residents maintain their integrity in the face of human demands for housing or sheep-fodder or ski-slopes might be expected to unite animal and environmental campaigners.

In fact, many animal welfare groups find themselves strongly opposed to the practices of Scottish Natural Heritage (Scotland's official conservation body), whose management strategies include an annual deer cull. During the cull, thousands of deer are shot. In some areas, the carcasses are slung together in canvas and carried out by helicopter. The image is for many a disturbing one, and some British animal welfare groups have used it to allege the impropriety of mass destruction of living creatures in the name of conservation. Conservationists respond that, with no natural predators since the demise of the wolf (the last wolf in Scotland was shot in 1743),[5] and with artificial restrictions on their range, deer populations rise to the point that great damage is done to habitat and crops, and the deer themselves face starvation in the course of hard Scottish winters. Similar issues arise in other parts of Britain and Europe with the culling of squirrels, greys being killed in large numbers in the attempt to arrest the retreat of the red. Conflict between welfarists and conservationists over culling has reached such a pitch that animal liberation organisations have claimed responsibility for arson attacks on property belonging to English Nature (the English equivalent of Scottish Natural Heritage), while conservationists are inclined to dismiss all animal welfarists as mad and sentimental terrorists.

ANALYSIS

Animal welfare

The term 'animal' is ambiguous. It is worth asking which creatures the word evokes. For many, it summons images of cats, dogs and cattle. On reflection, these might be joined by an elephant or perhaps a whale. Variations on this will typically remain within the class of mammals, and humans may or may not be included. Humans are of course animals, and most animals are not mammals. But the word is often used to mean all animals except humans, thereby drawing a neat line between humans and all other animals, while lumping together creatures as disparate as kangaroos and crustacea.

Those whose background includes biology or zoology will typically have a different set of images. There are between eight and eighty million species of animal on earth. These are divided into around thirty-three Phyla, of which only two are purely terrestrial. The Phylum Chordata, which includes mammals and birds, numbers around 45,000 species. The Phylum Arthropoda, which contains insects, molluscs and crustacea, contains between two and ten million species. As J. B. S. Haldane reputedly claimed, 'God had an inordinate fondness for beetles', while the biologist Robert May suggests that, 'as a rough approximation, everything on earth is an insect'.[6]

Most animal welfarists are not concerned with all animals, but with a small sub-class of them. They are often criticised for this, the criticism being that the sub-class is selected for dubious reasons, such as that the animals within it are furry, have large appealing eyes and are otherwise attractive to humans.

While it is true that welfarists are not concerned with all animals, their criterion is not, in fact, furriness. Welfarists are concerned with animals that are conscious; that can suffer pain and experience pleasure; that are in some sense aware of their lives and the fortunes and misfortunes involved in living them. This collection of capacities and characteristics is abbreviated as sentience. This is the sense in which I shall use the term.

Why these animals? There is a clear rationale behind the answer. First, it involves a particular view of morality. For example, it may be argued that to act morally is to consider the interests of others, and not just one's own; or that the essence of morality has to do with restraining from causing harm to others. Second, there is the belief that consciousness and the ability to suffer – sentience – are the capacities that make it possible for a creature to have interests, or to suffer harm. Thus sentience becomes, in effect, a criterion of moral significance, of being the kind of entity a moral agent can have moral obligations towards. This is why welfarists are concerned with these animals, and not with all animals, believing that not all animals are sentient. The distinction between sentient and non-sentient animals is presumably not a sharp one, and there may be cases where is it difficult to tell one way or another. Nevertheless, the criterion plays an important theoretical role and, in practice, the existence of grey areas does not affect the many cases where the sentience of an animal is undisputed.

Note that the welfarists' concern with individual, sentient animals will include domesticated and tamed animals as well as those which are wild. Welfarists argue that we have moral obligations towards these animals, and that these obligations clearly imply better treatment than is often found in many contemporary animal-using institutions, such as the farm, laboratory, zoo or pet-keeping household. Implications also follow for human activity that affects the lives of free-living animals not directly under our jurisdiction.

Conservation

Conservation bodies, like Scottish Natural Heritage, are concerned, not with individual animals, but with the environment in a broader sense. The focus of conservation concern varies, but will usually fix at the level of species, habitats and ecological systems and processes. That is, the conservationist is typically interested in ecological collectives or communities rather than individuals. Within this, there may well be a bias towards relatively natural rather than human-made landscapes, and wild rather than tamed or domesticated collections of animals and plants.

Why these entities? The justifications offered for conservation objectives are diverse, and the subject could easily occupy a paper in itself. One abbreviated thought is that the concern with ecological sustainability, with having ecosystems that endure, leads to a concern for biodiversity, given that resilience in ecosystems has been held to depend on the diversity of species implicated within them. There is much dissent over the truth of the diversity/resilience claim, and many now take it to be discredited. But the continuing debate about ecosystem durability, and how to protect it, relies on reference to species rather than to individuals, and the search for answers is taken to lie in the domain of biological science, which tends to operate at the species rather than the individual level. Ed Wilson writes in *The Diversity of Life* that:

Since antiquity biologists have felt a compelling need to posit an atomic unit by which diversity can be broken apart, then described, measured, and reassembled . . . the species concept is crucial to the study of biodiversity. It is the grail of systematic biology. Not to have a natural unit such as the species would be to abandon a large part of biology to free fall, all the way from the ecosystem down to the organism.[7]

In short, a recurring theme is the relationship between conservation and science. From a biological point of view at least, it is species rather than individuals which are considered to be unique. And the species rather than the individual is held as key to our scientific understanding of ecosystems and biodiversity and hence to our ability to protect and preserve them.

Why the interest in biodiversity? Answers here also vary, but might be grouped into anthropocentric and non-anthropocentric varieties, the former justifying concern with biodiversity by reference to human economic, aesthetic, scientific or survival interest in it, the latter insisting that non-human life forms have some value which is independent of human needs and desires. Much more needs to be said here, and reasonable doubts may be cast over the merits of such a distinction. For now my point is simply that, whether or not the ultimate justification for concern is human-centred, the focus of this concern still lies with the so-called 'units' of biodiversity – species and ecosystems – rather than with individuals.

Key differences

We can now summarise two key differences between welfarists and conservationists.

Scope of primary concern

The first difference is with regard to the scope of concern that the two groups acknowledge. Welfarists are concerned with individual, sentient animals. Any concern for habitats, ecological systems and processes is derivative; it is not for the habitat itself but only in so far as the habitat is necessary for the welfare of the sentient individuals within it.

The primary concern of conservationists is with habitats, species, ecological systems and processes: in short with ecological collectives. Concern for individuals – sentient or otherwise – will be derivative. For example, the preservation of very rare species may involve the investment of a great deal of effort directed towards individuals. The ospreys on Loch Garten in Scotland are guarded from trophy-hunters twenty-four hours a day during the nesting season. Black rhinos in Hwange National Park are fitted with radio-monitoring collars and dehorned to discourage poachers. But in both cases the aim is to preserve the species and the concern for particular individuals is a means to this end. Or perhaps one might say that concern for individuals and for species elides in these kinds of cases. Were ospreys to become more common, however, the guard would be removed, though the impact of nest raids on the lives and welfare of the individuals involved would no doubt remain the same.

Welfarists, then, are concerned primarily with individual, sentient animals and with ecological collectives only in a derivative sense. For conservationists, the situation is reversed. It might be objected that, if justification for conservation objectives is ultimately human-centred, then the conservation concern with species and systems is itself derivative. Thus the contrast with welfarists is dissolved. But here a distinction needs to be made between objectives and the justifications offered for them. The justification for concern with species might appeal to the interests of humans, and even to those of individual humans. This would soften one contrast between welfarists and conservationists while heightening another. For, although both would be concerned with individuals, welfarists recognise obligations towards individuals who are not human, while conservationists (of this variety) insist that our obligations are, in the end, to humans alone. At the level of objectives, however, the contrast between concern for sentient individuals on the one hand and ecological collectives on the other remains intact.

Fundamental objective or guiding principles

The second difference is between the fundamental objectives or guiding principles of the two groups. Welfarists aim to protect the lives and welfare of individual sentient animals. They are particularly concerned with reducing unnecessary suffering, especially when this results from the actions and practices of humans.

The fundamental objective of conservation is, roughly, the preservation of species diversity and ecological integrity. This does not seem to entail that suffering should be reduced. Indeed, conservationists may argue that suffering is an inevitable part of natural life, and that it is not up to humans to interfere with this.

These two differences in the theoretical substructure of animal welfare and con-servationist groups – which we might now paraphrase as differences in the scope of their concern and in the content of their objectives – may occasionally complement each other at a practical level. For example, the Royal Society for the Protection of Birds (RSPB), while working to preserve diversity in bird species, declines to become involved with the treatment or rehabilitation of injured, individual birds – unless they are especially rare. They would never undertake to care for injured domesticated hens or tamed parrots or wild but common birds such as house-sparrows. On the other hand, the Royal Society for the Protection of Animals (RSPCA), a welfare organisation, will take on the care of injured individuals of any species, rare or common, wild, domesticated or tame. It has a number of rehabilitation centres specifically for wild animals, and the RSPB, if consulted about an injured wild bird, may well recommend that it be taken to such a centre. Here, there is in effect a rather practical division of labour – though the RSPB would not, I think, be interested in the welfare of individual birds even were it able to take this on in addition to its other commitments. It would certainly constitute a change of policy were they to do so, and would need an additional brief from members and those who finance them.[8]

But there are many cases of conflict rather than albeit uneasy complementarity. Conservationists may be actively hostile towards some sentient animals, particularly those which are domesticated or introduced. J. Baird Callicott famously describes sheep as hooved locusts and cattle as living artifacts and writes that, from a conservation perspective, there is little difference between a flock of sheep and a fleet of four-wheel drive vehicles.[9] Controversy over introduced species is common, that currently raging between welfarists and conservationists over the fate of the cats introduced to the islands of St Helena and now threatening indigenous species being but one example. Zoos are typically condemned by animal welfare groups, in so far as the individuals incarcerated there suffer boredom, other psychological distress or physical discomfort. Conservationists may consider that zoos are justified by the role they play in the preservation of species or by the value of research designed to aid species conservation in the field that they facilitate. Similarly, wildlife parks which provide excellent conditions for individual animals may be subsidised by selling hunting permits. And, to return to the Scottish deer, the conflict is stark. While welfarists recommend that the deer be fed supplementary hay, conservationists recommend that they should be shot in large numbers.

In sum, from the conservationists' point of view, the preservation of species, habitats and ecological communities may justify killing individual animals, or keeping them in captivity, or compromising their welfare in other ways. From the welfarists' point of view, since the lives and welfare of individual animals are paramount, overriding this in the interest of broader environmental goals seems unacceptable. From this point of view, an analogy would be overriding human welfare in order to protect something that has value only in so far as it is useful to humans, or perhaps killing humans to save their houses.

The disparities in the theoretical commitments of welfarists and conservationists throw at least some light on these and other examples where strong policy differences persist. But what might be done with this conflict?

DISMISSING ANIMAL WELFARE

One response is to argue that the animal welfare position should be rejected. A cheap and not very convincing try might dismiss it because, as a movement, it contains some violent fanatics. More credibly, it could be argued that animal welfarism rests on a mistaken view about the scope of morality. Individual animals are not, whatever the welfarists say, significant from a moral point of view. To simplify the issue, I will focus on wild animals rather than domesticated or tamed ones. It may be reasonably clear that we have responsibilities towards animals we have tamed. But is the same true of wild creatures? In the conservation context, the question often arises in this form: should we be concerned about wild animals as individuals, or only as species?

From the perspective of conservation or biology, this question may appear to be a strange one. From this perspective, it can seem quite obvious that concern for non-human animals is appropriately directed towards animals as species. Consider this extract from Primack's *Essentials of Conservation Biology*.

> [O]n both biological and ethical grounds, species rather than individual organisms are the appropriate target of conservation efforts. All individuals eventually

die, but it is the species that continues, evolves and sometimes forms new species. In a sense, individuals are just the temporary representatives of the species.[10]

Someone who does not recognise this is rather suspect. They are probably senti-mental about animals, or perhaps have an allegiance to animal rights. They are almost certainly not scientists. This is not to suggest that cruelty to animals is acceptable. And there are circumstances in which conservationists have to have an understanding of the roles individual animals play in order to be successful in preserving the species. For example, if a matriarchal elephant is killed, younger generations of elephants in that family may be handicapped by lack of certain kinds of knowledge. In this kind of case, the conservationist may need knowledge about animals as individuals. But the primary concern is still for the species.

There is a strong temptation to go along with this. It is often difficult to resist pressure to conform with an accepted point of view, and the risk of being labelled sentimental in a scientific community is rarely an alluring one. But there are a number of things worth noting here.

First, the sentimental appeal that some individual animals have for some humans can lead to a broader concern for habitats and species, and may be deliberately harnessed as an effective source of motivation for conservation objectives. People who adopt whales or dolphins, for example, may initially be drawn to pictures of particular animals and encouraged with progress reports of their named adoptees. But concern for William Whale is likely to lead to concern for William's habitat and peers, and hence to enhanced awareness of marine conservation issues.

Secondly, the notion of sentimentality is worth looking at. The term is often used in a derogatory way, as in 'he is (merely) sentimental about animals'. To be sentimental about animals is to have a response towards them that is rooted in emotions. A sentimental attitude towards animals is often contrasted with a detached, objective, scientific one, the assumption being that the scientific attitude is superior. This assumption, however, is questionable. A scientific approach to animals may be the best approach in some contexts but not others. It will greatly help if you are trying to figure out the mating strategies of spiders, but may need supplementation if you are trying to persuade spiderphobes to favour their conservation. Here, enhanced empathy may prove to be more effective than scientific data. Moreover, the thought that an empathetic response to animals is in some sense illegitimate is itself rather odd. Sometimes empathy is perfectly appropriate, and its lack can amount to a failure if imagination. The same can be said about other sentimental or emotion-based responses to animals. There are circumstances in which such a response is called for. Witnessing cruelty would be a good example. Inappropriate emotional responses to animals, like inappropriate extrapolations from humans to animals, are another matter, and may be open to legitimate criticism. But it would be a mistake to assume that emotional responses to animals are always out of place.

The third and most important point refers to our attitude towards humans. Our notion of inter-human ethics is strongly individualistic. We struggle to keep individuals alive, even when they are very elderly or extremely ill. Premature death is considered a tragedy. Treating people as if preservation of the human species were the primary concern might suggest that the very old and the very ill be allowed to die. It would lead to a number of recommendations that are, in the human context, utterly unacceptable. Even as human population growth threatens to overwhelm habitats and other species, no one suggests that humans should be culled. While birth control may be recommended, the language used to describe methods of controlling non-human animals sounds appalling if translated into the human context. To discuss sustainable human culling would be to abandon the essence of human morality rather than accord with it.

But why might it be necessary to think about humans at the individual level, and yet a mistake to do so with any other species of animal? The conservationist who recognises obligations towards humans as individuals, yet deals with all other animals only at the species level, has to show how this view of things can be justified. It should be emphasised that the claim to be defended is that we have no obligations at all to the individuals of any other species besides the human one. Whether or not our obligations to human individuals are stronger than those we have to the individuals of other species remains open for further debate.

One attempt to justify this position claims that, unlike humans, other animals do not possess individuality. They do not have distinct character traits, appearances, personalities. Hence we cannot be required to treat them as individuals. But this view does not survive exposure to animals. It is never held by those who work with them, particularly if the work involves training. Vicki Hearne shows in *Adam's Task* the extent to which successful training of dogs and horses required detailed and intimate knowledge of the particular preferences, fears and inclinations of the dog or horse in question.[11] Even if there is no interaction between humans and animals, the sort of familiarity with a group of animals that ethologists, for example, acquire soon results in the ability to recognise and distinguish between individuals – and this by reference to their behaviour as well as their appearance.

This is, of course, particularly true of the higher animals. I do not know where on the evolutionary scale individuality is likely to peter out, or even if it does. There is plenty of anecdotal evidence of researchers who come to recognise members of various insect species, for example, as individuals. This in turn has sometimes led to the expression of affection towards initially unlikely recipients. The early nineteenth-century British Lord Chancellor, Lord Erskine, reputedly had:

> two leeches which had saved his life when he had been bled by them. He kept the latter in his library, insisted that they had quite different personalities, gave them the names of two prominent surgeons, and brought them out at dinner parties to entertain his guests.[12]

Individuality in micro-organisms may seem unlikely, but this may be because it is hard to spot. In any case, the individuality of sentient animals is rarely in doubt.

A second response is to claim that humans are different from other animals in some morally relevant way. This response, like the one above, might be offered as much by the 'humans only' conservationist as by the 'humans as individuals, other animals as species' variety. The argument would be that we owe concern to individual humans, but not to individuals of other species, or that we only owe concern to humans, because humans, unlike other animals, are self-conscious, or have a unique linguistic ability, or are rational or intelligent. In short, some characteristic of humans is identified and appealed to. But two problems immediately arise.

First, it is very hard to find a characteristic which all humans enjoy and all non-humans lack. Self-consciousness has arguably been identified in primates and intelligence and rationality (at least in some senses of the word) are characteristics enjoyed by many animals besides humans. Nevertheless, it has been argued, for example by Alan Holland, that autonomy, rationality and self-consciousness are characteristics which are both distinctively human, and more or less exclusively human. Certainly they are possessed to a significantly greater degree by humans than by any other creatures.[13] But here the second problem arises. Suppose that we agree with Holland that a characteristic possessed in significantly greater measure by humans than by other animals is all we need; or suppose that a characteristic which clearly distinguishes between human and non-humans could in fact be found. Humans are, for example, the only creatures to wear socks, and toast sandwiches (though presumably not all humans do these things). But it must now be shown why this characteristic is relevant to the question in hand. This applies to the apparently more sensible criteria of autonomy, rationality, intelligence and linguistic ability as much as to the crazy ones, and turns out to be just as difficult to do. These characteristics are in effect being used as criteria of moral significance and yet, as Baird Callicott succinctly puts it, the criteria seem unrelated to the benefit for which they select.[14] The sort of non-sequitur involved has been paraphrased by Mary Midgley as the claim that it is alright to inflict pain on other animals because they cannot form grammatical sentences.[15]

A different version of the same basic strategy claims that non-human animals, unlike humans, do not have souls. This is why we have obligations to the individual humans, but to the individuals of no other species. Problems abound. The view is common in Europe and in Anglo-American cultures, but there are plenty of cultures who find souls in non-human animals, in trees, rivers and rocks. It is not clear what would count as evidence in an attempt to adjudicate between different views. Even if it could be established that humans alone possess souls, it is not obvious that a diminished concern for individuals of other species would reasonably follow. If souls bestow eternal life, our obligations to ensouled beings might be thought to be less urgent than to those whose brief existence on earth will be all the life they get.

Of course, there are many attempts to show why possession of characteristics such as autonomy and rationality, if not souls, are relevant to the issue of moral significance. Holland argues that they underpin moral capacities such as the ability to love and to respect, and that this is why we owe moral consideration to individual humans – because of the possibility that humans may reciprocate. This is not a possibility with individuals of other species. Even allowing the truth of this claim (though again see Vicki Hearne's *Adam's Task*) familiar problems arise in virtue of those humans who are, for whatever reason, incapable of reciprocation but who we nevertheless recognise obligations towards. Holland's response is that we recognise obligations towards, for example, severely retarded humans because they are members of a species whose normal members can reciprocate moral obligations. But while he thinks that this may justify humans giving preferential treatment to the interests of fellow humans over those of other animals it does not, in his view, justify the claim that we have no obligations at all towards non-human individuals. In his view, the injunction to avoid inflicting unnecessary pain, for example, applies to at least some animals as clearly as it does towards humans.

At this point I want to, as it were, intervene in the argument. Many of the attempts to justify the view that the only individuals we have moral obligations towards are human individuals look for a characteristic or set of characteristics which either grants moral significance or denies it, wholesale. Autonomy and rationality are often evoked in this fashion. Welfarists may counter with a preferred criterion, such as sentience, arguing that, whereas rationality and the rest have no bearing on the question of moral significance, sentience does, and that this is a characteristic which unites humans and other animals rather than distinguishes between them.

My own view, and that of James Rachels,[16] is that the question, 'which characteristic(s) qualifies a being as one which moral agents have moral obligations towards?' in fact makes little sense. It makes much more sense to discuss specific moral obligations than to discuss moral obligations in general. This is hinted at in the Midgley paraphrase given above. The claim 'we can inflict pain on animals because they cannot form grammatical sentences' is indeed a daft one: but the claim 'we have no need to ensure freedom of speech for animals because they cannot speak' is perfectly sensible. Similarly, the question of the characteristic(s) a creature would need to possess in order for moral agents to have an obligation not to inflict pain on it may be answered by sentience, while an obligation to protect freedom of religion would be linked with the tendency to worship, and so on.[17]

On this view, the claim that we have at least some obligations to at least some non-human individuals is hard to deny. If it is difficult to explain why a being must be rational before we owe it moral consideration *per se* it is even harder to explain why a being must be rational, or linguistically competent, before we are obliged to refrain from inflicting unnecessary pain upon it. Alternatively, it may be insisted that a common denominator for all ethically significant beings should be located. In this case, if it is accepted that the capacity to experience suffering is a necessary and sufficient condition of having interests, then sentience will appear to be a stronger candidate than rationality and the rest.

The above is a highly abbreviated account of the arguments. Nevertheless, I suggest that the 'species only' conservationist is left with a dilemma. Impaled on one horn is the view that morality requires moral agents to concern themselves, not with the welfare of individuals, but solely with the well-being of species and ecological communities. This fits well with conservation concerns and objectives. But it has unacceptable implications for our dealings with humans.

Taking the other horn, conservationists can agree that morality in the human sphere is deeply and fundamentally concerned with humans as individuals, and rightly so. It is just that individuals of other species do not have this status. But this position invites the observation that, since Darwin, we have had to accept that a sharp line between humans and non-humans cannot be drawn in biology. Yet regular attempts are still made to do so in ethics. I have suggested that these attempts are unsuccessful.

In sum, concern for individuals plays a crucial part in our dealings with other humans. If the claims of human individuals are to be counted it is hard to see why those of sentient animals, strikingly similar in many relevant respects, are not to be considered at all.

I want, then, to defend a fairly minimal animal welfare claim: that we have at least some moral obligations to individual, wild, sentient animals, and that these obligations involve a concern for their lives and welfare. Do conservationists ever in fact deny this? The view is tacitly endorsed by conservationists who argue that, while culling may be necessary, it should be done humanely. But it may be implicitly denied by conservationists whose reservations about culling arise not from ethical worries but ones about public relations. In some cases, implicit denial of the welfare claim can also be detected in the way the issue is discussed. In a recent edition of the *New Scientist* John Bonner outlines the threat that grey squirrels in the Italian Roero hills present both to red squirrels and the local human community, to whom the hazel-nut harvest is worth around ten million pounds. The author argues that a means of controlling their numbers is urgently required. Of the various possibilities, warfarin is recommended as the only one whose effect will be sufficiently rapid. The problem is that public opinion is opposed to warfarin, because '[most people have never seen a red squirrel and have come to like its American Cousin . . . They do not like the idea of these creatures dying a slow and painful death.]'[18] Bonner dismisses this as squeamishness that the Italians literally do not have time for.[19] At no point in the article does he acknowledge that killing grey squirrels in a manner that causes them protracted suffering raises genuine ethical issues which merit at least some consideration. It is this sort of position that I believe needs to be revised in the light of the animal welfare claim.

DEEPER DIVERGENCES

Suppose it is agreed that we have obligations to individual, wild sentient animals. How strong are these obligations? How do they compare to those that we have to humans on the one hand and ecological collectives on the other?

On the Singer/Regan type view, a relatively small sub-class of animals is accorded the same moral significance as humans. On Singer's view we are required to give equal consideration to the similar interests of all sentient beings; on Regan's to acknowledge that all subjects-of-a-life have equal rights to life and well-being. Both deny that we have any obligations to ecological collectives as such.

In my view this is problematic: not, or not just, in terms of the content of the answer but also with regard to a number of the assumptions and commitments on which it rests. These include the assumption that moral significance depends upon the possession of a particular characteristic. In so far as they take moral significance to rest on this alone, animal welfarists are, I think, mistaken. In the last section, I want to sketch this and other criticisms of welfarism. I will use these criticisms to introduce a number of further areas where the philosophical foundations of welfarism differ markedly from those which underpin conservation. These differences can be detected most readily between welfarists and those environmental philosophers who, in their analysis of conservation policy, recognise direct obligations to ecological collectives. These have been called deep, holistic environmentalists. During this last section, then, my point of contrast will move from welfarists and conservationists to welfarists and environmental philosophers of this particular kind. (It is my view that much conservation policy is underpinned by holistic, deep environmental philosophy, but I do not have space to make the case for that here.)

Extensionism

The welfarists' position relies heavily on an extension of human ethics into the non-human world. This, in essence, is their argument. Assuming that we owe moral obligations to humans then, in the absence of relevant differences between all humans and all animals and given some relevant similarities between humans and some animals, sheer consistency forces us to conclude that we owe moral obligations to some animals too. Our assumed obligations to humans are thus used as the foundation upon which concern for non-humans can be established.

Environmental philosophers may be critical of this kind of attempt to establish moral obligations to the non-human world. They may look for ways of grounding respect for the non-human world which is independent of, and does not rely upon, our respect for humans. In doing so they may offer a number of reservations about the implications of the so-called extensionist approach.

The emphasis on characteristics and consistency

Many welfarists assume that moral significance rests on the possession of a characteristic, such as sentience. They argue, moreover, that consistency is central to our dealings with all those who qualify. In Singer's view, for example, we should give equal consideration to the interests of all sentient animals. We should not give extra weight to the interests of those we know and love, just because we know and love them.[20]

In so far as this is taken to give a comprehensive account of our moral obligations, the position is immensely problematic. Singer, for example, imagines coming across a child whose toes are being gnawed by a rat, and expresses serious and apparently genuine doubt about what a moral agent should do in this situation. The problem is that both rat and child have a serious interest in survival and so, on the face of it, it seems that the agent is just as obliged to protect the rat's dinner as the child's feet.[21]

Clearly, something has gone badly wrong here. One wants to insist that some obligations derive from particular relationships between moral agents and others, and that some relationships create moral obligations that legitimately pull against sheer consistency. In the rat case, the relationship between mother and child or between human and young of the same species may reasonably be held to override those obligations that derive simply from the sentience of the animals involved. This raises the question of whether humans have special obligations to other humans simply because we are all human. Singer's view is that this is mere speciesism: a prejudice, like racism, that we should strive to overcome. But this strikes a deeply discordant note. Of course, Singer may nonetheless be correct. Here I will only suggest that questions about the felicity of Singer's speciesism analogy are among the most interesting raised by the animal welfare debate. Many welfarists fail to do them justice.

In my view, then, while the sentience of a creature has considerable bearing on the question of how a moral agent should treat it, the question cannot be answered comprehensively by reference to this, or any other, characteristic. Nor can it necessarily be answered in the same way for all moral agents. The relationship between the agent and others may also be relevant, as well as the context in which they find themselves. Singer's insistence that, when thinking morally, we must deliberately and carefully disregard the special relationships that we have with family, friends, members of our community is in effect an exhortation to unravel what it is to lead a human life. The fabric of such a life is constituted by relationships whose significance is often a moral one. It might even be argued that the good life for humans involves fostering precisely the kind of involvement with others within which moral obligations can arise.

This criticism of welfarism indicates a significant further difference in the theoretical foundations of welfarism and conservation. For, while the welfarists derive much of the power of their position from the emphasis on characteristics and consistency, environmental philosophers are likely to resist this approach. While it is sometimes argued that life itself is the characteristic which bestows moral significance on an entity, the claim that all living things should be treated equally is seldom held to have more than rhetorical force. The environmental philosopher is more likely to emphasise difference in the obligations we have towards beings who, judged by their sentience alone, are rather similar. For example, most environmental philosophers will recognise different obligations towards wild and domesticated animals in virtue of the different relationships we enjoy with them, or between living things which are rare as opposed to common. Thus, from the animal welfare perspective, two creatures with the same capacity to experience pleasure and pain will be held to exert the same moral pull on all moral agents. From a conservation perspective, of two equivalently sentient animals, a rare one might well be considered to have priority over a common one because of its significance in the network of ecological relationships around it.

The 'no trespass' view of morality

A related difference between the philosophical commitments of animal welfare and conservation arises from a further implication of the extension of conventional theory to non-humans. It concerns what might be called the 'no trespass' view of morality. Within the animal welfare movement, particularly where the concepts of rights is appealed to, there is a tendency to suppose that to recognise the moral status of a being is to recognise that it is morally sacrosanct, that almost all interference with its life and welfare is prohibited. Tom Regan, for example, argues that once we recognise the moral status of animals, we realise that the problem with intensive farming is not that animals are misused in such systems, but that they are used at all.[22]

We can understand this thinking, because it is often applied in the human context. This 'no trespass' view of morality divides sharply between the morally sacrosanct and those who are fair game, and lends great importance to the distinction between beings which have moral significance and those which do not. The animal welfare movement extends the boundary of the fence behind which the morally sacrosanct take shelter beyond humans to include some animals. But they retain the fence. Those on the far side will include most of the entities environmental philosophers are primarily concerned with.

One response would be to argue that plants and ecosystems should be brought within its bounds. But it can also be argued that the no-trespass view of ethics is, speaking very loosely, unecological. A more ecological ethics would not try to divide the moral universe in this way, recognising instead that we are all both users and used, coexisting in complex systems of interdependence. The important question from this perspective is not how do we distinguish the users from the used, but what constitutes acceptable and unacceptable use of different living things. Again, this moves us away from any attempt to establish a principle of equality that applies to all morally significant beings, towards a much more contextual notion of ethics, in which the importance of relationships is emphasised. It also opens up the possibility of discussing projects like Zimbabwe's CAMPFIRE initiative, which promotes the utilisation of animals for conservation objectives in ways that so-called preservationists and the Singer/Regan-style welfarists would have to reject outright. (These projects aim to benefit the people that often suffer from living alongside animals like elephants, by bringing revenue into local communities from, for example, hunting safaris. In this way, they give people reason to be interested in the conservation of elephants and other animals that they would not necessarily have otherwise).

Conventional ethical theories and individualism in ethics

The extension of moral concern advocated by animal welfarists usually takes place within the framework of conventional ethical theories. Welfare and environmental philosophers are typically divided in their affection for these theories. Conventional approaches to ethics may be insightful when it is the treatment of individual people that is under discussion. And they have been helpful in considering our obligations to animals, for example in the context of medical research or veterinary medicine. Welfarists are largely in favour of retaining existing ethical systems, at least in part because of their potential for delivering powerful indictments against the mistreatment of animals.

The environmental philosopher may have significant reservations about conventional ethical theories. These stem from the observation that these theories, utilitarianism and rights theory being good examples, take the individual, adult human as the paradigm case of the kind of being we have moral obligations towards. The animal welfare movement uses these theories to explore our obligations to non-humans. But the environmental philosopher is concerned that, if the process of trying to extend ethical obligations to non-humans is carried out within the framework of these theories, the emphasis on individuals will be carried over from the human to the non-human world in a problematic way.

What are the problems? First, the attempt to articulate and explore the nature of our obligations to ecological collectives is not facilitated by conventional, individualistic ethical theories. Talk of the rights of species or the interests of habitats quickly becomes absurd; as does speculation about their suffering. The welfarist may suggest that this is because species and systems have neither rights, interests nor the capacity to suffer. The environmental philosopher may argue that the conceptual apparatus of conventional ethical theory is inadequate to the task of developing environmental ethics, and needs to be supplemented or even replaced. The concerns of conservationists are not adequately captured by individualistic accounts of ethics, even if these are extended to include sentient non-human animals. For, while indirect concern for habitats may be generated, it is much harder to see what sense can be made of the conservationists, commitment to the well-being of species or ecosystems *per se*, given that this does not always amount to the same thing as the aggregated interests of their members.

Secondly, the environmental philosopher seeking to articulate conservation concerns may have independent reservations about the primacy of the individual in conventional accounts of ethics. Given the intimate connection between individuals in the case of herd and pack animals, and between them and their habitat in the case of all wild animals, the singling out of the individual as the appropriate unit for attention can come to look both artificial and unhelpful. I am sympathetic to this criticism, and think it may have similarities with that offered to liberals by communitarian political thinkers. Here the thought is, roughly, that the characteristics such as autonomy and rationality which underpin liberal views about the rights of individuals, are not naturally existing properties of human beings as individuals, but the products of social and cultural contexts in which individuals are embedded.[23] Thus to single out the individual as the locus of moral attention is in some sense mistaken. Similarly, to single out individual animals for moral attention, by reference to characteristics such as sentience which they possess, is to neglect the way in which these characteristics result from, and can only exist in the context of, the ongoing processes of evolutionary ecology.

Metaphysics

The environmental philosopher, then, may criticise the welfarist on grounds which are as much metaphysical as ethical. Differences in the metaphysical commitments that underpin the ethical views of welfarists and environmental philosophers may be identified as a further and significant difference between them.

Specifically, the environmental philosopher may claim that the animal welfare position implies a metaphysics, or world-view, that is unsatisfactory both in its over-emphasis on individuals and in the view it presupposes about the relationship between humans and the rest of the world.

Individuals

The basic criticism of animal welfarism would be that it rests on a metaphysics or world-view in which individuals are sharply in focus. That this is the only or most appropriate way of seeing the world may be challenged from a number of directions. As above, it can be argued that individuals and their characteristics do not exist in abstraction from the evolutionary and ecological processes from which they emerge. Discussion of the Gaia theory and its implications may shift attention from the individual to the biosphere.[24]

From the perspective of ecological science, or some interpretations of it, emphasis on relations between living and non-living components of ecosystems also softens the focus on individuals, while biological science may seem to focus at the level of species in a metaphysical as well as an ethical sense.

At the other end of the scale, Richard Dawkins in *River Out of Eden*[25] talks powerfully of the river of life as a river of DNA – encoded information, flowing through the transient bodies of the entities we think of as individuals. His description suggests that information is 'more real' than individuals, and his views can, at least temporarily, rather unsettle any assumption that individuals are obviously the ontologically primary units in existence, or that individuals are the obvious focus for moral concern.

Humans and the world

Here, the criticism of welfarism goes something like this. In asking the question, which creatures on the planet have moral status and which do not – in, as it were, standing back from nature and asking whether and why we should value it – there is a sense in which welfarists are supposing themselves to be separate and detached from nature, rather than a part of it. This depiction of humans as detached observers, recognising a category of morally sacrosanct beings to which they belong and occasionally deigning to allow that a few other creatures join them there, is held to be mistaken. An alternative sketch shows humans as one species amongst many, immersed in a network of moral and ecological relationships.

In both cases, I think that the criticisms of welfarism would be worth developing. Clearly I cannot do that now, but I suggest that a discussion about appropriate metaphysical positions, and what will count as criteria of propriety, will tend to divide welfarists from deep environmentalists, and hence welfarists from conservationists whose policies stem from a deep environmental position.

TAKING STOCK

I began this chapter by arguing that the policy differences between animal welfarists and conservationists are underpinned by differences in the scope of their primary concern and the content of their fundamental objectives. I then tried to defend a fairly minimal animal welfare claim. This is that we have at least some moral obligations to individual, wild, sentient animals, and that these obligations involve a concern for their lives and welfare. Conservationists, I argue, should accept this. If this were to happen, a certain amount of progress towards the resolution of the welfare/conservation debate would be achieved.

How much? A first point to note in answering this is that while conservationists may be persuaded of direct obligations to individual animals, animal welfarists are inclined to doubt that any sense can be made of the notion that we have direct moral obligations to ecological collectives. But they are likely to acknowledge concern about habitats and ecosystems which, while indirect, is nevertheless substantial. This, in many cases, will generate similar policy prescriptions, at least at a general level. It rarely makes sense to be concerned about forest animals and not about forests. Thus, if conservationists recognise some concern for animals as individuals and animal welfarists demonstrate indirect concern for habitats, reasonable potential for practical cooperation is created.

In particular cases, however, dispute is likely to persist because of the difference in the relative priorities the groups attach to individuals over collectives. Conservationists will put the well-being of ecological collectives over that of individual animals; welfarists are likely to do the reverse. Hence, Scottish conservationists show their commitment to animal welfare concerns by trying to ensure that deer are shot painlessly. Animal welfarists may agree that deer numbers need to be controlled but insist that alternatives to culling must be found.

Nevertheless, what has been said above at least opens the way for reasonable debate about conservation policies which infringe on the lives and welfare of animals, and about animal welfare practices which have undesirable ecological implications. This may be particularly important in Europe, where there has been polarisation of the welfare-conservation views, and a tendency for the poles to dismiss each other's view out of hand.

We are left with the difficult business of weighing the claims of individuals against the claims of species and other ecological collectives. But these kinds of difficulties are at least familiar from the human context, where claims of particular individuals must constantly be weighed against claims of family, local community, nation and so on. And, as in the human case, issues like deer-culling raise genuine moral dilemmas. Such dilemmas are not resolved by dismissing one or other point of view, and no general or algorithmic solutions may be found to them. They seem to be characteristic of a moral life which recognises multiple sources of value. As Martha Nussbaum puts it.

> '[t]he richer our scheme of values, the harder it will prove to effect a harmony within it. The more open we are to the presence of value ... in the world, the more surely conflict closes us in. The price of harmonisation seems to be impoverishment, the price of richness disharmony.'[26]

If this is true, the appropriate response is to learn how to live with disharmony rather than to force a false harmony upon our decision-making procedures.

So far, then, animal welfarists and conservationists may be able to acknowledge each other's position as complementary to their own at a general level, and agree to work through disagreements as they arise in particular cases. But I also argued that there is a second level at which theoretical disagreements exist. This level may run deeper than the first. Thus welfarists tend to be committed to traditional notions of morality, while many environmental philosophers hold that traditional moral theories obscure rather than clarify the nature of our moral obligations to the non-human world. There may also be significant differences in the metaphysical foundations of the two groups. In the latter part of this paper, I outlined some of these differences, and suggested that they give rise to a number of significant criticisms of the animal welfare position. These differences raise difficult and fundamental problems in ethical theory and their resolution may be harder to achieve. Here, more work is required.

As to the initial dispute over the scope and content of the principles which guide conservation and welfarism, my view is that there is an important core of truth in the claim that we have obligations to individual sentient animals, including wild ones. However, the way this claim has been articulated and developed by philosophers in Europe, North America and Australia is deeply problematic and cannot do justice to the complexity of some of the issues involved. I think that this is revealed in discussions about conservation issues, and that it becomes even clearer if we leave European examples and change continents. To this end I will close with a few remarks about elephants.

POSTSCRIPT

I have become increasingly interested in elephant-culling, an issue as complex as it is non-European. I will not pretend to know a great deal about the subject. But it does seem to embody a similar welfare/conservation split. When elephants are restricted in their range, as the pressure of human numbers means they must be, there is evidence to suggest that they have an adverse impact on woody vegetation, that they block other animals' access to water-holes and that, in general, they have a deleterious effect on their habitat and other species within it. Culling has often been recommended for these and other reasons.

Yet it is hard not to be moved by accounts of elephant culls given, for example, by Iain and Oria Douglas-Hamilton.[27] Those I have spoken to who work with elephants offer convincing testimony to their individuality, the complex social relations that exist within elephant families and so on. The idea of shooting entire families of elephants or, perhaps worse, shooting members of families, appears very differently when the animals are known as individuals as opposed to statistics in a park management plan.

I have not yet met anyone who wholeheartedly endorses culling rather than regards it as a necessary evil. Nevertheless, conservation and welfare perspectives conflict over the issue. In addition, the elephant issue raises questions of human/animal conflict more sharply than do most of the European examples. Grey squirrels do represent a threat to human crops, but it is hard to see the squirrel as dangerous in the immediate sort of way that elephants can be. It is here, where animals of one species threaten, not just their own habitats, but human livelihoods, or where animals represent income for people and projects who sorely need it, that a commitment to animal welfare is tested most acutely. I have argued in defence of the view that we owe concern to animals as individuals, and I think that the killing of intelligent and social animals must always be a regretted last resort. But I also think that the standard approaches to animal welfare have failed to do justice to the real dilemmas and difficulties involved. As a result, they may very reasonably be charged with trying to transfer views evolved in contexts in which humans are threatened neither by animals nor by poverty, to situations in which these threats are prevalent. A revised account of our obligations to individual animals needs to take these criticisms to heart.

NOTES

1. *Environmental Values*, ed. Alan Holland, Lancaster University (The White Horse Press).
2. *Ecos*, journal of the British Association of Nature Conservationists, ed. Rick Minter, Cheltenham, Glos.
3. *Biodiversity and Conservation*, ed.
4. Information offered in this paragraph was taken from the following sources:
   - United Nations Environment Programme, *Global Biodiversity Assessment*, 14 November 1995, reported by Nicholas Schoon, 'Half all birds and mammals extinct within 300 years', *The Independent*, 15 November 1995;
   - United Nations Environment Programme, *Global Biodiversity Assessment. Summary for Policy Makers* (Cambridge: Cambridge University Press, 1995);
   - Norman Myers, 'Bugs in the system', *The Guardian*, 19 October 1995;
   - R. Sylvan and D. Bennett, *The Greening of Ethics: From Human Chauvinism to Deep Green Theory* (Cambridge, UK: White Horse Press/Tucson, AZR, USA: University of Arizona Press, 1994);
   - P. Vitonsek, P. R. Erlich, A. H. Erlich and P. A. Matson, 'Human appropriation of the products of photosynthesis', *BioScience* 36, pp. 368–93.
5. Oliver Tickell, 'Return to the wild', *Geographical Magazine*, February 1995.
6. Green College lectures, 1994, *The Origin of Species*: Professor Robert May, 'The fire this time: biological diversity yesterday, today and tomorrow', Monday 24th January, 1994.
7. Edward O. Wilson, *The Diversity of Life* (London: Penguin, 1992), pp. 37–8.
8. I am grateful to Gill Aitken for information about RSPCA and RSPB.
9. J. Baird Callicott, 'Animal liberation, a triangular affair', in *In Defence of the Land Ethic*. (New York). SUNY Press, 1989), p. 19.
10. Primack is paraphrasing views attributed to Holmes Rolston. See R. B. Primack, *Essentials of Conservation Biology* (Sunderland, MA. Sinauer Associates, 1993).
11. Vicki Hearne, *Adams Task: Calling Animals by Name*.
12. Christine Kenyon Jones, 'Our dumb favourites and their protectors', *Times Literary Supplement*, 5 January 1996.
13. Alan Holland, 'On behalf of moderate speciesism', *Journal of Applied Philosophy* 1 (2), 1984.
14. J. Baird Callicott, 'Animal liberation'.
15. Midgley quotes from Richard Sorabji, *Animal Minds and Human Morals: The Origins of the Western Debate* (London: Duckworth, 1993) as follows: 'It sounded grand enough when Aristotle and the Stoics declared that man had reason and animals had not. But, as the debate progressed, it began to appear that animals might lack only certain kinds of reasoning, and a stand was taken on their not having speech. When this defence too began to be questioned, a retreat was made to the position that they lacked syntax "They lack syntax, so we can eat them", was supposed to be the conclusion.' Mary Midgley, 'Beastly beliefs', a review of Sorabji in *Nature* 36B, 24 March, 1994.
16. James Rachels, 'Do animals have a right to life?', in H. Miller and W. Williams (eds), *Ethics and Animals* (NJ: Humana Press, 1983).
17. Ibid.
18. John Bonner, 'Red or dead?', *New Scientist* 2013, 20 January 1996, p. 30.
19. Ibid.
20. Peter Singer, *Animal Liberation*, 2nd ed (London: Thorsons, 1991), Chapter 1.
21. 'What, for instance, are we to do about genuine conflicts of interest like rats biting slum children? I am not quite sure of the answer . . .' Peter Singer, 'Animal liberation', *The New York Review of Books*, 5 April 1973. Quoted in Eve Browning Cole, *Philosophy and Feminist Criticism* (Paragon House, 1993), p. 46.

22. Tom Regan, *The Case of Animal Rights* (New York and London, Routledge, 1984 and 1988).
23. See Charles Taylor, 'Atomism' in *Philosophy and the Human Sciences, Philosophical Papers 2* (Cambridge. Cambridge University Press, 1985).
24. James Lovelock's *The Ages of Gaia* has just been revised (Oxford. Oxford University Press, 1995).
25. Richard Dawkins, *River Out of Eden* (Harper Collins, 1995)
26. Martha Nussbaum, *The Fragility of Goodness* (Cambridge. Cambridge University Press, 1986), p. 75.
27. Iain and Oria Douglas-Hamilton, *Battle for the Elephants* (London. Doubelday, (1992), Chapter 21.

9

WHALING IN SAND COUNTY: THE MORALITY OF NORWEGIAN MINKE WHALE CATCHING

J. Baird Callicott

INTRODUCTION

Jon Wetlesen, of the Department of Philosophy and Centre for Development and Environment at the University of Oslo, invited me to Norway to participate in one of a series of seminars examining various environmental controversies through the lens of various approaches to environmental ethics. 'No doubt,' he wrote, 'we have a case on hand with the charges that are being raised against the Norwegian government after it decided to allow the resumption of commercial whaling.'[1] In 1986, the International Whaling Commission declared a moratorium on commercial whaling. In the spring of 1993, the Brundtland administration – hoping to reverse its declining popularity in an election year – defied the moratorium and unilaterally allowed Norwegian whalers to take 160 minke whales. The political ploy was successful; Gro Harlem Brundtland was re-elected. Accordingly, during the summer of 1993, Norwegians killed 153 minke whales.[2] And I can personally attest to the fact that whale steaks and chops were unabashedly advertised on the menu of at least one Oslo restaurant in the fall of the year.

Wetlesen asked me to examine the controversial decision of the Norwegian government to allow the resumption of commercial whaling, in defiance of the IWC moratorium, through the lens of the Aldo Leopold 'land ethic'. An earlier version of this paper was read to an audience that included, in addition to members of the academic community at the University of Oslo, representatives of the Norwegian government. Lars Wallöe of the UO Department of Physiology and chief adviser on whaling policy to Prime Minister Brundtland responded formally. This revised version takes account of some of the more salient concerns that Wallöe and others expressed.

Off-shore whaling is a miniscule and insignificant component of the Norwegian economy. The votes of a few sub-arctic fishermen, their families and friends could hardly, by themselves, determine the outcome of a national election. Evidently, the resumption of whaling has become very popular in Norway. Are Norwegians so fond of whale meat that they will vote for politicians who promise to satisfy their craving? One hundred and fifty-three minke whales would not go very far among four million Norwegians – unless Ms Brundtland could also work a loaves and fishes type miracle. Somehow, Norwegian national pride seems bound up with the right to kill whales. To get some sense of Norwegian sentiments, I was asked to imagine that India was the world's most powerful and influential country, and that the government of India rammed a resolution banning the slaughter of cattle through the United Nations. How would people in beef-eating nations feel about that? The comparison, of course, is not entirely apt. Bovids and other species of domestic animals are not at risk of extinction. Whales are not the sacred cows of any traditional religion. And, freely roaming the seven seas, whales are no one's private property.

Why, in any case, did the Norwegian government allow only the resumption of minke whaling? For two reasons, one bio-economic, the other bio-cultural.

First, the bio-economic reason. Unlike the sperm, the bowhead, the right, the blue, sei, fin and humpback whales, the minke whale was not driven to near extinction during the cetacean holocaust – the century and a half of intensive, unregulated slaughter of great whales in all the world's oceans. Minke whales are the smallest species of the rorqual family, yielding less meat, oil and baleen per unit of capture-effort than their larger cousins (one blue whale, the largest of the rorquals, yields as many barrels of oil as thirty-two minke whales); they are fast swimmers; and their carcasses sink.[3] So, modern commercial whalers did not concentrate their efforts on minkes until the mid-1970s – after the preferred species populations had become so depleted and technologies of capture so improved that minke whales were worth pursuing.[4] Fortunately, the minke whale *species* came through its decade of global persecution numerically diminished, but not endangered. Therefore, some believe, it can and should sustain further killing.

Second, the bio-cultural reason for limiting the kill in 1993 to minke whales. People living in Norway have killed minke whales for centuries. Other species occasionally frequent coastal waters in the northern summer, but the minke whale is so often seen close to shore and up the long fjords that in Norwegian it is called the *vågehval* – the whale of the fjord.[5] Thus long before Norwegian peoples had learned to build even the most primitive boats they could have opportunistically speared or trapped and drowned a minke whale that had strayed too far up a narrow inlet. After the Vikings learned to build seaworthy boats, minke whales were regularly hunted as part of the coastal subsistence regime in Norway. In short, minke whales are locally available and killing them is a long local tradition.

One might think that the Aldo Leopold land ethic – the prototype for all subsequent environmental ethics – could shed a lot of light on the morality of commercial whaling. But whales live in the sea, not on land. Therefore, if one wants to make an informed moral judgement about commercial whaling, one should consult the 'sea ethic', not the *land* ethic.

Of course, I'm joking – lamely. But under the surface of many a joke – good as well as bad – lies a serious point. The land ethic has its limits. The name itself reveals a kind of parochialism. Nearly three-quarters of the (misnamed) planet Earth is covered by water. Elsewhere I have argued that the land ethic would be utterly incapable of providing moral guidance should we human beings discover, and be in a position to affect, life on Mars – or anywhere else off what my colleague Holmes Rolston, III likes to call 'the home planet'.[6] Why? Because the linchpin of the land ethic is what Leopold called the 'community concept'. And, by definition, we human beings are not evolutionarily kin or ecologically related to unearthly forms of life. We would share no community with them.

Certainly we are evolutionarily kin to cetaceans – indeed, fairly close kin, phylogenetically speaking, since they are mammals no less than are we. But the evolutionary ancestors of cetaceans returned to live in and adapt to the sea long before we latecomers showed up on the land – for them a long-abandoned environment.[7] Unlike cetaceans, we *Homo sapiens* evolved on land. And, for most of our short tenure on this planet, we went to sea only for so long and so far as we could swim. Thus human beings, on the one hand, and whales and dolphins, on the other, belong, biohistorically speaking, to very different biotic communities. Perhaps that very difference – the mysterious otherness of marine life – might be the point of departure for the yet-to-be-formulated sea ethic. But that is a moral ship that I shall not attempt to launch.

Instead, I steer a course in the opposite direction. My compass star will be an ethic of caring and community, rather than an ethic of Otherness and *différance*.

ABOUT THE LAND ETHIC

I have been at pains to point out at every opportunity that, as a moral philosophy, the Leopold land ethic is neither imperialistic nor isolationistic – to employ political metaphors. Although Leopold carelessly wrote:

> A thing is right *when* it tends to preserve the integrity, stability, and beauty of the biotic community. It is wrong *when* it tends otherwise.[8]

we can be sure that he did not intend the logically ambiguous word 'when' to be interpreted to mean 'if and only if.' Preserving the integrity, stability and beauty of the biotic community is a sufficient condition for an action to be right, not a necessary condition. Actions that tend to further other goods may also be right. How can we be so sure about this? Well, in the first place, Leopold frequently acknowledges the legitimacy of other goods, such as human material well-being. He says, for example, that 'A land ethic of course cannot prevent the alteration, management, and use of these "resources"' (referring to soils, waters, plants and animals).[9] And, in the second place, Leopold characterised the land ethic as an 'accretion'.[10] That implies that he understood the land ethic to be an addition to, not a substitute for, our more venerable and familiar social ethics. Thus the land ethic was never meant to oust traditional human-oriented morality and reign supreme. It was intended, rather, to supplement traditional human-oriented morality.

Further, as an additional domain of ethics, the land ethic is not unrelated to our more familiar social ethics. It is not an ethic that is isolated, standing apart from our other ethics and incommensurable with them, any more than it is an ethic that would supplant them. 'Accretion' suggests another layer of the same substance forming a structure like that of an onion. According to the general theory underlying the land ethic, the substance, the common denominator, of all our ethics is community. About this, Leopold is quite emphatic. Indeed, his words seem almost dogmatic: 'All ethics so far evolved rest upon a single premise: that the individual is a member of a community of interdependent parts.'[11] Thus, as we see, the land ethic was not conceived to be an *ad hoc* add-on to our traditional social ethics, based upon altogether new and unfamiliar premises and principles. It is, rather, the most recently born sibling in a family of ethics – the family of ethics generated by and relative to our various community entanglements. Hence, in applying the land ethic to the present question, the morality of whaling, we needn't confine ourselves to the land ethic as such – that is, to the land ethic, narrowly defined – we can reach more deeply into its generic communitarian premises and principles for guidance.

Finally, let me address another potential misconception of the land ethic, invited by the casual exposition of its author. It may seem to provide moral considerability only for environmental *wholes*, to the neglect, altogether, of *individual* non-human natural entities. In the land ethic's summary moral maxim that I just quoted, Leopold mentions only an action's tendency to preserve the integrity, stability and beauty of the biotic *community* as the criterion of its rightness or wrongness. But the land ethic accommodates concern for individual non-human beings no less surely than it coheres and peacefully coexists with our more venerable and familiar human-oriented ethics. When Leopold first crystallises the implications of the land ethic he mentions individual non-human natural entities alongside biological wholes: 'In short,' he writes, 'a land ethic changes the role of *Homo sapiens* from conqueror of the land-community to plain member and citizen of it. It implies respect for his *fellow-members*, [as well as] respect for the community as such.'[12]

A HOLISTIC LAND-ETHICAL TAKE ON MINKE WHALE HUNTING

Suppose things are just what the Norwegian whaling industry and the Norwegian government say that they are: the minke whale is not an endangered or threatened species, and its populations may be harvested sustainably.[13] Assume also that we can translate Leopold's ethic *mutatis mutandis* from the landscape into the seascape. And further grant that we human beings, now a seafaring pelagic primate, may choose to abjure conquest and become plain members and citizens of marine biotic communities as well as of terrestrial ones. What does the land ethic permit us and not permit us to do? To hunt the minke whale or not to hunt the minke whale? That is the policy question put to the land ethic.

Though it cannot prevent the alteration, management and use of these 'resources', a land ethic, according to Leopold, would guarantee other forms of life a 'biotic right' to continuance.[14] If to hunt the minke whale threatened or endangered the species, then the imperative of the land ethic would be categorical: minke whales should not be hunted. Marine conservation organisations such as Greenpeace dispute the Norwegian government's claim that the minke whale is plentiful and could sustain a strictly regulated annual catch.[15] But, for the sake of argument, let us stipulate that carefully regulated minke whale hunting would not endanger the species. Then what?

Given the incontestable – though not unmitigated – holism of the land ethic, we might direct our moral attention next to the effect of minke whale hunting on marine biotic communities. What effect, for example, would an annual reduction of the number of adult minke whales have on the populations of krill that the whales eat? Presumably a reduction of the number of adult minke whales would cause an increase in the krill population. That, in turn, might cause a reduction in the phytoplankton population that the krill eat, resulting next in a crash in the abnormally inflated krill population, . . . and eventually in the starvation of whales.[16]

The second-most famous essay in *A Sand County Almanac*, 'Thinking like a mountain', is a homily about the dangers of ignorant human meddling with animal and plant populations in complex dynamic equilibria:

> I was young then and full of trigger-itch; I thought that because fewer wolves meant more deer, that no wolves would mean hunters' paradise . . . Since then I have lived to see state after state extirpate its wolves. I have watched the face of many a newly wolfless mountain, and seen the south-facing slopes wrinkle with a maze of new deer trails. I have seen every edible bush and seedling browsed, first to anaemic desuetude, and then to death. I have seen every edible tree defoliated to the height of a saddlehorn . . . In the end the starved bones of the hoped-for deer herd, dead of its own too-much, bleach with the bones of the dead sage or molder under the high-lined junipers.[17]

Transposing this land ethical parable from a terrestrial to a marine milieu, let the wolves stand for the whales, the deer for the krill and the browse for the phytoplankton. Note that the analogy is not perfect. The young, pre-ecological Leopold hoped for an abundance of deer not wolves, while whalers hope for an abundance of whales not krill. But whatever link in the food chain one hopes sustainably to exploit, the putative ecological principle remains the same: significantly interfering with poorly understood complex population equilibria courts disaster.[18]

But the argument against minke whale hunting based upon its possible deleterious effect on the marine biotic community to which minke whales belong is weak.[19] In general, arguments against human enterprises with demonstrable economic benefits based upon speculative ecological risks are weak. Further, not only are ecologists incapable of certainly predicting what specific effect sustainable minke whale hunting will have on poorly understood marine biotic communities, the general ecological principle that Leopold so poignantly illustrates in 'Thinking like a mountain' has been more recently impugned in ecology. In a widely cited and influential book, *Discordant Harmonies*, Daniel Botkin attacks and dismisses the balance-of-nature notion prevailing in ecology at mid-century – with direct reference, incidentally, to the historic case of the deer irruption on the Kaibab plateau in northern Arizona that Leopold dramatised in 'Thinking like a mountain'.[20] And Botkin expressly denies that classic notions of predator–prey equilibria are useful in the management of marine 'fisheries'.[21] (Presumably his reservations would apply equally well to 'whaleries'.) I might add that, upon close critical scrutiny, Botkin's arguments prove inconclusive and unpersuasive. But his book has been so warmly received because he so effectively popularises the current mass movement in ecological theory from holism to individualism, from stasis to change, from elegant order to stochastic chaos, and from stability to perturbation as the normal state of nature.

If sustainable commercial minke whale hunting would not adversely affect the integrity of marine biotic communities (that is, if it would not threaten or endanger the species), and probably not affect their stability (supposing that stability remains an operative idea in ecology), what effect would it have on their beauty? Leopold writes:

> The physics of beauty is one department of natural science still in the Dark Ages. Not even the manipulators of bent space have tried to solve its equations. Everybody knows, for example, that the autumn landscape in the north woods is the land, plus a red maple, plus a ruffed grouse. In terms of conventional physics, the grouse represents only a millionth of either the mass or the energy of an acre. Yet subtract the grouse and the whole thing is dead. An enormous amount of some kind of motive power has been lost.
>
> It is easy to say that the loss is all in our mind's eye, but is there any sober ecologist who will agree? He knows full well that there has been an ecological death, the significance of which is inexpressible in terms of contemporary science. A philosopher has called this imponderable essence the *noumenon* of material things. It stands in contradistinction to *phenomenon*, which is ponderable and predictable, even to the tossings and turnings of the remotest star.
>
> The grouse is the noumenon of the north woods, the blue jay of the hickory groves, the whiskey-jack of the muskegs, the piñonero of the juniper foothills . . . [22]

To a historian of philosophy, Leopold's appropriation of Immanuel Kant's distinction between noumena and phenomena may appear sophomoric at best. But the 'philosopher' to whom Leopold here refers was, as a matter of fact, not Kant. Leopold actually became aware of this technical, philosophical distinction already corrupted in the work of P. D. Ouspensky – if that is any excuse. By *noumena*, in any event, Kant referred to metaphysical objects, things-in-themselves, which are beyond human ken. Only phenomena are present to human consciousness, according to Kant. As Leopold employs the term here, however, the noumena of land are quite actual or physical – and therefore, strictly speaking, phenomenal. Nonetheless, in a metaphorical way, they constitute the 'essence' of the landscape. In this sense, Leopold's usage observes the spirit of Kant's definition, if not the letter.

A good case could be made that whales are the noumena of the high seas. They are for me. On more than one occasion I have braved the winter winds at the Point Reyes Light House staring out to sea for a fleeting glimpse of migrating California gray whales. Whales are noumenal beings for so many other people that together we have managed to secure the fragile international moratorium on whaling – now defiantly flouted by the government of Norway – to prevent their 'loss'.

But here at issue is not 'an ecological death' – which no responsible party to the debate would countenance. At issue, rather, is *sustainable* commercial minke whale hunting. Leopold believed that the ruffed grouse was the noumenon of the north woods, and unequivocally opposed its loss – that is, its extirpation. But in those biotic communities where grouse were abundant, Leopold himself enthusiastically hunted them.[23]

What can we conclude from this initial pass of the general problem at hand – the morality of commercial whaling – before the tribunal of the land ethic? Certainly commercial whaling is environmentally unethical if it threatens or endangers species of whales. And when sustainably harvesting species populations that are not threatened or endangered – as when engaging in any other human exploitation of 'natural resources' – certainly people should take care not to disorganise biotic communities (assuming that current ecology still recognises the existence of organised biotic communities). And what can we conclude about this initial pass of the specific question at hand – to hunt or not to hunt the minke whale? – before the tribunal of the land ethic? Regrettably, that cautious commercial minke whale hunting is permissible – *if* the species population is as robust as alleged, and *if* strict quotas are observed so as to prevent over-harvesting.

AN INDIVIDUALISTIC LAND-ETHICAL TAKE ON MINKE WHALE HUNTING

So says the Leopold land ethic if we scrutinise the matter only in the light of its holistic golden rule or summary moral maxim: 'A thing is right when it tends to preserve the integrity, stability, and beauty of the biotic community. It is wrong when it tends otherwise.' Sustainable commercial minke whale hunting may not be right. That is, no one supposes that it would positively tend to preserve the integrity, stability and beauty of the biotic community. But neither is sustainable commercial minke whale hunting wrong, since, so far as we know, it would not positively tend otherwise. Other things being equal, if minke whales are plentiful, then strictly regulated commercial minke whale hunting is land-ethically permissible.

But are other things equal? As I suggested earlier, the summary moral maxim of the land ethic is incomplete, for it says nothing about duties to 'fellow-members' of the biotic community. And, in fact, elsewhere in 'the land ethic' Leopold has rather little directly to say about fellow-members – about how we should treat individual nonhuman beings – except that we owe them 'respect'.

From the point of view of modern ethical principles, respect for fellow-members of the *human* community implies, at the very least, non-interference. Invading the homes of other people and making slaves of them or slaughtering them for profit would, certainly, be inconsistent with our generally acknowledged duty to respect fellow human beings. Indeed, we can think of no more heinous crime than to kill and eat a fellow human being. Now, as we explore what it might mean to add a new accretion to our set of community-generated ethics, an environmental ethic, surely to kill and eat a fellow-member of the *biotic* community would be prima facie suspect. Wouldn't *that*, if anything would, violate our duty to respect our fellow-members of the biotic community? In *Respect for Nature*, Paul W. Taylor actually draws just such a conclusion and finds himself having awkwardly to justify violently interfering with fellow-members of the biotic community in our pursuit of the desiccated human well-being that he could approve.[24] Repeatedly, however, I have argued that the theoretical foundations of the land ethic do not warrant a simple extension of our familiar human ethics to the environment.[25] Also Leopold himself found respecting deer and hunting them (no less enthusiastically than he hunted ruffed grouse) to be perfectly consistent.

How so? Because, as I have also repeatedly explained, the structures of our human communities, on the one hand, and of our biotic communities, on the other, are very different.[26] Hence, we should expect the ethics correlative to these very different kinds of communities to be correspondingly very different. Human communities are organised around mutual security and mutually beneficial, cooperative exchanges of goods and services among members. Biotic communities are organised around a flow of energy through food webs. Human communities thrive when fellow-members peacefully and equitably give and receive, buy and sell. Biotic communities thrive when fellow-members photosynthesise, graze, browse and prey, live, reproduce, die and decay. Here is Leopold's thumbnail sketch of the biotic community:

> Plants absorb energy from the sun. This energy flows through a circuit called the biota, which may be represented by a pyramid consisting of layers. The bottom layer is the soil. A plant layer rests on the soil, an insect layer on the plants, a bird and rodent layer on the insects, and so on up through the various animal groups to the apex layer, which consists of the larger carnivores.[27]

In the biotic community, human beings are omnivores. If the land ethic condemned one species killing and eating another, it would condemn the very heart and soul of the biotic community that it was originally conceived to foster and preserve. In nature's economy, 'the only certain truth', Leopold observes, 'is that its creatures must suck hard, live fast, and die often.'[28]

Is 'respect for fellow-members', therefore, a hollow phrase, empty of moral significance in the land ethic? Is the land ethic devoid, after all, of any meaningful provision of moral consideration for individuals? No, I don't think so. However, Leopold himself, as far as I am aware, never attempts directly to cash out 'respect for fellow-members' in the hard currency of appropriate behaviour. I have suggested elsewhere that we might get a clue from the way peoples who are indigenous to various biotic communities, and who profess respect for their fellow-members, comport themselves toward soils and waters, plants and animals. Practitioners of those traditional American Indian cultures with which I am most familiar expressed respect for violently appropriated fellow-members of their biotic communities in various ways. Least subtle was care not to waste them accompanied by an overt expression of gratitude to the individual plants and animals whose lives were taken only for genuine human need. More indirect expressions of respect were the many and seemingly whimsical and arbitrary 'rules' surrounding the seduction, capture, dispatch and disposal of various plants and animals: tobacco should be offered to birch trees from whom bark was to be stripped; laughter at a moose's funny face was prohibited; the meat of bears had to be eaten up all at one feast; the bones of beavers should not to be burned or fed to dogs; and so on.[29]

Above all, respect for game animals requires land-ethical hunters to dispatch them with care, skill and humanity. Human beings should not cause other forms of life to suffer gratuitously.

So what light does this attempt to cash out land-ethical 'respect for fellow-members' in behavioural currency shed on the problem at hand, the morality of sustainably harvesting robust species populations of whales? From what I have just written, one might infer that it illuminates the politically correct seam between good environmentalism and good cultural pluralism. Indigenous peoples, such as the North American Inuit and Eskimo – who have respectfully (I presume) hunted whales for generations – might land-ethically go on doing so, while modern Europeans, Euro-Americans and Japanese (the Ainu excepted) may not.[30] But I do not think that that is the right inference to draw. Certainly I do not think that that is the inference Leopold himself would have drawn. We know for a fact that he did not think that it was land-ethically OK for indigenous peoples to hunt deer and other 'game' animals, but not OK for modern Europeans and Euro-Americans to do so. Modern Europeans and Euro-Americans might land-ethically hunt robust species populations of game so long as they too – in their own fashion – demonstrated respect. Leopold himself demonstrated respect for game in no less subtle and complicated a manner than did the Lakota or the Ojibwa. A modern Western – or perhaps I should rather say *post*modern Western – demonstration of respect for hunted fellow-members of the biotic community, as sketched by Leopold, included learning the biology of one's quarry; voluntarily limiting one's means of capture (preferring, for example, to use a compound bow and arrow instead of a gun, or a double-barrelled instead of an automatic shotgun); good markspersonship; not shooting when one cannot be sure of making a quick, clean, kill; strict obedience to statutory regulations (such as bag limits and closed seasons); and, in general, assiduously following a code of sporting conduct. In writing about these matters, Leopold employed an unusually strong moral vocabulary: 'Voluntary adherence to an ethical code elevates the self-respect of the sportsman, but it should not be forgotten that voluntary disregard of the code degenerates and depraves him.'[31]

Norway is a well ordered and governed country in which whale hunting is closely monitored. Thus Norwegian whalers may be counted on strictly to observe the quotas set by the Brundtland administration. Moreover, Norway (after some resistence in the early 1980s) now requires that exploding harpoons be used in minke whale hunting – to spare the quarry as much suffering as possible.[32] Referring to Norwegian cannoneers, Egil Ole Öen notes, very much in the spirit of Aldo Leopold, that 'the hunter's attitude to hunting, experience, and competence are extremely important. Training, accuracy, ability to judge the exact moment to shoot are all factors that separate good hunters from lesser ones.'[33] Norway has taken steps to assure that Norwegian minke whale hunters are among the good ones. The gunners on Norwegian whale boats are formally trained and must pass a markspersonship test with the harpoon cannon in addition to an ordinary weapons-use examination for big game hunting (since wounded minke whales may sometimes be dispatched with a rifle).[34] And we may suppose that Norwegian whalers sincerely cultivate an attitude of genuine regard for their quarry and that they really feel remorse for taking the lives of whales, which they believe they must do because of dire economic necessity. Upon land ethical principles, why would this postmodern expression of respect for the minke whale be any less justificatory than the respect expressed by premodern whale hunters? Upon land ethical principles, why would *sustainable* minke whale hunting, provided it be done *respectfully*, be any less justifiable than sustainable deer hunting, respectfully done?

In the opinion of Norwegian whaler Björn Hugo Bendiksen, as reported in the *New York Times*, 'There is no reason to protect them. They're plentiful. Killing a minke is no different from killing a deer.'[35] Personally, I think that killing whales is abominable, however it is done and by whomever it is done. But I do not think that killing deer is abominable. And I have no qualms about eating venison. On the contrary, I relish it. But I would consider eating whale meat only a little less loathsome and obnoxious than eating human flesh. As a philosopher, I also think that inconsistency is abominable. I consider tolerating inconsistency among my own moral judgements to be only a little less loathsome and obnoxious than eating whale meat. Therefore, unless I can mount a convincing case for a significant difference between hunting whales and hunting deer, I should approve the former with the same alacrity as I do the latter or I should censure the latter with the same fervour as I do the former.

Here is one obvious difference. Standing on *terra firma* it is perfectly possible to kill a deer quickly and cleanly. Now think about shooting a whale with a harpoon tethered to a rope. The whale is rolling on the surface of the water, while the bow of the boat is pitching up and down and back and forth with the swells. As Joseph Horwood comments, 'It can be appreciated that great skill is required of the gunners to even hit the whale, let alone the target areas behind the skull.'[36] It can also be appreciated that, as a matter of fact, in more than half of all cases the whale's death is prolonged and its agony proportionately protracted.[37] Thus, for reasons not of logical but of practical necessity, whaling violates the first land-ethical rule of respect for non-human fellow-members of the biotic community. It is inherently inhumane for more than half the minke whales taken.

A THICKENED DESCRIPTION OF RESPECT FOR FELLOW-MEMBERS

Consider further how one might cash out 'respect for fellow-members' in the hard currency of appropriate behaviour. A United States President should behave presidentially, and a citizen of the United States should behave deferentially toward the President – even the notoriously incompetent or improbable ones of recent history. As we Americans say, such behaviour expresses our 'respect for the office', and we address the occupant of the White House as 'Mr President' – even though we may think the man himself to be a buffoon or worse. The same sort of thing goes of course for the Prime Minister and prime ministers, the Royal Family and the royals, the Senate and senators, the Parliament and MPs, and so on and so forth. Though one's grandparents may be undistinguished and have learned nothing worth sharing in the course of their long and meaningless lives, we believe that one should treat them, nevertheless, with the deference due a senior member of the family. In general, then, one important and familiar aspect of the ethical concept of respect, as we know it in our various human communities, is behaviour appropriate to various social roles. One does not respect a waitress if one treats her as another dinner guest, any more than she would respect the guests were she to behave as one of them. We do not respect a student if we treat him as a colleague, any more than he would respect us as professors were he to behave as if he were our peer. And this thickened description of respectful behaviour holds, even if the waitress in the first example were a talented jazz musician holding down a day-job or the student in the second example were a budding genius far brighter than we, his mentors. Part of being a member of a community is to play multiple social roles, and each of them has its peculiar sort of competency and its corresponding due respect.

In contemporary human society there is a good deal of social mobility. Anyone, as we Americans like to boast, can grow up to be President of the United States – as several recent ones have proved. But in the biotic community one is born to one's social role. Social mobility is achieved, if achieved at all, only by species and only over many generations through natural selection and adaptation. Now, in the economy of nature, deer are herbivores and the prey of omnivores (such as bears) and carnivores (such as wolves). That is their social role. They seem to know it. And they seem to accept it. Human beings are also omnivores, with a decided preference for meat if and when it can be obtained. Human beings have hunted deer, antelope and other ungulates ever since human beings became human. According to standard (perhaps male-biased, but standard nevertheless) anthropology, hunting terrestrial game helped shape human anatomy, physiology, psychology and society. And according to standard evolutionary biology, being hunted helped shape the anatomy, physiology, psychology and society of prey species. Deer are alert, cryptic, evasive and fleet. They reach sexual maturity within a year and a half of birth; they reproduce prolifically; and they do not live, in any event, more than a dozen years.[38] The great twentieth-century Spanish philosopher José Ortega y Gasset insisted that 'the only adequate response to a being that lives obsessed with avoiding capture is to try to catch it.'[39]

Is it permissible – as Ortega, Leopold and Paul Shepard have variously argued – to hunt deer and other game animals?[40] Few would argue that tribal peoples presently living in continuity with traditional ways should not hunt traditional game as part of their traditional means of subsistence. It is not politically correct to censure the folkways of traditional peoples, provided those folkways do not adversely affect vocal human victim-groups. But many have argued that contemporary industrialised folk should not hunt deer and other traditional game animals. What's the difference, one wonders – especially from the point of view of the game. Perhaps it's a matter of technology: deer hunting with Stone Age technologies is fair; with modern technologies it's not. But Stone Age hunting technologies are also less efficient and may therefore cause game animals more suffering than would modern technologies. However that may be, few contemporary aboriginal subsistence hunters still employ Stone Age means. Most contemporary North American Indian hunters, for example, use a plethora of modern gadgets to make their hunting more convenient and efficient – everything from steel-jawed traps and breech-loading rifles to snowmobiles and outboard motors. And many contemporary hunters living in industrial societies use contemporary versions of Stone Age weapons – most obviously, bows and arrows. In any case, the whole point of game laws in countries that have them is artificially to limit the overwhelming destructive power that people can now bring to bear upon traditional game animals. Perhaps it's a matter of necessity. But must contemporary traditional peoples hunt to survive? Perhaps they must to survive culturally. But that's the very argument that Leopold and Shepard have advanced to justify their own hunting. Hunting, they claim, is their biological and cultural birthright. And indeed Norwegians justify whaling, especially minke whaling, by just such an argument from tradition and culture. Perhaps it's a matter of appropriate attitude and intention.

But all this is a digression. Wherever the absolute truth may lie concerning the morality of contemporary, multicultural human beings hunting deer and other prey animals in the various biotic communities that human beings can claim to be plain members and citizens of, clearly hunting is conditionally OK by the land ethic. What are those conditions? There are two general ones, both already noticed here. The first, holistic, general condition is that hunting should not threaten or endanger species populations or the integrity, stability and beauty of biotic communities. The second, individualistic, general condition is that game animals should be respected. And a more specific aspect of respect – to go directly to my present point – is treating a member of the biotic community in a manner appropriate to its role in the economy of nature. If Ortega goes too far in suggesting that one ought to hunt prey animals, at least we can be confident that the land ethic permits one to hunt them. But the land ethic, I suggest, would morally censure hunting animals that are not proper prey animals. To do so would violate the general imperative of the land ethic to respect fellow-members.

Thus, for instance, the land ethic would not permit hunting sharp-tailed grouse (or prairie chickens as they are often called) in Wisconsin. Why? They are, biologically speaking, a prey species, but habitat destruction has endangered Wisconsin's species populations. The land ethic would not countenance much of the actual hunting that goes on in the United States of white-tailed deer, our paradigm case of a prey species, because few American hunters are skilled markspersons or would pass up the chance to shoot a deer when they could not be sure of killing it quickly and cleanly, and fewer still know the natural history of, or demonstrate a properly respectful attitude toward, their living targets. Further – and now to illustrate my present point – examined through the lens of the land ethic, even in Alaska or Siberia where the species populations are not endangered, hunting timber wolves is wrong because these animals are top carnivores in their biotic communities, and to treat them as if they were prey is not appropriate.

I feel the same way (and without knowing exactly why, so must many of my fellow Wisconsonians) about the proposal (perennially broached by wildlife managers and perennially rejected by an outraged citizenry) to open a hunting season on sandhill cranes in the Lake States.[41] Sandhill cranes were shot to near oblivion by several generations of Euro-American pioneers and their descendants east of the Mississippi River. The species population has recovered and cranes now trumpet over all the fields and woods near extensive wetlands in the upper Midwest. They could be hunted sustainably. But they should not be. Sandhill cranes mate for life, hatch only two eggs and rear only one offspring per season, spend several years as non-reproductive juveniles and can live to be nearly fifty years old.[42] They do not manifest the life history of a prey species.[43] To treat them as prey is not, therefore, appropriate.

Of course the drift of my argument should now be plain. The great whales have few natural enemies, and none that attack them from above the surface of the water. I have seen film footage of whale hunting on television (not of minke whales, but of one of the larger rorqual species, as I recall). When the catcher boat pulled along side the hapless victim, she did nothing to evade her fate. She was not wary and evasive like a deer. She just went on swimming at the same speed in the same direction until she was harpooned. Death did not come to her for many minutes. Whales nearby – lovers, relatives and friends of the stricken one – did not scatter in all directions to avoid being harpooned themselves, like caribou when a pack of wolves rush the herd and hamstring one of its members. The other whales swam around in distress and tried to help their mate, mother, sister or companion – making easy targets of themselves.

I am opposed to hunting sandhill cranes by anyone regardless of their cultural identity. Cranes do not manifest the life history of a prey species and for us human beings to treat them as such is, therefore, land-ethically wrong. I am even more opposed to whale hunting. The great whales are – even more demonstrably than cranes – not prey species. And, even if they were, we would not be among their proper predators, being aliens in pelagic environments. Therefore, for us to hunt whales is *more* land-ethically wrong – worse, if that is possible – than for us to hunt cranes.

But Both Orcas and the Old Norse Long Preyed on Minke Whales

The specific policy question here, however, is not whale hunting in general, but Norwegian minke whale hunting in particular. And, as a matter of fact, minke whales *are* a prey species, however long-lived (more than fifty years) and slow (six to eight years) to reach sexual maturity.[44] They are regularly attacked and eaten by orcas, especially in the Southern Hemisphere.[45] Furthermore, as already noted, people living on the western coast of Norway have trapped and killed minke whales that ventured into the fjords centuries before they mastered the craft of building seaworthy ships, which enabled them eventually to pursue whales far off-shore.[46]

What can be said in defence of the minke whales to this powerful argument?

First, if Norwegians argue that they are justified in killing and eating minke whales because orcas kill and eat minke whales, that would put them on a precipitous slippery slope sliding toward wholesale resumption of whaling, irrespective of species. Though orca attacks on bowheads, humpbacks, right, sei, fin and blue whales are not unknown, they are rare. These much larger baleen whales are virtually free of natural enemies. Will the Norwegians insist on resuming indiscriminate whaling if and when the populations of these species recover from the excessive slaughter of the recent past? Probably.

Indeed, the Norwegian government doubtless would argue that if the community of nations could tolerate a resumption of minke whale hunting in the 1990s, why resist hunting any species of whale in 2025? – or whenever population estimates indicate that a commercial harvest of presently endangered species can be sustained.

Second, a long Norwegian tradition of human predation on minke whales may not be long enough to matter land ethically. Though human beings living in Norway may have killed and eaten whales for a 'long time' by cultural or historical frames of temporal reference, human predation on minke whales is 'recent' by evolutionary frames of temporal reference. Unlike deer, minke whales have not had time to evolve defensive responses to a new (evolutionarily speaking) land-based predator. So, no matter how traditional, even venerable, the culture of minke-whale hunting may be in Norway, human beings are not co-evolved predators of minke whales as orcas are.

Third, there is another slippery slope to be wary of. If, standing upon a venerable tradition of whaling, the Norwegian government feels justified in flouting international agreements and allowing its citizens to kill the number of minke whales that it believes to be sustainable, surely the governments of Iceland, Russia, Portugal, Brazil, South Africa, Japan and all the other countries with a whaling 'tradition' will soon feel equally justified in doing the same thing. The number of minke whales killed annually by Norwegians may be sustainable. But what will happen to the global minke whale population when other governments, following Norway's lead, unilaterally allot their would-be whalers comparable numbers? At the bottom of this slippery slope lies a tragedy of the commons.

Fourth, though this is a strictly prudential, not a land-ethical argument, Norwegians might want to think about yet another slippery slope. Lawless behaviour begets lawless behaviour. Today nation states are asserting all sorts of claims based on culture and tradition, and acting on them in defiance of international conventions. By obdurately asserting a right on behalf of its citizens to kill minke whales, the Brundtland administration may be spending precious moral capital. The post-Cold War world is rife with nationalism and land-grabbing. Norway has not always been an independent state. Either Sweden or Denmark might in future decide to assert a right, based on tradition, to reclaim Norway. The chance of that happening seems remote, now. But a decade ago the chance that the Soviet Union would break up seemed, if anything, even more remote. The Norwegian government's defiance of the international moratorium on whaling contributes to the general breakdown of international law and order. And that would seem to be a most imprudent policy for a small and vulnerable country to pursue in an increasingly dangerous and capricious world.

THE MORAL COMMUNITY OF INTELLIGENT LIFE ON EARTH

Yes, whale hunting is land-ethically wrong, absolutely and categorically – even if the target species can sustain an annual commercial harvest and even if the whalers go about their grim work obsequiously. But killing whales is morally wrong for another reason that is not exactly land ethical.   The land ethic is a moral accretion beginning to take form in human culture correlatively with our recognition that we human beings are members of hierarchically ordered biotic communities no less than of hierarchically ordered conspecific communities. But we share another kind of community with whales. Orcas – killer whales – have been compared with wolves, the 'wolves of the sea'. They are top carnivores and hunt in pods, similar to wolves in this respect, who also hunt cooperatively, in packs.[47] When they're not feasting on minke whales, they prey mostly upon fish, birds, and non-cetacean marine mammals – pinnipeds, such as sea lions, walruses and seals. But is that the only or most illuminating comparison we might make? Perhaps a better comparison might be to our Stone Age ancestors who also hunted in bands and preyed mostly upon non-primate terrestrial animals – deer, antelope, bison and beaver. Wouldn't it be better to say that orcas are the 'people of the sea'?[48]

Why? Because the lifespan of an orca is more comparable to that of a human being; orca social behaviour appears to be more complicated than that of wolves; orca social vocalisations seem to convey more information than wolf howls – indeed, orcas seem to have evolved a system of communicative sounds as complex as human language, though we have as yet no way to comprehend it; and orca brains are large, indeed much larger than ours, and, like ours, they are richly fissured.[49]

But notice that many of these and similar things could be said about all the toothed whales and dolphins. And the really astonishing and morally relevant comparisons with ourselves – complex social organisation and relationship, information-rich vocal communication and large cerebral cortexes – are characteristic of many of the mysticeti as well as all the odontoceti. We human beings and the cetaceans are fellow-members of the global biotic community, and we are fellow mammals with few natural enemies. They are warm-blooded, live-birthing, long-lived, suckling, nurturing, playful, curious, learning beings inhabiting an element as alien from our own as any can be on Earth. But we also may share a fellowship with them of a much more sympathetic sort. We and the cetaceans may have evolved quite different, but equally expansive, mental lives. What do whales do with those big brains? We don't know. But brains such as theirs must have some grand, neocortical, brainy function. Else why would large, deeply convoluted cetacean neocortexes have evolved?[50]

With reaching arms and grasping hands, we human beings evolved a primarily practical, manipulative, problem-solving intelligence that is only secondarily reflective and speculative. As the cetaceans have no similar appendages, their intelligence, we may imagine, is primarily devoted to more philosophical and contemplative applications.[51] Here of course I'm going way out on a limb. How can we assess whale intelligence? More fundamentally, can we even meaningfully attribute 'intelligence' to whales?[52]

To answer the latter question first, one could so narrowly define 'intelligence' that only human beings can be said, properly, to have it. But, except for a few analytic philosophers, everyone seems to know what is meant when someone says that one dog is more intelligent than another or that on the whole specimens of one non-human species, say the elephant, are more intelligent than specimens of some other, say the giraffe. And now to answer the former question, we make comparative assessments of intelligence between and among species – just as we make them between and among ourselves – on the basis of performance. Everyone knows that the odontoceti are as intelligent as dogs and chimpanzees because they are famous for the wonderful 'tricks' they perform in aquaria.[53]

But that is not the kind of 'performance' or the kind of manifestation of intelligence to which I mean to call attention. We know empirically that whales utter quite complex and sophisticated vocal signals which we have not yet deciphered – nor may we ever be able to.[54] One well-known example is the annually changing 'song' of the humpbacks, which contains more bits of information than the *Iliad*.[55] Could the humpbacks' progressively developing, rhyming song be an epic history of their race? Could it articulate a dialectical cetacean metaphysic? These are questions no one can answer. But at the very least we can confidently believe that we share a select community-of-intelligent-life-on-Earth with whales and dolphins. There exists a cetacean mind in the waters as well as a human mind on the land. And membership in that community – the community of minding organisms – no less than in other communities, carries with it special ethical duties and obligations. After all, the whales seem to recognise us as fellow intelligent beings and assiduously refrain from harming us.[56] Shouldn't we, at the very least, reciprocate?

Wolves of the sea? People of the sea? Neither comparison really seems quite right. There is something altogether too precocious, too adolescent, too reckless about our human intelligence to dignify it by comparing it to the ancient intelligence of the cetaceans.[57] Here at last I think that I have sounded the depths of my aversion and disgust at the resumption of whaling. The cetaceans are the first super-intelligent species to have evolved on the planet, though 'intelligent' connotes something altogether too thin, too superficial for my meaning.[58] To look upon commercial whaling with approval seems to me to be like looking with approval on a horde of cunning but illiterate vandals looting and plundering the art galleries and libraries of an ancient and peaceful civilisation in the name of gathering fuel for cooking fires. Should we be killing beings who may be, for all we know, the most highly evolved form of intelligent life on the planet?[59]

BUT ARE WHALES REALLY SO SMART?

In *A Thousand Mile Walk to the Gulf,* John Muir notes that 'The fearfully good, the orthodox of this laborious patchwork of modern civilization cry "heresy" on everyone whose sympathies reach a single hair's breadth beyond the boundary epidermis of our own species.'[60] So one should not be surprised to find a few fearfully good modern mammologists and cetologists now crying 'heresy' on an earlier generation of scientists – such as John Lilly and Peter Morgane – who had the temerity to suggest that there may indeed be a mind in the waters that is equal in capacity, though very different in content, to the human mind on land. The defensive anthropocentrism of two guardians of orthodox opinion, D. E. Gaskin and Margaret Klinowska, is evident in their rhetoric and their sophistries.

As to rhetoric, Gaskin writes, 'Are we then in a position to draw some tentative conclusions about cetacean social structure, behaviour, communication and intelligence? There is a tendency for authors to continue *prevaricating*, suggesting that more and more information is needed before decisions can be made. I think that certain broad conclusions, however, *can* be drawn at this time.'[61] Here Gaskin labels a liar (in plain English) any scientist who has the humility to think that the current state of human knowledge about such extremely complex and difficult questions may be limited. According to Klinowska, belief that cetaceans are highly intelligent is a 'dogma' – suggesting that such a belief is a religious, not a scientific, tenet.[62]

As to sophistries (and sarcasm – to wit, 'sadly' in the following quotation), Gaskin observes that 'Studies to date of [cetacean] sound production do not, sadly, even begin to produce evidence of the existence of a "language" that parallels those of *Homo sapiens*, with their rich variety of syntax.'[63] He concludes that since cetaceans have no true (that is, anthropomorphic) language, they have no true (that is, anthropomorphic) intelligence. But no one who has noted that complex vocal communication exists among cetaceans suggests that such communication is structured by means of syntaxes similar to those of human languages. Stirling Bunnel, for example, points out that 'The cetacean auditory system is predominantly spatial [analog, in other words, rather than digital], like our eyesight, with much simultaneous information and poor temporal resolution. So dolphin language apparently consists of extremely complex sounds which are perceived as a unit.'[64] Correspondingly, cetacean intelligence may be comparably rich without being structurally parallel.

Klinowska's sophistries are more numerous. First she argues that gross brain size is a poor indicator of intelligence because – get this – the brains of extraordinarily intelligent human beings (such as Albert Einstein) proved to be no larger than those of ordinarily intelligent human beings. If, she argues to the same point, relative average brain size were indicative of relative average intelligence among various species, then the African elephant (brain weight = *circa* 7,500 grams), along with various kinds of cetaceans (sperm whale: *circa* 7,820 grams; fin whale: *circa* 6,930 grams; orca: *circa* 5,620 grams; bottlenose dolphin: *circa* 1,600 grams), would have to be regarded as more intelligent than *Homo sapiens* (*circa* 1,500 grams).[65] Just so.[66] However, we shouldn't correlate large absolute brain size with great mental capacity, Klinowska cautions, because 'it might be that large animals just need larger brains to control their larger bodies,' leaving little brain power over for non-somatic functions.[67] Since *Homo sapiens* scores the highest if intelligence is indicated by brain to body weight ratio, Klinowska is herself willing to entertain this correlation. The human brain averages 2.10 per cent of the human body weight, the bottlenose dolphin 0.94 per cent, the African elephant 0.15 per cent, the orca 0.09 per cent.[68] But subtract the more or less inert weight of blubber and bone, count only the organs and muscle tissue, and the relevant body weight of cetaceans is reduced dramatically. Consider, further, that cetaceans have no appendages and digits to control. How decisively then does the brain-to-body-weight-ratio argument undermine claims of cetacean intelligence?

Klinowska moves on from 'brain quantity' to 'brain quality' and cites studies indicating that cetacean brains lack one of six layers in the neocortexes of most 'higher' land mammals as well as the 'anatomical structural heterogeneity characteristic of more evolved brains such as those of primates'.[69] According to Klinowska 'this means that cetaceans have no true neocortex, or only a pre-neocortex. If a neocortex is really essential for the development of "intelligence," cetaceans are clearly disqualified.'[70]

It would be impossible here to compare Klinowska's claims against all the relevant literature on the arcane subject of cetacean neuroanatomy and neuro-physiology. Space, however, does permit cross checking Klinowska's conclusions against the recent research of one student of comparative neurology, Peter Morgane. Morgane's generosity of spirit is as indubitable as his scientific credibility. For in 1974 Morgane wrote, 'the enormous surface area of the whale cortex and its luxuriant and highly convoluted appearance still appear to be sound arguments for considering the Cetaceans as potentially intelligent and highly developed fellow beings.'[71] Does Morgane continue to think so?

The short answer is no. Histological studies of the cytoarchitecture of cetacean brains reveal:

> Poor transitional boundaries between architectonic areas, giving a sense of over-all monotony or homogeneity with a low degree of structural heterogeneity; only slight differentiation of cortical layers (weakly expressed stratification) and cells (poor neuronal differentiation); weak cellular specialization with predominance of simple, generalized neuronal forms over complicated forms [. . .] in other words, a general absence of diverse collections of neuronal families.[72]

Morgane (writing with Ilya Glezer) appears to agree, further, with those who regard the cetacean brain as pre-neocortical: 'In fact, the absence of Layer IV can be considered as a sign of intermediate-type cortex. This feature defines the neocortex of the dolphin as showing transitional type cortical features and, therefore, not reaching the highest developmental stage of neocortical organization' that appears in the mammalian carnivores and primates.[73] (By 'intermediate-type' and 'transitional' Morgane means intermediate between reptiles and mammals, and transitional from the one class to the other. Rather, the cetacean brain is more similar in structure to those of hedgehogs and bats. (Hedgehogs are 'survivors from the Eocene' and thus represent living fossils for comparison.)

But Morgane and Glezer add a scientific caveat that has decisive moral significance:

> Cetaceans are thought to have descended back to the sea some 50–70 million years ago. They adapted themselves to the new aquatic conditions and appear to have preserved characteristic features of the original structure of the brain of primitive mammals extant at that time in greater measure than land animals. *At the same time the cetaceans were in a new environment* conducive to developing specific features of brain adaptation not characteristic of mammals that remained on land.[74]

And what are those specific features? Unlike hedgehogs which have changed little since the Eocene, the contemporary cetacean brain has become very large. 'There is an extremely vigorous expansion of neocortex,' as Morgane and Glezer put it.[75] And what are the functions of the large structures in the aquatic mammalian brain

– however 'conservative' the cytoarchitecture – which followed a path of evolution different from that of land mammals? According to Morgane and Glezer, 'much of the massive development seen in cetacean neocortex may represent non-sensory areas and the significance of these vast expansions is unknown.'[76]

Klinowska tries to convince us that these vast expanses are in effect a garbage dump. Rapid eye movement during sleep is correlated with dreaming. And one theory of the function of dreams is clearing the sensory experience accumulated during the day from the brain's memory banks – sort of like deleting unimportant data from the hard-drive of a computer. According to Klinowska, 'Animals which cannot use this system need another way to avoid overloading the neural network, for example by having bigger brains.'[77] Cetaceans exhibit no rapid eye movement during sleep and hence *presumably* do not dream. 'So,' concludes Klinowska, 'following this line of argument dolphins would have to have big brains because they cannot dream.'[78]

Such a line of argument seems to be an almost desperate attempt to demean cetacean mental capacity. Morgane and Glezer, by contrast, exhibit a humility in the face of abject ignorance that is the mark of the true scientist:

> The effect of the aquatic medium on the neocortex is not clear, given the many resemblances between the dolphin neocortex and that of the bat and hedge-hog . . . The differences between the dolphin neocortex and that of hedgehogs and bats is not so much in the cortices that are directly comparable, i.e., the known sensory and motor areas, but is due to the fact that, as opposed to the hedgehog and bat neocortex, *the dolphin neocortex consists of vast cortical fields for which we have no ascribable functions.*[79]

So, should we follow Bunnel and ascribe contemplative functions to these vast cortical fields? Or should we follow Klinowska and ascribe waste storage functions to them? Morgane and Glezer respond with the appropriate scientific answer: 'Only future work can give possible answers to these intriguing questions.'[80]

And what about whaling in the meantime? And again, more especially, what about commercial minke whaling? Morgane and Glezer's study, cited here, is of the brains of small-toothed whales (bottlenose dolphin, harbour porpoise, striped dolphin, pilot whale and beluga whale). In Joseph Horwood's *Biology and Exploitation of the Minke Whale* there is no discussion of the minke whale brain – quantitatively or qualitatively. The minke is one of the least social of cetacean species, rarely found in groups of more than two or three individuals.[81] But from this even Lars Walløe – as earlier noted, Gro Harlem Brundtland's chief scientific adviser on whaling policy – is unwilling to conclude that the minke whale is therefore less intelligent than other species of whale.[82] Evidently, we are as ignorant about the mind of the minke whale as about that of any other cetacean species and know much less about the minke whale mind than about that of better studied species. Knowing so little about this creature, should we abandon it to the harpoon? Shouldn't we human beings, rather, give the minke whale, as well as all other cetacean species, the benefit of the doubt until we have more certain answers to fundamental questions about what sort of beings we are proposing to kill with so very little reason?

NOTES

1. John Wetlesen, letter, 15 March 1993.
2. John Darnton, 'Norwegians claim their whaling rights', *New York Times*, 6 August 1993, pp. 1 and 2.
3. Joseph Horwood, *Biology and Exploitation of the Minke Whale* (Boca Raton, FL: CRC Press, 1990).
4. The whaling industry did not react to the dangerously declining populations of preferred species in an enlightened way. According to Justin Cook, 'Introduction and overview', in Margaret Klinowska (ed.), *Dolphins, Porpoises and Whales of the World: The IUCN Red Data Book* (Gland: IUCN, 1991):

   > A major landmark year was 1974, when the IWC adopted a procedure to regulate whaling according to principles of sustainable utilization (IWC, 1976). The New Management Procedure (NMP) set out to manage each whale population separately. Populations depleted to below their level of maximum sustainable yield (MSY) were to be protected, while catches from populations above were limited so as not to deplete them below this level. *The NMP was introduced in response to outside pressure, including moves in the United Nations to call for a complete suspension of commercial whaling.* Although some of the major whaling nations voted against the introduction of the NMP, they abided by most of the catch limits set under the NMP in its first few years of operation. (p. 10, emphasis added)

   Cook cites 'Chairman's Report on the Twenty-Sixth Meeting', *Report of the International Whaling Commission* 26, 1976: 25–26. As a result of the NMP, the industry turned its attention to the minke whale.
5. Horwood, *Biology and Exploitation*.
6. J. Baird Callicott, 'Moral considerability and extraterrestrial life', in Eugene C. Hargrove (ed.), *Beyond Spaceship Earth: Environmental Ethics and the Solar System* (San Francisco: Sierra Club Books, 1986), pp. 227–59. Here, it may be worth noting, I write:

   > In the face of [the] giddy enthusiasm for communicating with 'intelligent life' on other planets, it is both sobering and irritating to observe that those involved in SETI, the search for extraterrestrial intelligence, have not first established – as a kind of preliminary benchmark or data base, so that they would have some idea of what communicating with an exotic intelligence would be like – communication with nonhuman forms of intelligent life on Earth. Cetaceans carry the biggest brains on this planet, with richly fissured cerebral cortexes . . . Like us, they are social animals. But they live in environments, relatively speaking, very different from ours. Hence, theirs is a world apart from ours, a terrestrial analog of an extraterrestrial environment. And they engage, apparently, in complex vocal communication, of which we to date understand not one word – or rather click, grunt, or whistle. (pp. 231–2)

   See also Holmes Rolston, III, *Environmental Ethics: Duties to and Values in the Natural World* (Philadelphia: Temple University Press, 1988).
7. G. A. Mchedlidze, *General Features of the Paleobiological Evolution of Cetacea*, anonymously translated from Russian for the Smithsonian Institution Libraries and the National Science Foundation (New Delhi: Amerind Publishing, 1984). The most ancient known fossil whales date from the Eocene, fifty million years ago.
8. Aldo Leopold, *A Sand County Almanac and Sketches Here and There* (New York: Oxford University Press, 1949), pp. 224–5.
9. Ibid., p. 204.
10. Ibid., p. 202.
11. Ibid., p. 203.
12. Ibid., p. 204, emphasis added.
13. Gro Harlem Brundtland, 'Whales and sustainable ocean management', *The Network*, April 1993; and Darnton, 'Norwegians claim'.
14. Leopold, *Sand County*, p. 211.
15. Kieran Mulvaney, 'Norway's whaling and Agenda 21', *The Network*, April 1993; and Darnton, 'Norwegians Claim'. According to Klinowska, *Dolphins, Porpoises and Whales*, p. 377, the International Whaling Commission's Scientific Committee estimates a Northeastern Atlantic population of some 80,000 minke whales, recalculated to an estimate of some

50,000. The Norwegian government, as reported by Darnton, assumes the accuracy of the former figure.

16. According to Cook, 'Introduction', this issue is taken quite seriously by credible conservationists: 'The World Conservation Strategy (IUCN/UNEP/WWF, 1980) states the view that commercial whaling should remain suspended until [among other conditions] the consequences for the ecosystems concerned of removing large portions of the whales' populations . . . can be predicted' (p. 10). Cook cites *World Conservation Strategy* (Gland: IUCN, 1980).

17. Leopold, *Sand County*, pp. 130–2.

18. George Small, 'Why man needs the whales', in Tom Wilkes (ed.), *Project Interspeak* (Portland, OR: Project Interspeak, 1979), pp. 17–18, offers the following ecological caveat:

> 70% of the oxygen added to the atmosphere each year comes from plankton in the sea. Serious damage to the world ocean therefore could endanger the entire atmosphere of the earth. During the last two decades man has killed so many of the large whales that four species have been rendered commercially as well as almost biologically extinct. These are the blue whale, the fin whale, the humpback, and the sei whale. Their population has been reduced from a total of several million to just a few thousand. Every one of those vanished millions of whales used to consume several hundred tons of a large species of zooplankton a year. That plankton now is undergoing a classic population explosion for want of a predator. What will be the effect on the oxygen-producing smaller plankton in the world ocean? What will be the effect on the color and reflectivity of vast areas of the oceans? What will be the effect on the average water temperature of the oceans, on its dissolved oxygen content, and subsequently on the earth's atmosphere? No one knows. (p. 17)

19. According to Cook, 'Introduction', 'the results of work by the IWC Scientific Committee to date suggest that successful management of cetacean populations may be achieved in the absence of a full understanding of the relevant ecological interactions' (p. 10).

20. Daniel B. Botkin, *Discordant Harmonies: A New Ecology for the Twenty-first Century* (New York: Oxford University Press, 1990), pp. 76–80.

21. Ibid., pp. 19–23.

22. Leopold, *Sand County*, pp. 137–38.

23. See ibid., pp. 62–5.

24. Paul W. Taylor, *Respect for Nature: A Theory of Environmental Ethics* (Princeton, NJ: Princeton University Press, 1986).

25. J. Baird Callicott, *In Defense of the Land Ethic: Essays in Environmental Philosophy* (Albany, NY: State University of New York Press, 1987).

26. Ibid.

27. Leopold, *Sand County*, p. 215.

28. Ibid., p. 107.

29. See Thomas W. Overholt and J. Baird Callicott, *Clothed-in-Fur and Other Tales: An Introduction to an Ojibwa World View* (Washington, DC: University Press of America, 1982).

30. As Cook, 'Introduction', explains:

> The current suspension of commercial whaling does not apply to 'aboriginal subsistence whaling to satisfy aboriginal subsistence need', for which the IWC continues to set catch limits. This type of whaling includes catches of bowhead whales off Alaska, catches of gray whales off the Arctic Siberian coast, and catches of fin and minke whales off Greenland. The IWC does not attempt to define what is meant by aboriginal subsistence whaling, but it also includes whaling on behalf of aboriginal people to cover cases where the vessels are not necessarily operated by aboriginal people. (p. 13)

31. Leopold, *Sand County*, p. 178.

32. Egil Ole Öen, '*Norwegian Penthrite Grenade for Minke Whales: hunting Trials with Prototypes of Penthrite Grenades in 1984 and results from 1984, 1985, and 1986 Seasons*,' paper for the Workshop on Humane Killing Methods, Glasgow, 20–23 June 1992.

33. Ibid., p. 9.

34. Öen, '*Norwegian Penthrite Grenade.*'

35. Darnton, 'Norwegians claim', p. 1.

36. Horwood, *Biology and Exploitation*, p. 151.

37. Öen, 'Norwegian Penthrite Grenade' reports 45.1 percent of the minke whales hit with the explosive harpoon specially developed for Norwegian minke whaling died 'instantly' (within ten seconds). For *all* whales in the sample (including those that died 'instantly' the median survival time was 1 minute 15 seconds and the mean survival time was 6 minutes 34 seconds. In an article entitled 'Whaling and emotions' printed in the 12 May 1993 morning issue of the Oslo newspaper *Aftenposten*, the authors (Svenn Conradi, Hans A. Eglund, Kåre Elgmork, Knut Kloster, Ivan Nötnes, and Vigger Ree) draw the following analogy. Hunting whales from boats is like hunting elephants from moving trucks with penthrite harpoons in which circumstances about half the elephants would live for five, ten, fifteen, thirty or forty-five minutes, pulling the truck after them, until they collapsed from exhaustion and agony. Such elephant hunting would be unacceptably inhumane to most people in Norway as elsewhere, they argue, and would be banned by law.
38. Rory Putman, *The Natural History of Deer* (Ithaca, NY: Comstock Publishing Associates, 1988).
39. José Ortega y Gasset, *Meditations on Hunting*, Trans. Howard B. Westcott (New York: Charles Scribner's Sons, 1972), p. 138.
40. See Paul Shepard, *The Tender Carnivore and the Sacred Game* (New York: Charles Scribner's Sons, 1973).
41. West of the Mississippi, I regret to say, sandhill cranes have been legally hunted in several states with a less enlightened citizenry, beginning in 1961, and in Mexico and western Canada.
42. Paul A. Johnsgard, *Cranes of the World* (Bloomington, IN: Indiana University Press, 1983).
43. Johnsgard, *Cranes of the World*, notes that:

    only about a quarter of the nonjuvenile population of cranes represents successfully breeding pairs, with the other 75 percent of adult birds either nonbreeders or unsuccessful breeders. Few if any other legally hunted game species in North America have such a low recruitment rate as this, and it poses serious and complex problems of management if cranes are to be legally hunted. (p. 38)

    He also notes that 'figures indicate an astonishingly high rate of first-year band recoveries for a species with a . . . very low natural mortality rate, and it is very possible that they reflect a serious degree of hunting overkill in sandhill cranes' (p. 40).
44. Joseph Horwood, *Biology and Exploitation*.
45. According to Horwood, *Biology and Exploitation*: 'Stomach contents have demonstrated the extent of this predator–prey relationship. From 49 stomachs, Shevchenko found that 84% had eaten minke whales . . . It shows that the frequency varies with location, but in some places that killer whales were feeding predominantly on minke whales' (p. 102). One wonders how this could be so, if it is also true that: 'A recent estimate, based on sighting data, of the number of killer whales in Antarctic Areas II to V (60' 7" W to 180' 7"), south of approximately 60' 7", is 200,000 [and] the estimated population of minke whales in the same area is 450,000' (p. 102). With only 2.25 minke whales per killer whale, it would seem that the latter would soon eat up the former, if the latter were indeed feeding 'predominantly' on the former.
46. Lars Walöe, personal communication. Wallöe, the chief scientific adviser of Gro Harlem Brundtland on the whaling issue, claims that this has been going on for 1,500 years.
47. Barbara C. Kirkevold and Joan S. Lockard (eds), *Behavioral Biology of Killer Whales* (New York: Alan R. Liss, 1986).
48. Randall L. Eaton, 'The view from Samish Flats', in *Project Interspeak*: 13–15 explicitly draws this comparison: 'The orca is to the ocean what man is to the land . . . Like man, orca rules its domain, or did until recently challenged by man. Man and the killer whale . . . are the two most formidable, successful, and intelligent social predators to live on earth' (p. 14).
49. Ibid.
50. Stirling Bunnell, 'The evolution of cetacean intelligence', in Joan McIntyre (ed.), *Mind in the Waters: A Book to Celebrate the Consciousness of Whales and Dolphins* (New York: Charles Scribner's Sons, 1974), pp. 52–9, observes, 'Though we know very little about what cetaceans do with their large brains, we can be sure that such impressive structures would not have evolved if they were not being used. They are highly organized and well-maintained systems, clearly not vestigial structures or non-adaptive systems' (p. 59).

51. Bunnell, ibid., also points out that 'The Cetaceans' system appears to be a more integrated and contemplative one, evolved in conditions where immediate danger was not so likely as it was for most mammals.'

52. Peter Morgane, 'The whale brain: the anatomical basis of intelligence', in McIntyre, *Mind in the Waters*, pp. 84–93, observes:
> It certainly would be presumptuous and naive to presume that at the present time we are able to measure the 'intelligence' or intellectual capacity of whales, and no serious student of brain function, to this writer's knowledge, makes such claims. In dealing with such nonmanipulators as whales, we have continued to be obsessed with the necessity of our own nature to search for an analogue of the hand and the manipulative ability. Clearly we should find a more general principle than merely 'handedness' and its use! . . . As [Loren] Eisley has so well stated, 'Man expresses himself upon his environment through the use of tools. We therefore tend to equate the use of tools in a one-to-one relationship to intelligence.' Is it not well to examine other possible modes of the expression of intelligence or intellectual capacity? (pp. 92–3)

53. Bunnell, 'Evolution of cetacean intelligence', notes:
> Extreme playfulness and humor are conspicuous in dolphins and may be found in whales also, although they are harder to observe. Despite its low status in puritanical value systems, play is a hallmark of intelligence and is indispensable for creativity and flexibility. Its marked development in cetaceans makes it likely that they will frolic with their minds as well as their bodies. (p. 58)

54. Jeanette A. Thomas and Ronald A. Kastelein (eds), *Sensory Abilities of Cetaceans: Laboratory and Field Evidence* (New York: Plenum Press, 1990).

55. Roger Payne and Scott McVay, 'Songs of humpback whales', *Science* 173, 1971: 583–97.

56. John C. Lilly, 'Communication between man and dolphin', in *Project Interspeak*: 7–11, claims that:
> The Cetacea realize that man is incredibly dangerous in concert. It is such considerations as these that may give rise to their behavioral ethic that the bodies of men are not to be injured or destroyed, even under extreme provocation. If whales and dolphins began to injure and kill humans in the water, I am sure that the Cetacea realize that our navies would then wipe them out totally, at a faster rate than the whaling industry is doing at the present time. (p. 11)

Randall L. Eaton, 'The view from Samish Flats', draws a similar conclusion from the remarkable fact that orcas, in contradistinction to sharks, do not attack *Homo sapiens*:
> Much of the orca's behavior and interaction with man suggest that orcas make sophisticated decisions and that they are surprisingly aware of us. For example, we believe orcas avoid killing people, even in defense of self or young, because they know that the long-term risks from harming humans are great. And, judging from human response to other dangerous predators, they would be right! Even an accidental killing of humans by orcas could mean wholesale slaughter for orcas. (p. 14)

57. Lilly, 'Communication between man and dolphin', notes:
> Paleontological evidence shows that the whales and the dolphins have been here on this planet a lot longer than has man. Dolphins (like the current *Tursiops*) have been here in the order of fifteen million years with brain sizes equal to and greater than that of modern man. Apparently some whale and dolphin brains became the equal of that of present-day man and then passed man's current size about thirty million years ago. Secure human skulls in large numbers with a cranial capacity equal to present man are found only as far back as one hundred and fifty thousand years. Thus we see that man is a still evolving latecomer to this planet. (p. 11)

And Bunnel, 'Evolution of cetacean intelligence', comments:
> It is interesting to reflect that Cetaceans reached this point [a brain size between that of *Australopithecus* and *Homo erectus*] perhaps thirty million years ago, while we got there only a million years ago, which in turn leads to the issue of whether this indicates anything as to the relative subtlety, complexity, and balance of mind between these two life-forms. (p. 55)

58. Joan McIntyre, 'On Awareness', in McIntyre, *Mind in the Waters*, pp. 69–70, prefers 'awareness' to 'intelligence'.

59. Similar ethical conclusions informed by similar observation are drawn by John Lilly, 'Communication between man and dolphin':

Those who believe that they are killing to provide huge reservoirs of flesh for industrial use rather than killing the largest, most sophisticated brains on the planet, somehow must change their beliefs; their killing must be prevented by giving the cetaceans the same legal protection as humans . . . Seventy-one percent of the surface of our planet is covered with oceans, inhabited by the Cetacea. Let us learn to live in harmony with that seventy-one percent of the planet and its intelligent, sensitive, sensible, and long-surviving species of dolphins, whales, and porpoises. (pp. 7 and 11)

And Peter Morgane, 'The whale brain':

It is unthinkable for us to sit idly by and let such unique beings wantonly be destroyed by selfish and short-sighted men. This is a resource and kinship that belongs to us all. Our very training and deepest feelings make us respect these wondrous creatures. Would that the brains of men could lead them to live in harmony with Nature instead of ruthlessly plundering the seas that nurtured us. (p. 93)

60. John Muir, *A Thousand Mile Walk to the Gulf*, ed. William Frederic Badè (Boston, MA: Houghton Mifflin, 1916), p. 139.
61. D. E. Gaskin, *The Ecology of Whales and Dolphins* (London: Heinemann, 1982), p. 151. The emphasis on 'prevaricating' is added; the emphasis on 'can' is in the original.
62. Margaret Klinowska, 'Brains, behavior, and intelligence in cetaceans (whales, dolphins, and porpoises)', in Fisheries Research Institute (eds), *Whales and Ethics* (Reykjavik: University of Iceland, 1992), p. 21.
63. Gaskin, *Ecology*, p. 152.
64. Bunnel, 'The evolution of cetacean intelligence', p. 58.
65. Klinowska, 'Brains, behavior, and intelligence', p. 21.
66. Bunnel, 'The evolution of cetacean intelligence', writes: 'While elephants have very large brains (thirteen pounds as compared to three pounds of *Homo sapiens*) and give evidence of considerable rational and conceptual ability, their communication systems appear to be much less elaborate than the ones which Cetaceans use' (p. 53). That may still be true, but in the meantime an ultrasonic 'elephant language' – a system of calls in a frequency range so low as to be inaudible to human ears – has been discovered. See Jane E. Brody, 'Picking up Mammals' deep notes', *New York Times*, 2 November 1993: B5–B6.
67. Ibid.
68. Ibid., p. 22.
69. Ibid., p. 23.
70. Ibid., p. 24.
71. Morgane, 'The whale brain', p. 89.
72. Peter Morgane and Ilya I. Glezer, 'Sensory neocortex in dolphin brain', in Jeanette A. Thomas and Ronald A. Kastelein (eds), *Sensory Abilities of Cetaceans: Laboratory and Field Evidence* (New York: Plenum Press, 1990), p. 131.
73. Ibid.: p. 120.
74. Ibid., p. 116, emphasis added.
75. Ibid., p. 118.
76. Ibid., p. 124.
77. Klinowska, 'Brains, behavior, and intelligence', p. 25.
78. Ibid.
79. Morgane and Glezer, 'Sensory neocortex', p. 132, emphasis added.
80. Ibid.
81. Horwood, *Biology and Exploitation*.
82. Letter from Jon Wetlesen, 10 October 1993.

10

ZOOS REVISITED

Dale Jamieson

The possibility of perpetual reinvention is deeply embedded in the American psyche. Waiters can become movie stars, gangsters can be transformed into respectable businessmen, and corrupt White House officials can return as fundamentalist preachers. One California governor, who signed the most liberal abortion law in the nation, became a fiercely born-again anti-abortionist; another former California governor, one of the leading political fund-raisers of his generation, ran for president on a platform that denounced political fund-raising as the root of all evil. Despite its attractions, reinvention is not always successful. In F. Scott Fitzgerald's *The Great Gatsby*, the title character emerges from a shady past to assume the life of a Long Island gentleman. Yet despite the trappings of wealth and power, his new identity is fragile. In the end he succumbs to his past.

In their drive to reinvent themselves American zoos are very American. Early zoos were explicitly meant to demonstrate and celebrate the domination of nature by man. They included all sorts of exotics, both human and non-human.[1] As the control of zoos moved from rich and powerful individuals to communities and governments, they increasingly were seen as sources of urban amusement. But in these enlightened times many zoo professionals no longer see amusement and entertainment as roles that are worthy of zoos. Indeed, in this spirit, the New York Zoological Society has abolished its zoos; however, wildlife conservation parks have risen, phoenix-like, to replace them. In their current reinvention zoos are being pitched as the last best hope for endangered wildlife. For advocates of zoos, as for Jay Gatsby, the past is evil but fortunately always behind us. The present is good, and the future promises to be even better – assuming the money holds out.

Critics of zoos rightly see this attitude as self-serving and disingenuous. Most zoos are still in the business of entertainment rather than species preservation. Despite protestations to the contrary, most zoos are still more or less random collections of animals kept under largely bad conditions. Although the best zoos have been concerned to position themselves as environmental heroes, they have done little to promote this ethic in the zoo industry as a whole. There are many bad exhibits and many bad zoos, but not much is being done to shut them down. Even the best zoos have problems with preventable mortality and morbidity due to accidents or abuse and are too often in league, wittingly or unwittingly, with people whose idea of a good animal is one that turns a quick profit. The rhetoric of science, favoured by the best people in the best zoos, has not yet penetrated the reality of most zoos and indeed carries with it new possibilities for abuse. Even now, with the bad old days presumably behind us, there is not much ground for complacency.

Still, it is clear that zoos are changing. They are becoming more naturalistic in environment, focusing more on species preservation and scientific research and less on entertainment. Zoos in the future, at least the better ones, will increasingly become more like parks.

Parks and preserves are changing as well. They are becoming more like zoos. In 1987 Kenya's Lake Nakuru National Park was completely fenced (Conway, 1990). It is only a matter of time until large East African mammals are managed in much the same way as domestic animals, as already has been suggested by the World Conservation Union (see Conway, 1995; Hutchins et al., 1995). This tendency toward management is also at work in the national parks in the USA.

What will become of wild nature in this proliferation of mini-parks or mega-zoos (Conway, 1990)? Wild nature may be done for. Human population growth remains out of control. The effects of human consumption and production are modifying fundamental planetary systems in what may be irreversible ways. We are probably already committed to a climate change that will have profound effects on both nature and human society. Extremely remote areas in the Arctic and Antarctic regions are suffering the effects of human-induced ozone depletion. Today no part of the planet is unaffected by human action. Nature may not yet be tamed, but she is no longer wild (McKibben, 1989). The evolution of every animal species, to some degree, is now affected by human action (Borza and Jamieson, 1990; Jamieson, 1990, 1992).

One of the most dramatic effects of human action is the epidemic of extinctions currently sweeping the earth. Increasingly zoos have attempted to position themselves as the guardians of wild nature, as the boy with his thumb in the dike trying to hold back the floodwaters. I do not believe that zoos can successfully play this role. Establishing genetic warehouses is not the same as preserving wild animals. Highly managed theme parks are not wild nature.

Although in the bad old days zoos may have made their contributions to extinction, they are not responsible for the current wave. Nor are they directly to blame for our pathetic response to it. What is to blame is the peculiar moral schizophrenia of a culture that drives a species to the edge of extinction and then romanticises the remnants. Until a species is on the brink of extinction it seems to have little claim on our moral sensibility.

Consider the northern spotted owl. Most people probably agree with the Denver newspaper, the *Rocky Mountain News*, which editorialised (16 March 1992) that loggers need jobs as much as the spotted owls need trees. This is what passes for a moderate position, carefully balancing the unsustainable lifestyle of a few thousand humans against the very existence of another form of life. Once the owl is extinct or a few stragglers have been moved indoors, people will sing a different song. No steps will be too extreme to save this endangered species.

In the bad old days I published a paper with the subtle, highly nuanced title 'Against zoos' (Jamieson, 1985). For my effort I was virtually accused of child abuse by a local television station. Its correspondents interviewed children visiting the Denver Zoo, eliciting their reactions to some pointy-headed philosopher who wanted to take their fun away. The responses were predictable. A column in the *Chicago Tribune* (28 April 1991) said that my ideas were so absurd that 'only an intellectual could believe them.' No less a journal than *Time Magazine* (24 June 1991) called me a 'zoophobe' and suggested that I am indifferent to the fate of endangered species.

What I tried to do in that much-maligned paper was to set forth as rationally as possible the case against zoos. I examined the arguments that have been given on their behalf: that they provide amusement, education, opportunities for scientific research and help in preserving species. I saw some merit in each argument, but in the end I concluded that these benefits were outweighed by the moral presumption against keeping animals in captivity. I also claimed that despite the best intentions of zoo personnel, the profound message of zoos is that it is permissible for humans to dominate animals, for the entire experience of a zoo is framed by the fact of captivity.

Serious people have taken issue with my claims and arguments (see, for example, Chiszar et al., 1990; Hutchins et al., 1995). Because some of my critics place more weight on the role of zoos in preserving endangered species than I do, I want to discuss that issue in some detail. However, I first want to reconsider whether there is a presumption against keeping animals in captivity, since this claim is foundational to my argument against zoos.[2]

IS THERE A PRESUMPTION AGAINST KEEPING ANIMALS IN CAPTIVITY?

In my 1985 paper I argued that there is a presumption against keeping animals in captivity. My argument was rather intuitive. Keeping animals in captivity usually involves restricting their liberty in ways that deny them many goods including gathering their own food, developing their own social orders and generally behaving in ways that are natural to them. In the case of many animals captivity also involves removing them from their native habitats and conditions. If animals have any moral standing at all, then it is plausible to suppose that depriving them of liberty is presumptively wrong, since an interest in liberty is central to most creatures that matter morally.

My claim that there is such a presumption has recently been challenged (Leahy, 1991). If Leahy is correct in thinking that there is no such presumption, then there is no general reason for being opposed to zoos. The acceptability of keeping animals in captivity would turn entirely on a case-by-case examination of the conditions under which various animals are kept. Before considering Leahy's arguments against this presumption, let us first consider the view to which he is committed.

The idea that there is a presumption against keeping animals in captivity implies that it is not a matter of moral indifference whether animals are kept captive. But it carries no implication about how strong the presumption is. People who agree that there is a presumption against keeping animals in captivity can disagree about the strength of the presumption or about whether it is permissible to keep an animal in captivity in a particular case. What Leahy is committed to is the view that, everything else being equal, it is a matter of moral indifference as to whether animals are kept in captivity; we might as well flip a coin. I believe that this view is implausible.

Although it is difficult to perform this thought experiment, imagine that we could guarantee the same or better quality of life for an animal in a zoo that the animal would enjoy in the wild. Suppose further that there are no additional benefits to humans or animals that would be gained by keeping the animal in captivity. The only difference between these two cases that might be relevant is that in one case the animal is confined to a zoo and in the other case the animal is free to pursue its own life. Would we say that the fact of confinement is a morally relevant consideration? I believe that most people would say that it is, and that it would be morally preferable for the animal to be free rather than captive. In my opinion this shows that most of us believe that there is a moral presumption against keeping animals in captivity. That we believe that there is such a presumption is indicated in various ways. For example, sometimes it is said that keeping an animal in captivity is a privilege that involves assuming special obligations for the animal's welfare. This expresses the sense, I believe, that in confining an animal we are in some way wronging it, and thus owe it some compensation.

With this result in mind, let us consider Leahy's arguments. He appears to offer two. The first (following Hediger, 1964) involves the claim that animals are not truly free in the wild. They are constrained by ecological and social pressures and are 'struck down by natural predators and diseases which, quite reasonably, can be said to limit their freedom' (Leahy, 1991: 242). Since animals are not truly free in the wild, keeping them in captivity does not deprive them of liberty. The second argument is a conceptual one. According to Leahy, animals do not have language and are not self-conscious; therefore they cannot make choices or raise objections. Since they cannot make choices or raise objections, they cannot be said to live their own lives. Since they cannot live their own lives, they can never really be free. Since animals can never really be free, confining them in zoos does not deprive them of their freedom.

The first argument is intended to show that as a matter of fact animals are not free in their natural habitats while the second argument is intended to show that animals can never be free under any circumstances. There is no presumption against keeping them in captivity because in neither case does captivity deprive them of something that they have in the wild.

We should see first that these arguments do not really question the view that there is a presumption against depriving animals of liberty. What these arguments are supposed to show is that animals do not or cannot have liberty, thus they are not deprived of it by captivity. If it could be shown that animals do have liberty in the wild but not in captivity, then Leahy might agree that there is a presumption against keeping animals in captivity on grounds that it deprives them of liberty. At least he has said nothing that counts against this view.

The core of the issue, then, is the plausibility of the commonsense view that animals lose their liberty when they are removed from the wild and kept in zoos. I affirm the commonsense view; Leahy denies it. Who is right?

Consider Leahy's second argument first. Two steps in the argument that invite objection are these: the claim that animals are not self-conscious, and the claim that self-consciousness or language is required for making choices.

The topic of self-consciousness is a difficult one. Philosophers and psychologists often use this concept in different ways. One approach, characteristic of Descartes and much of the philosophical tradition, associates self-consciousness with the ability to use language or other complex symbol systems. But even if it were agreed that the use of complex symbol systems is required for self-consciousness, it would appear that various primates and cetaceans satisfy this criterion and thus would be excluded from the scope of Leahy's conclusion (Herman and Morrel-Samuels, 1990; Savage-Rumbaugh and Brakke, 1990). For those animals who use complex symbol systems, Leahy would have no argument for supposing that they are not free in the wild. Thus with respect to those animals at least, my claim that there is a presumption in favour of liberty would appear to survive unscathed. A second approach, characteristic of work in cognitive ethology, regards attributions of self-consciousness as underwritten by such factors as behaviour, evolutionary continuity and structural similarity. Researchers have argued that a wide range of behaviours in a variety of animals involve self-consciousness, including social play, deception and vigilance (Mitchell and Thompson, 1986; Byrne and Whiten, 1988; Griffin, 1992; Jamieson and Bekoff, 1993). Whichever approach is adopted, the claim that only humans are self-conscious appears doubtful.

The second dubious step in this argument involves the claim that self-consciousness is required for making choices. The philosopher's paradigm of choice may involve listing alternatives on a yellow pad with the pros and cons of each fully described in the margins, but this is only one way of making choices. Many of our choices are made without explicitly representing alternatives and totting up pluses and minuses – for example, when we choose coffee rather than tea, hit the brake rather than the gas, or immediately agree to give a lecture in Iowa in response to a telephone call. In these kinds of cases it is hard to see exactly how self-consciousness is supposed to be involved. Moreover, important work on animal behaviour has purported to address such topics as mate choice (Bateson, 1983), habitat choice (Rosenzweig, 1990), and the choice of nest sites (Bekoff et al., 1989). For the most part this work has been done without presupposing that animals are self-conscious. It may be that these researchers misuse the term 'choice' or are simply wrong in supposing that animals make choices in these situations. However, I believe that it is more plausible to suppose that it is Leahy's claim that is false and that self-consciousness is not required for choice. Since at least two steps in Leahy's second argument appear dubious, it is plausible to suppose that the argument fails.

Leahy's first argument attempts to show not that animals cannot be free under any conditions but that as a matter of fact they are not free in the wild. The idea is that if they are not free in the wild, then they lose nothing when they are confined in zoos. The evidence for the claim that animals are not free in the wild is that they are constrained by ecological and social pressures and are struck down by natural predators and disease.

If pointing to ecological and social pressures were sufficient for showing that an animal is not free, it would prove too much, for all organisms, including humans, are constrained by ecological and social pressures. The most that this claim could establish is that social and ecological pressures restrict animals to such an extent that they are more free in captivity than they are in the wild.

Are animals more free in zoos than in the wild? On the face of it, this claim is wildly implausible. It is like saying that humans are more free in prison than on the street because they are not subject to the same pressures as people on the street. The argument seems to overlook the fact that social pressures exist in zoos as well as in the wild, and in many cases such pressures are more intense in zoos because individuals are inhibited from responding to them in the ways in which they would in the wild. But more important, even if it could be shown that caged animals, whether human or non-human, live longer than those who are uncaged, this would not provide evidence for the claim about freedom. Nor could the claim be established by showing that caged animals are happier than uncaged animals. Liberty is not the same as longevity or happiness, nor does it always manifest in these ways. Moreover, there is very little evidence for supposing that captive animals live longer or are happier in zoos than they are in the wild. It seems plain that most animals have less freedom in zoos than in the wild. Indeed, the very point of systems of confinement is to deprive them of freedom.

For reasons that I have given it seems to me that Leahy's arguments fail. The commonsense position, that everything else being equal it is better for animals to be free, is vindicated. However, there is another line of argument that might be thought to be more challenging than those pursued thus far. It might be granted that there is a presumption of liberty with respect to animals who are born in the wild, but denied that there is any such presumption with respect to those who are born in captivity. It might be argued that captive-bred animals have never known freedom, so they are denied nothing by captivity.

In my view there is a presumption in favour of liberty with respect to all animals, whether bred in captivity or in the wild. Imagine humans who have never known liberty. Would it be plausible to deny that there is a presumption of liberty for them on the grounds that they do not miss what they have never known? An affirmative answer would be absurd. Indeed, we might think that the tragedy of their captivity is all the greater because they have never known liberty. Transferring these intuitions to non-human animals, we can see that there is a presumption in favour of liberty even with respect to animals born in captivity. Indeed, the presumption may even be stronger in their case. Still, some people would argue against this presumption, pointing out that many animals bred in captivity would not survive liberation, despite attempts at preparation. Their lives in nature would be nasty, brutish and short. Even if this is true it fails to show that there is no presumption in favour of liberty for these animals. At most it shows that in these cases the presumption in favour of liberty is outweighed by concerns about the welfare of these animals. The presumption for liberty exists, but it may be wrong to release these animals into the wild.

What I have argued in this section is that a basic claim of my 1985 paper, that there is a presumption in favour of liberty for animals, still stands. The burden of proof rests on those who would confine animals in zoos. The most compelling reason for confining animals in zoos, in some people's eyes, is the need to preserve endangered species. It is to this justification that I now turn.[3]

CAN ZOOS PRESERVE ENDANGERED SPECIES?

There are a number of arguments against zoos as meaningful sites for preserving endangered species. First, such preservation is needed, it is rightly pointed out, because we are losing species at an enormous rate. But although estimates differ and not all the facts are known, it is obvious that not more than a tiny fraction of these species can be preserved in zoos. Ehrlich and Ehrlich estimate that American zoos could preserve about one hundred mammals under the best conditions (1981: 211). Second, only a small number of the species preserved in zoos could ever be reintroduced into their natural habitats. Indeed most attempts at reintroduction have failed (Beck, 1995). For many species, zoos are likely to be the last stop on the way to extinction. Finally, over many generations the genetic structure and behaviour of captive populations change. Captivity substitutes selection pressures imposed by humans, either intentionally or inadvertently, for those of an animal's natural habitat. Indeed, under some definitions of domestication, confining animals in zoos and breeding them in captivity transforms them into domesticated animals (see, for example, Rodd, 1990: 113; Clutton-Brock, 1992; but see also Norton, 1995). Whether we count zoo animals as domesticated or not, it is clear that in fifty, one hundred, or a thousand years we may not have the same animal that was placed in captivity, much less the animal that would have existed had it evolved in nature. Taken together these arguments show that the role that captive breeding and reintroduction can play in the preservation of endangered species is at best marginal. Thus the benefit of preservation is not significant enough to overcome the presumption against depriving an animal of its liberty.

Against arguments such as these (Jamieson, 1985; Varner and Monroe, 1991), it is sometimes objected that they are entirely hypothetical. Where are the data? it is sometimes asked, and then we hear anecdotes about species that have been saved by captive breeding programme. Such arguments are made against Varner and Monroe by Hutchins and Wemmer, who go on to assert that 'there are many problems facing captive breeding and reintroduction programs, but they are not insurmountable' (1991: 10). But how do they know that? Where are the data that show that such problems are not insurmountable? Is this a scientific statement or the expression of a quasi-religious faith in the idea that humans have the ability to technofix everything, even the threatened extinction of other species?[4]

The point is that demands for data can be made by either party to the dispute. The fact is that there are anecdotes on both sides, qualitative material that different people evaluate in different ways, but very little that looks like hard data. The sceptic about captive breeding programme will say that the defender of zoos has the burden to show that such programme really can be successful. If there is a presumption against keeping animals in captivity, then it is wrong to do so unless a case can be made that the benefits outweigh this presumption. From the perspective of a sceptic, an inconclusive argument on this point is one that the sceptic wins.

Defenders of zoos say that the burden is on the other side, for captive breeding keeps options open. True enough. We ought to keep options open, not only for ourselves but for future people as well. But at what cost? Unless the presumption that animals should not be kept in captivity can be overcome by the moral case for keeping options open, this observation does not carry much weight. It certainly does not establish a burden of proof.

There is another dimension to this dispute. The critics of zoos point out that breeding and reintroduction programme can be extremely invasive, involving not just denials of liberty but sometimes pain and suffering for individuals. Defenders of zoos sometimes say that this suffering is for the good of the species. This is the manoeuvre that in my 1985 paper I called sacrificing the interests of the lower-case gorilla for those of the upper-case Gorilla.

There is a lot of confusion about the concept of species and its proper role in our biological and moral thinking (Ereshefsky, 1992; Hargrove, 1992). Yet law, policy and common morality take the concept very seriously. An animal that is part of an endangered species may have millions spent to protect it, but if it is a member of an endangered subspecies or a hybrid it may be exterminated as a pest. Some of these issues are explored by May (1990), O'Brien and Mayr (1991), Vane-Wright et al. (1991), Geist (1992) and Rojas (1992).

One confusion in our biological thinking concerns the relation between variability and species diversity. Species diversity is one kind of variability but not the only kind. Within most species there is an enormous amount of variability – think of dogs or coyotes, for example (Bekoff and Wells, 1986). The evolutionary story requires variability, but it is not clear that it requires a very strong conception of species. Dawkins writes that '"the species" [is] an arbitrary stretch of continuously flowing river, with no particular reason to draw lines delimiting its beginning and end' (1986: 264). Darwin himself was quite conventionalist about the concept of species, writing that 'I look at the term species, as one arbitrarily given for the sake of convenience to a set of individuals closely resembling one another' (Darwin, 1958: 67). The demotion of the concept of species from the exalted role that it played in Aristotelian biology was one consequence of the Darwinian revolution. Like other consequences of the Darwinian revolution, we are still struggling to grasp its full significance (Dewey, 1910; Rachels, 1990).

Variability is important to us as well as to the evolutionary process. We value variability, but just as we often focus on the charismatic mega-fauna and overlook other creatures that are as important to nature, so we often fix on species variability as the only kind of diversity that matters. We compound the problem when we think that it is species to which we have obligations rather than the creatures themselves. This is an instance of the general fallacy of attributing to species the properties of individual creatures. Individual creatures have hearts and lungs; species do not. Individual creatures often have welfares, but species never do. The notion of a species is an abstraction; the idea of its welfare is a human construction. While there is something that it is like to be an animal there is nothing that it is like to be a species.

I am a Darwinian about the concept of species, but I am not callous about the survival of nature. I am as concerned about saving wild nature as any defender of zoo breeding programmes. But I believe that the only hope for doing this is to put large tracts of the earth's surface off-limits to human beings and to alter radically our present lifestyles.[5] I agree with Ehrenfeld that 'the true prospects for conservation ultimately depend not on the conservation manipulations of scientists but on the overarching consideration of how many people there will be in the world in the next century, the way they live, and the ways in which they come to regard and use nature' (1991: 39).

I believe further that attempts at preserving wild nature through zoo breeding programmes are a cruel hoax. If zoo breeding programmes are successful they will not preserve species but rather transform animals into exhibits in a living museum. 'This is what used to exist in the wild,' we can say to our children while pointing at some rare creature alienated from its environment, 'before the K-Mart and the biotechnology factory went in.' Zoo professionals like to say that they are the Noahs of the modern world and that zoos are their arks. But Noah found a place to land his animals where they could thrive and multiply. If zoos are like arks, then rare animals are like passengers on a voyage of the damned, never to find a port that will let them dock or a land in which they can live their lives in peace and freedom. If we are serious about preserving wild nature we must preserve the land, and not pretend that we can bring nature indoors.

In my darker moments I believe, not just that zoos are in the business of perpetuating fraud with their rhetoric about preserving animals, but that, knowingly or not, they are deeply implicated in causing the problem that they purport to be addressing. Zoo professionals are often eager to remove animals from the wild to more controlled environments where they can be studied. But as more and more animals are taken out of the wild, the case for preserving wild nature erodes. Why save a habitat if there is nothing to inhabit it? Advocates of zoos like to point out that they are not just in the business of removing animals from the wild, but increasingly they are also involved in trying to preserve animals in nature as well. Although zoos boast of their programmes in the developing world, very few can withstand scrutiny.[6] The truth is that very few zoos make meaningful attempts to preserve animals in nature, and most zoos spend more on publicity and public relations than they do on animals. This is especially appalling because in many cases programmes to perserve animals in situ are relatively cheap. For example, the Bonobo Protection Fund estimates that the bonobo population in Zaire could be effectively protected for an initial investment of $185,000 and $60,000 per year thereafter. This is a small amount to spend for the protection of the rarest of ape species.

In my opinion we should have the honesty to recognise that zoos are for us rather than for the animals. Perhaps they do something to alleviate our sense of guilt for what we are doing to the planet, but they do little to help the animals we are driving to extinction. Our feeble attempts at preservation are a matter of our own interests, values and preoccupations rather than acts of generosity toward those animals whom we destroy and then try to save. In so far as zoos distract us from the truth about ourselves and what we are doing to nature, they are part of the problem rather than part of the solution.

SUMMARY AND CONCLUSIONS

Much of what I have said may sound like an aggravating stew of idealism and curmudgeonliness. Hutchins and Wemmer speak for many people when they say that philosophers seem 'more concerned with logical arguments than with practical solutions to real problems' (1991: 5). Although I wish non-philosophers were more concerned with logical arguments, I sympathise with their sentiments. It is a fact that despite the arguments that I and others have given, zoos are not going to go away. It is easier to try to change large institutions that are adept at fund-raising than it is to abolish them. At any rate we are responsible for the lives of a great many animals, and more are being bred all the time. Given that zoos exist, there is a great difference between good ones and bad ones. I would like to close by expressing some of my hopes and fears about how zoos may develop in the future.

As I have already said, the best zoos in the future will be increasingly indistinguishable from small parks. The conditions under which animals will be kept for breeding purposes and scientific study will be naturalistic. While the idea of a *naturalistic* environment should not be confused with a *natural* environment, it is clear that human-designed naturalistic environments rule out some of the worst of the abuses to which captive animals traditionally have been subject. For example, naturalistic environments would not permit animals to be constantly observed by hundreds of small boys who feed them Cracker Jacks and hurl various objects at them. This obviously would be an improvement over many exhibits that exist today.

In my opinion there will be increasing tension between what zoos do to gain public support (entertain) and what they must do in order to justify themselves (preserve species). This tension will emerge within zoos as those who are interested in animals and science will increasingly come into conflict with those whose charge is budgets and public relations. This conflict already prevents zoos from being as good as they can be, and it will become more pronounced in the future. This is a fear.

One hope that I have for the future is that we will recognise that if we keep animals in captivity, then what we owe them is everything. Whatever else we may believe about the morality of zoos, I hope we can come to a consensus that these animals are in our custody through no wish or fault of their own. They are refugees from a holocaust that humans have unleashed against nature. There should be no question of culling these animals or trading off their interests against those of humans. If we are to keep animals in captivity, then we must conform to the highest standards of treatment and respect.

My hope is that zoo professionals will accept this principle and that an enlightened and aggressive public will keep them to it, for the animals themselves have no voice in human affairs, and as nature recedes their voices become ever more silent.

ACKNOWLEDGEMENTS

This is a slightly revised version of a paper that first appeared in Norton *et al.* (1995). I gratefully acknowledge the Smithsonian Institution Press for permission to reprint much of this article. I also thank Tim Chappell for his useful comments on the previous version. Over the years I have learned a great deal about various topics touched on in this paper from Marc Bekoff, Anna Goebbel, Sue Townsend and John Wortman, and Don Lindburg has been an intellectual and moral inspiration. Despite my debts to these people, I alone am responsible for the views that I have expressed.

NOTES

1. For a moving account of an African Pygmy who was confined to the New York City Zoo, see Bradford and Bloom (1992).
2. Although I prefer to avoid the language of rights, my work on zoos has been greatly influenced by Rachels (1976). For a good discussion of the concept of freedom, see Taylor (1986: 105–11). It should also be noted that for the purposes of this essay I use the terms 'liberty' and 'freedom' interchangeably.
3. In a recent book Bostock agrees that there is a presumption against keeping animals in captivity, but claims that 'we can go a long way towards providing good conditions in zoos' (1993: 50). For the presumption to be overcome, however, it must be shown that the benefits of confining animals in zoos are greater than the burdens. This is not established by speculative claims about the possibility of creating good conditions for animals in zoos.
4. Proponents of zoos seem especially given to making unsubstantiated, sweeping claims. Wolfe attacks my 1985 paper for failing to consider 'that one function of zoos may be to help children make symbolic sense of the world around them.' He then goes on to conclude, 'Children learn to use their powers of fantasy and imagination – to love animals – by going to the zoo. Strip them of this rich source of their interpretive life and, as adults, they will likely be more unfeeling, not less' (Wolfe, 1991: 116–17). This is all very nice, high-minded rhetoric, and may even be true. But what I claimed in my 1985 paper is that there are very few data to support the educational claims that are made on behalf of zoos. Whether zoos indeed have the uplifting effects on children claimed by Wolfe is an empirical question. I ask again: where are the data?
5. For this reason I endorse the general concepts put forward by the Wildlands Project, PO Box 5365, Tucson, Arizona 85703.
6. *Newsweek*, 12 April 1993 documents the ineffectiveness and corruption of various programmes to save endangered species, several of them involving major zoos. For a case study, see Schaller (1993).

REFERENCES

Bateson, P. (1983) *Mate Choice* (New York: Cambridge University Press).
Beck, B. (1995) 'Reintroduction: zoos, conservation, and animal welfare', in B. Norton, M. Hutchins, E. Stevens and T. Maple (eds), *Ethics on the Ark* (Washington, DC: The Smithsonian Institution Press), pp. 155–63.
Bekoff, M., Scott, A. and Connor, D. (1989) 'Ecological analyses of nesting success in evening grosbeaks', *Ecologia* 81: 67–74.
Bekoff, M. and Wells, M. (1986) 'Social ecology and behavior of coyotes', *Advances in the Study of Behavior* 16: 251–338.

Borza, K. and Jamieson, D. (1990) *Global Change and Biodiversity Loss: Some Impediments to Response* (Boulder, CO: Center for Space and Geosciences Policy, University of Colorado).

Bostock, S. (1993) *Zoos and Animal Rights* (London: Routledge).

Bradford, P. and Bloom, H. (1992) *Ota Benga: The Pygmy in the Zoo* (New York: St Martin's Press).

Byrne, R. and Whiten, A. (eds) (1988) *Machiavellian Intelligence: Social Expertise and the Evolution of Intellect in Monkeys, Apes, and Humans* (Oxford: Oxford University Press).

Chiszar, D., Murphy, J. B. and Iliff, W. (1990) 'For zoos', *Psychological Record* 40: 3–13.

Clutton-Brock, J. (1992) 'How the beasts were tamed', *New Scientist*, 15 February, pp. 41–3.

Conway, W. (1990) *Miniparks and Megazoos: From Protecting Ecosystems to Saving Species*, Thomas Hall Lecture, presented at Washington University, St Louis.

Darwin, C. (1958) *The Origin of Species* (New York: Penguin).

Dawkins, R. (1986) *The Blind Watchmaker* (New York: Norton).

Dewey, J. (1910) *The Influence of Darwinism on Philosophy and Other Essays in Contemporary Thought* (New York: Henry Holt).

Ehrenfeld, D. (1991) 'The management of diversity', in F. Borman and S. Kellert (eds), *Ecology, Economics, Ethics: The Broken Circle* (New Haven, CT: Yale University Press).

Ehrlich, P. and Ehrlich, A. (1981) *Extinction: The Causes and Consequences of the Disappearance of Species* (New York: Random House).

Ereshefsky, M. (ed.) (1992) *The Units of Evolution: Essays on the Nature of Species* (Cambridge, MA: MIT Press).

Geist, V. (1992) 'Endangered species and the law', *Nature* 357: 274–6.

Griffin, D. (1992) *Animal Minds* (Chicago: University of Chicago Press).

Hargrove, E. (ed.) (1992) *The Animal Rights, Environmental Ethics Debate: The Environmental Perspective* (Albany, NY: SUNY Press).

Hediger, H. (1964) *Wild Animals in Captivity* (New York: Dover).

Herman, L. and Morrel-Samuels, P. (1990) 'Knowledge acquisition and asymmetry between language comprehension and production: dolphins and apes as general models for animals', in M. Bekoff and D. Jamieson (eds), *Interpretation and Explanation in the Study of Animal Behavior. Vol. 1: Interpretation, Intentionality, and Communication* (Boulder, CO: Westview Press), pp. 283–312.

Hutchins, M. and Wemmer, C. (1991) 'Response: in defense of captive breeding', *Endangered Species Update* 8: 5–6.

Hutchins, M., Dresser, B. and Wemmer, C. (1991) 'Ethical considerations in zoo and aquarium research', in B. Norton, M. Hutchins, E. Stevens and T. Maple (eds), *Ethics on the Ark* (Washington, DC: The Smithsonian Institution Press), pp. 253–76.

Jamieson, D. (1985) 'Against zoos', in P. Singer (ed.), *In Defense of Animals* (New York: Harper & Row), pp. 108–17.

Jamieson, D. (1990) 'Managing the future: public policy, scientific uncertainty, and global warming', in D. Scherer (ed.), *Upstream/Downstream: Essays in Environmental Ethics* (Philadelphia: Temple University Press), pp. 67–89.

Jamieson, D. (1992) 'Ethics, public policy, and global warming', *Science, Technology, and Human Values* 17: 139–53.

Jamieson, D. and Bekoff, M. (1993) 'On aims and methods in cognitive ethology', in D. Hull, M. Forbes and K. Okruhlik (eds), *PSA 1992*, Vol. 2 (Lansing, MI: Philosophy of Science Association); reprinted in M. Bekoff and D. Jamieson (eds), *Readings in Animal Cognition* (Cambridge, MA: MIT Press), pp. 65–78.

Leahy, M. (1991) *Against Liberation: Putting Animals in Perspective* (New York: Routledge).

McKibben, B. (1989) The End of Nature (New York: Random House).

May, R. (1990) 'Taxonomy as destiny', *Nature* 347: 129–30.

Mitchell, R. and Thompson, N. (eds) (1986) *Deception: Perspectives on Human and Nonhuman Deceit* (Albany, NY: SUNY Press).

Norton, B. (1995) 'Caring for nature: a broader look at animal stewardship', in B. Norton, M. Hutchins, E. Stevens and T. Maple (eds), *Ethics on the Ark* (Washington, DC: The Smithsonian Institution Press), pp. 102–21.

Norton, B., Hutchins, M., Stevens, E. and Maple, T. (eds) (1995) *Ethics on the Ark: Animal Welfare and Wildlife Conservation* (Washington, DC: The Smithsonian Institution Press).

O'Brien, S. J. and Mayr, E. (1991) 'Bureaucratic mischief: recognizing endangered species and subspecies', *Science* 251: 1187–8.

Rachels, J. (1976) 'Do animals have a right to liberty?', in T. Regan and P. Singer (eds), *Animal Rights and Human Obligations* (Englewood Cliffs, NJ: Prentice Hall).

Rachels, J. (1990) *Created from Animals: The Moral Implications of Darwinism* (New York: Oxford University Press).

Rodd, R. (1990) *Biology, Ethics, and Animals* (Oxford: Oxford University Press).

Rojas, M. (1992) 'The species problem and conservation: what are we protecting?', *Conservation Biology* 6: 170–8.

Rosenzweig, M. (1990) 'Do animals choose habitats?', in M. Bekoff and D. Jamieson (eds), *Interpretation and Explanation in the Study of Animal Behavior. Vol. 1: Interpretation, Intentionality, and Communication* (Boulder, CO: Westview Press).

Savage-Rumbaugh, S. and Brakke, K. (1990) 'Animal language: methodological and interpretive issues', in M. Bekoff and D. Jamieson (eds), *Interpretation and Explanation in the Study of Animal Behavior. Vol. 1: Interpretation, Intentionality, and Communication* (Boulder, CO: Westview Press), pp. 313–43; reprinted in M. Bekoff and D Jamieson (eds), *Readings in Animal Cognition* (Cambridge, MA: MIT Press), pp. 269–88.

Schaller, G. (1993) *The Last Panda* (Chicago: Chicago University Press).

Taylor, P. (1986) *Respect for Nature: A Theory of Environmental Ethics* (Princeton, NJ: Princeton University Press).

Vane-Wright, R., Humphries, C. and Williams, P. (1991) 'What to protect? Systematics and the agony of choice', *Biological Conservation* 55: 235–54.

Varner, G. and Monroe, M. (1991) 'Ethical perspectives on captive breeding: is it for the birds?', *Endangered Species Update* 8: 27–9.

Wolfe, A. (1991) 'Up from humanism', *American Prospect*, 112–25.

INDEX OF NAMES

Adorno, Theodor, 67, 72
Allchin, A., 30
Appleton, Jay, 85–7
Aquinas, St Thomas, 5, 25, 83–5, 87
Aristotle, 5, 24, 33, 87, 187
Augustine, St, 22, 26, 78

Bacon, Francis, 21
Bendiksen, Björn Hugo, 165
Berkeley, George, 24, 131
Berleant, Arnold, 39, 44, 86–7
Bernard, Claude, 33
Berry, Wendell, 45–6
Blake, William, 30
Bonner, John, 146
Botkin, Daniel, 160–1
Bourassa, Stephen, 85–7
Brundtland, Gro Harlem, 156–7, 164, 169, 174
Brundtland Report, 92, 95
Buchler, Justus, 76
Bunnel, Stirling, 172, 174
Burnet, T., 22

Callicott, J. Baird, 14–16, 141, 144
Cardenal, E., 21
Chandrashekhar, S., 34
Chappell, Timothy, 8–10
Chesterton, G. K., 20, 29, 32, 34
Clark, Stephen, 4–5
Coleridge, S. T., 67
Cooper, David, 44
Cupitt, Don, 50

Darwin, Charles, 17, 66, 146, 187
Dawkins, Richard, 51, 151, 187
Democritus, 32
Derrida, Jacques, 3, 39
Descartes, René, 9, 23, 31, 112, 184
Diamond, Jared, 93
Diogenes Laertius, 24
Douglas-Hamilton, Iain and Oria, 153
Dufrenne, Mikel, 67

Ehrenfeld, D., 188
Ehrlich, P. and A., 186
Einstein, Albert, 172
Epictetus, 23–4
Evernden, Neil, 42

Findlay, John, 71
Fitzgerald, F. Scott, 180
Fuller, Buckminster, 56

Gaskin, D. E., 171–2
Glezer, Ilya, 173–4
Gore, Al, 5, 20–1, 27
Graber, David, 47

Haldane, J. B. S., 137
Haldane, John, 5–6
Hardin, Garrett, 93
Hargrove, Eugene, 59
Hearne, Vicki, 143, 144
Hegel, G. W. F., 69
Hepburn, Ronald, 6–7
Heraclitus, 28, 33
Hobbes, Thomas, 8, 15, 92, 93–4
Holland, Allan, 144–5
Hopkins, G. M., 7, 79, 82
Horwood, Joseph, 165, 174
Hoyle, Fred, 57
Hume, David, 7, 15, 102, 113–14
Humphrey, N., 86

Jamieson, Dale, 16–17
Jesus, 97
Johnson, Dr Samuel, 79

Kant, Immanuel, 3, 8, 9, 14, 56, 59, 62, 67, 69, 73, 87, 121, 161
Keddy, Paul, 51, 53
Klinowska, Margaret, 171–4

Larrère, Catherine, 38
Leahy, M., 182–5
Leopold, Aldo, 15, 84–5, 156, 157–64, 166–7
Lewis, C. S., 50
Lilly, John, 71
Locke, John, 4, 15
Lovelock, James, 21, 29, 56
Lowenthal, David, 46–7

Marcus Aurelius, 119
May, Robert, 137
Midgley, Mary, 7–8, 144, 145
Mitchell, Edgar, 58
Moore, G. E., 97–8
Morgane, Peter, 171, 173–4
Muir, John, 171

Naess, Arne, 89, 95–6
Nagel, Thomas, 110
Nash, Roderick, 39, 47, 49
Nussbaum, Martha, 152

Öen, Egil Ole, 164
Ortega y Gasset, José, 166, 167
Orwell, George, 28
Ouspensky, P. D., 161

Pearce, David and Kerry Turner, 92, 97–8
Pepper, David, 50
Petrarch, 78–80, 83
Plato, 4, 20–36, 40
Plotinus, 22, 27, 30
Porphyry, 22
Primack, R. B., 141
Putnam, Hilary, 3–4, 6, 40, 53–5

Rachels, James, 145
Rawles, Kate, 12–14
Rawls, John, 99
Regan, Tom, 14, 146, 148–9
Rolston, Holmes, 1, 3–4, 124–6, 129, 158
Rorty, Richard, 3, 39, 45, 50, 51, 52, 56, 59–60
Rothenberg, David, 48
Ruskin, John, 73
Russell, Bertrand, 3

Schopenhauer, Artur, 67
Seneca, 78

Shepard, Paul, 166–7
Sikorski, Wade, 48–9
Singer, Peter, 14, 146–8
Smith, Adam, 8
Socrates, 28, 30
Spinoza, Baruch (Benedict de), 22, 31, 69
Sprat, Thomas, 31
Sprigge, Timothy, 10–12
Stoics, 22–4, 28, 34
Suger, Abbot, 29

Taylor, Paul, 124, 126, 163
Taylor, Richard, 128–9
Thoreau, H. D., 49
Traherne, Thomas, 29, 30

van Fraassen, Bas, 51
Voltaire (François-Marie Arouet), 95

Wallöe, Lars, 156, 174
Warren, Mary Anne, 102–16
Weil, Simone, 34
Wetlesen, Jon, 156
Williams, Bernard, 8, 114
Wilson, Alexander, 3, 39
Wilson, Edward, 138
Wilson, P. L., 30
Wittgenstein, Ludwig, 32
Wordsworth, William, 11, 69, 72, 73